LIBERATING LOMIE

Memoir of an Amish Childhood

Author featured in the *American Experience* documentaries
"The Amish" and "The Amish: Shunned"

~ For Sarah ~
Thank you for your important work.
May love and light shine on you
always!

Saloma

SALOMA MILLER FURLONG

MEMORY PAGES PRESS

Broadway, Virginia

To request permissions, contact the author at
saloma@salomafurlong.com

Paperback ISBN: 979-8-9861822-0-9
EBook ISBN: 979-8-9861822-1-6
Audio Book ISBN: 979-8-9861822-2-3

First paperback edition: June 2022

Cover design by Pamela Johnson
Book design by Saloma Miller Furlong
Edited by Marjorie Turner Hollman
Copyedited by Frances B. King
Proofread by April Sachs

Produced in the USA

MEMORY PAGES PRESS

Broadway, Virginia

Visit the author's website and blog at
https://salomafurlong.com
https://salomafurlong.com/aboutamish/

For Paul and Tim

To my loved sons, Paul and Tim, who inspired me to mindfully interrupt the unhealthy family patterns I inherited while still honoring the goodness in my Amish upbringing.

For Survivors of Abuse

If you have experienced or are experiencing abuse, know that you are not alone. May you find the courage to reach out for help from someone who cares. Know that you have the inner strength to carry you through the pain and to eventually transform it to make sure it does not get transmitted to the next generation. In the process, you find yourself becoming who you are meant to be.

CONTENTS

AUTHOR'S NOTES

Names: Some names have been changed.

Amish Customs: I chose not to break up the story line to explain Amish naming practices, modes of transportation or dress, courtship, or Amish-style shunning, so I've added an appendix at the end of the book to explain these customs. Please refer to these if you find yourself puzzling over certain terms I use in telling my stories.

Disclosure: For abuse survivors and those who find it hard to read about abuse, I want to be clear that this book is not an easy read. My childhood was a difficult one in which I endured abuses of all kinds, so my story wouldn't be complete if I omitted these hardships. I am grateful that I survived and eventually learned to thrive.

Note to the Abused: If you are experiencing abuse or its aftermath, know there is help from trained professionals at the National Domestic Violence Hotline (**1-800-799-7233**) and the National Sexual Assault Hotline (**1-800-656-4673**). Breaking the silence is the first step to stopping the abuse. It takes strength and courage to reach out for help. You have that courage, and you will find it.

PREFACE

In childhood there are frequently irreconcilable conflicts between loyalty to our parents and being true to our own selves. ~Alice Miller

My perspective about my childhood experiences has evolved and changed in the years since my first book, *Why I Left the Amish,* was published in 2011. Back then I was ecstatic about having that book published. It had taken me seventeen years, starting from the time I first began writing down stories about my Amish childhood, until the book was finally published. However, some years after launching the book, I began wishing I could take *Why I Left the Amish* off the market because of my changing perspective. When my contract with the publisher ended in January 2021, I chose not to renew it.

I had written then about the abuse I had endured at the hands of my paternal grandmother, my father, and my older brother. Some years after the book was published, I began asking myself why I had omitted the abuse I had endured at the hands of my mother (Mem). I realized I was still under the spell of believing that she was a martyr and a saint—a martyr for putting up with my father as her husband—and a saint for being the "good parent" to her children. She had promoted this view of herself for as long as I could remember.

Mem claimed that she'd had a happy childhood, surrounded by a loving family and a father who could do no wrong. Even in my teens, I sensed the happy-go-lucky story Mem wanted me to believe was fictional, and I became convinced of that as an adult. Yet however many times and in however many ways I asked for Mem's family history, she refused to relinquish her stories. At some point in her later years, I came to the realization that Mem had every intention of making sure her history and pain would be buried with her. I also realized that I would be left with the daunting task of reconciling my relationship with her, or my memories of her, on my own.

Not only did Mem refuse to relinquish her stories, but she also made repeated requests that I stay silent about my pain. When I was a young mother, I asked her questions in our letter correspondence about something that happened when I was a child. In her response, she wrote that I should "bury these things in the past and let them *stay* buried." These major differences in the way we approached our lives—Mem's determination to bury her pain and my need to voice mine, her attempts to silence me, and my attempts to draw out her story—were at the core of our longstanding battle of wills. The chasm between my worldview and the one Mem maintained to her death was never to be bridged.

For reasons I still don't understand, it took nearly a decade after Mem's death until I was finally ready to take an honest look at what had happened to me. *Liberating Lomie* revisits my childhood stories with this perspective.

When I began trying to reconcile my memories of Mem with what I felt was the truth, I started by writing a letter to her soul as a means of coming to terms with her, with the hope of eventually forgiving her. I often had to stop writing when I came to another traumatic event to allow myself a good cry. But I didn't stop writing until my letter grew to 150 pages long. This letter concluded naturally at the point when I had left home at twenty years old, which had forced our relationship to change.

After writing this long letter to Mem, I decided to braid a rug for a young friend who was getting married. Braiding rugs was one of the homespun arts I had learned from Mem when I was growing up. One day I was sitting in my attic room, braiding and looking out the window over the neighborhood. The flow of the traffic on the bridge that spanned the

Connecticut River in the background was like the flow of the water underneath it—the flow of life.

I felt Mem's presence as my hands folded in the edges of the soft, yielding strands of wool. I longed to reach a point of understanding Mem's life, forgiving her, and letting go of the past. Over and over I folded—right, then left, right, then left—while creating a braid of dark purple and gray. I thought of each strand as representing three parts of forgiveness: honesty, humility, and compassion. By braiding these three together, I felt I was braiding my way toward forgiveness.

Once I finished the rug, I braided another. And then another. I kept braiding until I had braided seven rugs over several months. Each creation added warmth and beauty to the home my husband David and I had renovated. They were a complement to the newly finished wood floors. They reminded me that even in the struggle to reach a reconciliation with Mem, I could still celebrate many of the things I'd learned from her, including how to create beauty in the form of braiding woolen rugs.

As I reflected on the two very different lives Mem and I had lived, I realized that my life would have resembled hers had I stayed and married someone I didn't love and then discovered he suffered from mental illness. I didn't know whether I would have had the kind of strength needed to raise a brood of children pretty much on my own. On the flip side of that, Mem could have had a life of her choosing had she decided to leave and strike out on her own. I often felt like Mem secretly coveted my life, even while condemning my choices to others in her community.

I wondered why I struggled with forgiving Mem as I had been taught I should do. The Amish definition of forgiveness is to forgive and forget. It seemed to me that Mem wanted to skip the forgiveness part—which first requires an admission of committing a wrong—and go directly to the forgetting part. I often wondered how I was supposed to choose which of my experiences to remember and which ones to forget. It seemed this was a natural process that I had no control over.

Mem's expectations that I should bear my struggles in silence mirrored those of our Amish community. These expectations had been handed down through the generations from mother to daughter as part of our cultural heritage. I had often wished I could meet such expectations and be a good Amish child and young woman. Growing up in this context, I couldn't understand where the desire came from to give voice to my experiences as a means of understanding my life and my world.

As I practiced the homespun art Mem had taught me by braiding woolen rugs, it dawned on me that I could choose which of the traditions I carried on, and which ones I could let go of. It didn't feel natural to me to remain silent about the pain I had endured in my childhood. I realized that forgiveness did not include bearing the burden of silence as Mem had done and as she wished for me to do. By remembering and writing my stories, I had to **for**go or **give** up the guilt of revealing what happened. Instead of forgiving and forgetting, I am remembering and relinquishing.

Mem with an "English" friend when she was still single, circa 1950

PROLOGUE

Freedom lies in being bold. ~Robert Frost

I did not sneak away in the dark of night. I left in broad daylight with a little blue overnight suitcase in hand. I was twenty years old, still a minor in the eyes of my parents and the state law in Ohio. If I got caught, there was one last resort for escaping the life I could no longer bear. I didn't even want to think about attempting suicide, so my life depended on making this work. I kept telling myself everything would work out all right. I'd laid my plans with care to ensure my success in leaving and my survival "out in the world." A friend was helping me to make arrangements to go to Vermont, the land of my dreams.

Throughout the night I had anticipated the moment when I'd walk out of my parents' home with no plans to return. I played the scene over and over in my mind. I'd wait in my room until my regular ride to work showed up and Mem would call up to let me know. By the sound of her voice, I'd know whether she was in the living room or in the kitchen. How I hoped she'd be in the living room so I could leave before she saw my suitcase!

As I heard Mr. Pell's car coming in the lane, Mem called from the

1

kitchen. My heart beat hard and fast. I grabbed my suitcase out of the closet and bounded down the stairs. I came face-to-face with Mem, sweeping the kitchen floor. She looked pointedly at my suitcase, then at me.

I said, "I'm babysitting tonight at the place where I work." It was not an outright lie, but it also wasn't telling Mem the whole truth.

Mem said severely, "Don't you let this happen too often."

"I won't," I said. I ran down the stairs and out the door to the yellow getaway car. I was leaving my Amish childhood behind, and Mem could not call it back.

This photo was taken after I left home, though it looks much like it did when I was growing up.

EARLY REMEMBRANCES

[O]ur memories are part of one great memory, the memory of Nature herself. ~William Butler Yeats

Twenty years before I left home with no plans to return, I was born the third child into an Amish family in northeastern Ohio. My parents lived on a farmette, with a barn, garden, fields, and a tiny four-room house taking up an acre of land. They also owned forty acres of woods surrounding the farmette.

I was born the day after my parents' fourth wedding anniversary. Mem once told me it was the only anniversary she had ever celebrated. But from what else she told me, those days sound more like a family crisis because a family member was leaving the world as I was entering it. My father's stepdad had died two days before I was born. He had been in a car and buggy accident the day before he died, and my grandmother believed the accident was the cause of his sudden death, though his obituary records the cause of his death as having been a stroke.

My father (Datt) was torn between being there for his bereaved mother and being present for his wife as she was about to give birth. I know he was at Mem's bedside when she arrived at the Amish midwife's home because the midwife had him administer the ether to Mem. Apparently, he gave her too much too soon, so she turned her head and ether got into one of her eyes. When she awoke, she wanted to know why her eye felt so strange, and the midwife told her what had happened. The way Mem told the story, Datt was to blame. But I wondered why the midwife had my father administer the ether instead of doing it herself.

After my birth, the Amish midwife, Mrs. Yoder, put me in a tiny basket, all wrapped in blankets, next to Mem's bed. Mem said I was a beautiful baby, with the thickest dark hair she'd ever seen on a newborn.

Some of Mem's recollections about my childhood came to me in the form of letters when I was a young mother myself. She once wrote:

> *The day that I was to come home was the funeral of dad's stepfather and [he] didn't come to pick me up until late and [I] remember how impatient Mrs. Yoder got. She said to me, "Must be he thinks more of his mother than he does of you." Which pretty well upset me for awhile.*

Mem returned home to her other two children, three-year-old Joey and one-year-old Lizzie. As was typical for Amish mothers in my community, Mem cared for me pretty exclusively for the first two weeks while a young woman in the community came and took care of Joey and Lizzie and the household chores so that Mem could get some rest.

Mem wrote to me about my babyhood:

> *You were a contented baby. I could sit you on the highchair, tied on, so you couldn't fall off, put the tray down and give you things to play with and you'd play for a long time. Sometimes by the east window and sometimes by me wherever I was working.*

I can imagine this. Even in the years I can recall, I often stared out that window when I was daydreaming, with Mem bustling about the kitchen. I loved looking out over the field to the east, where the sky met the tree line. It was the only horizon visible from any window in our home because we were otherwise surrounded by woods.

Mem breastfed all of us children, even though it was common for mothers to bottle-feed their babies at that time. Mem wrote this to me when my older son was a few weeks old:

Well, how is that little baby doing by now? Are you nursing him? What is more enjoyable? I can just feel the contentment sitting on my rocker and nursing my little ones. And wondering about their future. Now that is all over but I can still dream about it.

Mem stopped nursing me abruptly when I was seven months old because she became terribly ill with yellow jaundice and believed the illness could be passed on to me. I put her in a fix when I refused to take a bottle. Her mother-in-law came in and took control of the situation. "Humph! Never heard of a baby that wouldn't take a bottle!" she said. Mem told her she was welcome to try. And try she did. She stuck the bottle in my mouth and I spat out that nipple. She stuck it in. I spat it out. She had my other grandmother hold me down, and again she tried forcing me to take it. I still spat it out. Mem said it had been really hard for Grandmother to admit that she had to give up. Mem always told this story with a little satisfaction—as if I had defied my grandmother in a way she didn't dare to.

The only way to give me nourishment was by offering me milk and water from a cup, feeding me baby cereal mixed with warm milk, and other soft foods from a bowl. As Mem's health improved, she coaxed me to eat mashed potatoes, eggs, applesauce, and whatever else I'd eat. Despite these efforts, I showed signs of what today would be considered "failure to thrive." In Mem's words:

I remember I was worried because you wouldn't stand on your legs for so long. So I'd rub them every time I'd change your diaper. Momme, once when she was here saved the potato water, when we cooked potatoes for dinner. She then rubbed that on your legs and I guess I did too after that sometimes but I had more faith in just rubbing them, for therapy.

At the age when most children get up and walk, I was learning to crawl, but in my own way. I sat on my bottom and scooted around, using my legs to propel me—first one leg, then the other. I became very fast at it. Mem described how hard it was to keep my diapers clean because they picked up dirt from her pine floorboards as I went. In those days, she was still using a washboard to wash clothes. She boiled the diapers with lye soap in the water, added cold water, and scrubbed those diapers on the washboard until her knuckles bled.

Mem's fourth child, Sylvia, was born when I was eighteen months old. Not only did Mem have two in diapers, but she also had two babes-in-arms. Whenever Mem entered the place where women gathered for church with a child on each arm, someone would come to help her. When they reached for me, I screamed and cried until I was back in Mem's arms. They soon learned to take Sylvia instead.

Sylvia took her first steps only months after I did, when she was eleven months old, just three months after I'd turned two years old. Mem suddenly had her arms free—at least for a spell. When Sylvia was fifteen months old and I was almost three, Sadie was born.

I was talking in sentences by the time I was two years old, but I still wasn't walking. I gained the nickname "Chatter Box." Many years later, one of the other mothers in the community told the story of something that happened before I started walking. It took place during the Communion Service, which was held twice a year. Breaking and sharing the bread for Communion is a somber ritual in which all those who have been baptized eat bread and drink wine. Children are excluded from partaking in Communion bread because they are not yet baptized members of the church. On this particular Sunday, Mem was holding me in her arms, awaiting her turn to eat the bread, which the bishop would hand to her. At that point in the service, it was usually so quiet that people could hear themselves breathe. As Mem received her bread, I said out loud, in the middle of this solemn service, "*Ich will oh brot!*—I want some bread too!"

I try to imagine how Mem dealt with this situation. To have given me even a little bread would have been considered sacrilegious, yet leaving the service was also inappropriate. Perhaps she found a way to distract me so I wouldn't persist in embarrassing her further.

~

There are several incidents from when I was very young in which Mem's telling blends with my own memories. One night, when I was perhaps three years old, I sat on the woodbox next to the stove in the living room, surrounded by my family. I had a secret: I had a marble in my mouth. Mem had warned me many times not to put marbles in my mouth, but I could not resist the silky-smooth roundness as I turned it around and around with my tongue. Then, without warning, that marble slipped down my throat. I couldn't breathe. I didn't panic until I found myself being dangled upside down by one ankle and pounded on my back, hard. Mem had grabbed me, swung me upside down, and smacked my back. The marble popped out.

I wasn't old enough to realize that Mem had just saved my life. I thought she was punishing me for disobeying. I have an ever-so-dim memory of Mem gathering every marble she could find and getting rid of them. But there was no need as far as I was concerned. The feeling of dangling upside down in midair and being hit like that was enough to prevent me from putting marbles in my mouth ever again.

Another story Mem told me fuses with my memory. On a wintery Sunday morning when I was three, Mem bustled about, getting all five of us children ready for church. She discovered that my overshoes (boots that slipped on over my shoes) were too small for me to wear, but she remembered that there was a pair of boots in the box of used items that an English family had brought us as charity. There was one problem. They were red, a color we were forbidden to wear because it was too bright. But she had to keep my feet warm somehow, so she slipped them on over my shoes. Mem warned me that when we arrived at the home where church was being held, we needed to put them in the corner of the washhouse, so no one would notice.

I sat up a little straighter on the way to church that day. I couldn't easily look at my boots because they were under the buggy blanket that covered our laps to keep us warm, but I tried.

When we arrived at the service, Mem carried Baby Sadie into the washhouse, with Lizzie, Sylvia, and me walking by her side, bundled up in our black coats, capes, and bonnets. As I walked in, I looked around and spotted Mem's friend, Clara Yoder. I walked up to her and said, "Look, I have new boots!" I held one boot up for her to see.

Mem's face flushed with shame as all the women in the washhouse became completely still. After a long moment, she urged me into the corner and pulled my boots off so fast that my shoes came off with them.

As the women lined up to go into the service, Mem's friend Clara said, "It's okay. Don't be ashamed." Mem's grip on my hand relaxed a bit. Like many others in the community, she worried about what other people thought of her. I imagine her shame was lessened just a bit by Clara's reassurance.

I wore those red boots home that day and never saw them again.

In my early years, my parents created an environment that allowed us children to develop normal and happy memories. These are mixed with more traumatic ones.

None of Mem's recollections of my young childhood involve my father, so I have to rely on my memories of him. When we were babies and toddlers, Mem used to place us on Datt's lap after she changed our diapers and fed us. I remember rocking with Datt for hours on end, sometimes with toys in my hands. One day, I had just drunk a lot of water when Datt was rocking me. I could hear and feel the liquid sloshing in my tummy. I started giggling as Datt rocked back and forth and I heard the *doink, doink* that went with the motion. Datt realized what was happening, so he rocked back and forth, then stopped abruptly, and the sloshing inside tickled. I giggled and giggled. Datt had a wide grin as he played this game with me. It was the first time I remember the feeling of giggling so hard that the giggles tickled on their way up.

When I was a toddler, Datt sometimes placed my feet on top of his shoes, held onto my hands, and walked me around the house. I liked the feeling of being transported around on top of Datt's feet. Later, I saw him walking my younger siblings in the same way.

I also played a hand-stacking game with Datt, often after supper while we were still sitting at the table. He placed one of his hands on the table. I put one of my hands on his. He put his other hand down, and my other hand became the top of the stack. Then he took his bottom hand out and dropped it on top, and I followed his lead. If I forgot, he gently squeezed my bottom hand to remind me. We'd go faster and faster until our hands became like a threshing machine and we'd laugh. Sometimes Datt played the hand-stacking game with two of us at a time.

Mem had a red plastic Viewfinder that I loved to hold up to the light to view the magic pictures: mountains, fields of flowers, a huge dam, a waterfall, and images of what I now know to be the Grand Canyon. (I vaguely knew that Mem had been to some of those places. Later I understood that Mem had taken a cross-country trip before she was married.) There were also pictures of storybook characters from *Snow White and the Seven Dwarfs*, Mickey Mouse, Daffy Duck, and many others. It seemed that I should be able to reach out and touch what was in those three-dimensional pictures. I used to feel like using this toy was such a privilege because Mem didn't let us play with it often, making it all the more special.

A rope swing hung from a tall branch of an oak tree out next to the sandbox. I loved swinging high on it. Lizzie pushed me to get started, and then I pumped my legs until I was flying high above the woodshed roof. The wind swooshed past my ears, and butterflies fluttered inside my belly and made me giggle.

We played on the buggy that was in the shed attached to the barn. In our minds, we'd go places. I could even hear the horse hooves clopping along the pavement, as we clicked our tongues. We held the reins, which were made of braided twine, and once in a while called out, "Giddyap!" if we wanted the horse to go faster.

Behind the buggy was a pile of straw for bedding down the horses and cows. When the pile was high enough, we climbed into the haymow and took a flying leap into the pile of straw. Mem didn't like us doing that, but whenever there was a new pile of straw, it was too tempting not to.

I loved jumping rope. We had homemade jump ropes that were made of three strands of baling twine braided together. I counted the jumps as I twirled the rope over and over and over. Before I learned to count to one hundred, I'd count to twenty, then jumble numbers and yell, "One hundred!" when I was ready to stop. It was the highest number I knew, though I didn't comprehend it any more than I comprehend infinity as an adult.

I loved when Mem bathed my sisters and me on Saturday nights. I particularly remember bath nights in the winter. First Datt carried buckets of water in from the hand pump out by the barn and filled the copper boiler on the cookstove. While the water was heating, Mem brought up the tub from the basement and set it on a hand-crocheted rug next to the wood stove. She collected our clean clothes from the drawers in the upstairs bedroom and hung clean towels out to warm by the stove. When the water in the boiler was hot, she dipped it out into a bucket, then poured it into the tub, mixed it with cold water, and tested the temperature with her elbow. Then she helped my sisters and me strip off our clothes and get into the tub together. After she used a clean washcloth to wipe our faces, she bathed the youngest one, dried her off, dressed her in warm, clean clothes, and started again with the next oldest. I used to love the feeling of her washcloth bathing me down: first my face, then my neck, in and behind my ears, shoulders, arms, armpits, all the way down to my toes. Then she would dunk her washcloth into the warm water and rinse off my body before lifting me out and taking me into her ample lap. I can still feel what it was like to be enveloped in Mem's love. It was the closest thing to an embrace I ever experienced in my childhood. Like other Amish mothers, Mem did not show her affection for her children by hugging or kissing us. Still, on those Saturday nights when Mem wrapped me in that warm, dry towel and dried me off—all the way down to my feet and in between my toes—and dressed me in the fresh-smelling clothes she had laid out for me, I felt loved and cared for.

After bathing us, Mem braided our hair. She began by undoing the braids from the week before, brushing out our hair, and sectioning it into four parts—two front sections and two back. She dunked her hands into a bowl of water so they slid over my hair. She braided a front section and then braided that section into the back one. Toward the end, she braided a string into my hair. Once both sides were done, she looped the back braids through the front braids several times and tied them up with the strings she'd braided into the hair. She had a gentle touch, yet my hair felt tightly braided afterward.

On some Saturday nights, Mem would decide it was time to wash our hair. She'd put warm water in the wash basin and a pitcher, then one by one, she laid us on the counter next to the sink. All too soon it was my turn to lie down and move my head way out over the sink where Mem wet it down, added shampoo, and worked it through my long hair before rinsing it with the pitcher of warm water. I did not like having my hair washed and fussed as Mem did it. She tried soothing me by saying there were birdies in my hair as she was working in the shampoo. I didn't want birdies in my hair, and I didn't want to get my hair washed, either. After Mem rinsed out my hair, she dried it with a towel, and then came the painful part when she had to work out the tangles. Once that was done, I had to let my hair dry before Mem braided it. I was glad we didn't have to wash our hair every Saturday.

One morning, I watched out the window as Joey and Lizzie laughed and talked with the neighbor children, Susan and Brian Sakura. They were about to get on the school bus. I wished I could go to school.

Susan and Brian wore store-bought clothes because they were not Amish. Susan's shiny dark brown hair hung down her back.

When all four of them had climbed the bus steps and were sitting in their seats, they waved to me. Autumn leaves blew in swirls behind the bright yellow school bus as it pulled away and disappeared up the road.

Mem put the breadboard on the kitchen table. I asked, "Can I help?"

"Sure. Bring the *bankly* over," Mem said, gesturing at the little bench. She gave me a little of the dough to knead alongside hers. Mem kneaded her bread: turn, fold, push. Turn, fold, push. The table creaked with each push.

I asked, "Mem, can you tell me the elephant story?"

"But you already know that story."

"Will you tell it again?"

So Mem began. "It was a Sunday, and my aunt was taking care of us children. I was out in the front yard, playing in the sandbox. I heard a noise, and I looked up, and there was a big elephant walking in the yard. He was dragging a chain, and that was what was making the noise. The elephant had gotten loose from the circus, and it was coming right up our lane."

"Were you scared?"

"I would have been, except I had seen a picture of one in a book just a few days before. I had asked my mem if this was an animal to be afraid of, and she said no."

I looked into Mem's blue eyes and said, "Then what happened?"

"The elephant walked right past the sandbox and into the silage chute. My aunt let us look in through the window. The elephant picked up silage with its trunk and wiggled it around to get it into his mouth. Pretty soon two men came along, and they had a hard time getting him turned around and out of there because he kept stomping on the chain around his leg. But they finally did. Then they gave the elephant some water from the trough that our horses drank from. He stuck his trunk into the trough and swung it up into his mouth. Then the two men led him back out to the road and off to the circus."

Mem was greasing her bowl and turning the bread dough into it. She sprinkled flour on my fingers and rubbed them so the dough came off in little rolls. "Go get the little stainless steel bowl," she said. I found it and copied Mem. She covered the dough with a clean towel and set it near the stove to rise.

When I kneaded bread with Mem, I didn't know the difference between work and play because she had a clever way of combining the two. She allowed me to splash in the water to "help" her or my older sister Lizzie wash dishes. I had to stand on the *bankly* because I was too little to reach the kitchen sink.

I started making cookies and cakes before I could read the recipes. I would bring Mem the recipe when she was sewing in the living room, and she would tell me what to put in the batter next. She had shown me how to use measuring cups and big spoons (tablespoons) and little spoons (teaspoons) to measure the ingredients before mixing them together. She helped me pour the batter into the pan if it was a cake. I'd make oatmeal cake, spice cake, white cake, and applesauce cake. If I was making cookies, Mem stirred the last of the flour into the batter. Then I spooned the cookie dough onto a cookie sheet. We usually made buttermilk, molasses, or oatmeal cookies. I would add more variety to our baked goods later when I learned to read, but at first I did everything as Mem instructed. She was getting me ready to take on the responsibilities that I would experience as a burden later, but in the beginning it was all fun.

A summer picnic at our neighbors' house. I am on the right, Joey on the left, Sadie peeking from behind Joey's hand, and Sylvia looking over Sadie's head. Lizzie is missing from the photo.

IN THE SHADOWS

There is no despair so absolute as that which comes with the first moments of our first great sorrow... ~George Eliot

Interspersed with the "normal" memories of my young childhood are dark ones in which I experienced fear and sometimes terror.

Mem created a tight bond with me as a small child. She was my whole world. For the first three years, she was never far from my sight. Then one day she left my orbit.

Usually when Mem was going somewhere, she'd pick which of us children could go with her. On this day, we all got to go. We were going to go to the dentist's office. At least that is what I thought was going to happen.

We all piled into our next-door neighbor's car and headed up Hale Road, and then took a right on Burton-Windsor Road toward our little town of Burton. But then instead of going to Burton, Mrs. Sakura pulled in the lane of the Weaver family's home. Mem got out of the car and talked to the mom of the Weaver children.

I was standing on a sidewalk that led to their house when I realized that Mem wasn't next to me anymore. I looked around in panic. Then I saw that little red car with Mem and my siblings in it, heading up the hill and away. I thought the reason they had left me behind was because they'd forgotten me. I screamed out my panic and cried so hard I couldn't catch my breath. I must have blacked out because I fell backwards. I saw stars as the back of my head hit the sidewalk.

The next thing I knew, Ada Weaver was sending one of her children to fetch a little red wagon to give me a ride. But the longing to be with Mem and my family was too great for me to care about a wagon or anything else. When Ada said that Mem would come back, I realized that Mem had not forgotten me. Instead, she had purposely left me there. In my child's mind, I couldn't understand why the others all got to go to the dentist's office while I was left behind. For the first time in my life, I didn't know where Mem was, nor did I know if she would ever come back.

What seemed like an eternity passed before Mem and the others came back. By then I had no more tears left. I sucked in my breath and walked past Mem as if I didn't know her.

Sometimes Datt spent whole days on his hickory rocker, rocking slowly back and forth. Mem often tried coaxing him to do something else, but it seemed like it took more energy than he had to lift himself out of the rocker. He left it for meals, and sometimes when Mem demanded he needed to do something for her. Gradually I became aware that it wasn't normal for someone to spend as much time sitting in the house as Datt did.

More disturbing than Datt's inertia were his conversations with people who were not in the room. In the middle of his rocking, he'd stop, look up into the corner of the room, snap his dark eyes, and move his mouth as if he were talking to someone in an animated way. Then he'd pinch his lips together and slowly start rocking again, back and forth over the woven rug.

I'd look up into the corner of the living room, trying to comprehend who he was talking to. I knew something wasn't right, but I was too young to understand what it was.

Some nights Mem tried to urge Datt off his rocking chair to go do the farm chores, and it started an argument between them. Mem's voice became sharp, trying to command, cajole, or shame him into going out and doing the chores. Some nights Datt got up, put on his winter coat and hat, and stumped down the stairs and out the door. Other nights he wouldn't budge from his rocking chair.

One night I was playing on the floor with my sisters when Mem and Datt began arguing. Mem had been chastising Datt for what seemed like a long time. He stopped his rocking as Mem said, "I have enough to do without doing *your chores too!* It's time for you to do *your* share!"

"Yeah, well I do my share," Datt said.

"You do your share from your rocking chair, huh, while I do all the cooking, cleaning, washing, taking care of the children, and this isn't enough? Now I'm supposed to go out and milk the cow, feed the horses, the pigs, and the chickens, and then come in and make supper too? Why *should* I?"

"You wanted to have children... well, now you have them!" Datt retorted.

With this, Mem walked with angry footsteps toward the coats in the corner of the kitchen. I could feel her anger in the vibration of the floorboards. She wiggled her barn coat over her dress, pulled a scarf over her head and tied it under her chin, grabbed the only gas lantern we had, and headed out the door. Her last words before the door shut behind her were, "*Huck uff deah stuhl und less mich oll die eivet du dann!*—sit on your rocking chair and let me do all your work then!"

After the kitchen door closed behind Mem with a bang, we were left in the dim and flickering light of the oil lamp. Tension and anger crouched in all the shadows, like a beast ready to pounce. I was paralyzed by my terror.

Datt had stopped rocking as Mem slammed the door, but then he started rocking slowly back and forth. I moved into the small, yellow circle of light of the oil lamp next to Datt's rocking chair, to get out of the scary dark shadows. I was holding onto the arm of the rocking chair when I got too close and Datt rocked over my big toe. I heard the "crunch" just before the overwhelming pain slammed into my toe. I didn't know anything could hurt so bad. I wondered if my toe had been cut off. I screamed and sobbed so hard I couldn't catch my breath. I barely heard Datt say, "Lomie if you stop crying, I will give you a penny."

I couldn't stop crying. The pain in my toe was too big, and so was the fear when it dawned on me that Datt could not take care of me, no matter what happened. I wanted Mem to come in from outside and make everything okay.

Datt took his little metal cylinder matchbox out of his pocket. I used to love to watch him unscrew the top and see the blue tips of the matches, but not this time. I could not have stopped crying for anything. Datt turned away from me and picked up Sylvia and put her on his lap.

I was sitting on the floor in the living room, still sniffling from my sobs, when Mem finally came in from doing chores. I'd completely exhausted myself from crying. The searing pain had changed into a throbbing ache.

When Lizzie told Mem what had happened, Mem took my shoe and sock off. I saw with relief that my toe was still in one piece. There was blood oozing out from under my big toenail, and the whole toe had turned purple. Mem set about getting cold water in a wash basin to soak it, scolding Datt, "You could have gotten her water to soak her toe! Can't I even leave you with the children anymore?"

Datt sat there stock still on his rocking chair and said nothing. Mem continued to scold as she prepared supper and put it on the table.

After we had gathered around the table to eat, we bowed our heads in silence. Then Mem dipped vegetable soup into each of our bowls. Datt sat there, holding out his bowl, waiting to be served. Finally, when all of us children had been served, Mem served Datt his soup, and then her own. That's when quiet set in, the kind that made me wonder what would happen next. But I was too hungry to think about anything other than eating my soup.

That night, Mem and Datt's argument followed me into my dreams. Datt sat on his rocking chair with his arms folded over his chest as Mem kept on scolding. This time, instead of sitting there, Datt jumped up from his rocking chair, and with shuffled and hurried steps, he stomped out to the kitchen sink. He bent over and knocked his head into the sink, hard, several times. To my horror, the top of his head broke off and rocked back and forth, like a jagged piece of eggshell, in the white sink. He stood there without the top of his head and said, "Now are you happy?"

I screamed myself awake. I was hot under the covers, in the bed I shared with Lizzie and Sylvia. Mem got out of her bed and asked, "*Lomie, vas iss letz?*—Lomie, what is the matter?"

I was crying so hard that I couldn't catch my breath. Finally, between hiccups, I managed to tell Mem about my dream.

She tucked the covers around me, and said, "But it was only a dream. Go back to sleep." I couldn't tell Mem that it was like real life, so maybe it *could* happen.

Long after Mem had gone back to bed, I crouched in my bed, too afraid to go to sleep because I didn't want to go back into the dream. Mercifully, I eventually fell into a dreamless sleep.

~

Out of nowhere, Datt got a job. He helped with chores morning and night on the Hale farm up the road, hauling pails of milk from the barn to the milkhouse. He came home tired, which meant that Mem and Joey had to do our farm chores.

When Datt returned home one night, he told Mem at the supper table about an argument he'd had with a man who wasn't Amish. He was one of our egg customers, and we called him "The Yankee." On this night, The Yankee had gone to the Hale farm to buy milk, and he'd parked his car in the way of Datt hauling the heavy pails of milk. Datt had asked him to move the car, and The Yankee refused. Datt was agitated and upset.

Later that night, we'd all gone to bed, but I couldn't sleep. I was hot under the covers, and my nightie was sticking to me in the heat and humidity of late summer. I was looking at the chimney on the wall at the foot end of our bed when I saw it light up. A car had just come in our lane. The lights went off and a car door slammed. Someone yelled out in a raspy, harsh voice, "Simon!"

It was The Yankee calling my father's name.

Datt stayed still. He said in a whisper so we could all hear him, "Stay quiet and maybe he'll go away."

The Yankee didn't go away. He kept yelling louder, "Simon! Siii-monnn!" He knocked on the outside door and yelled my father's name. Mem and Datt were having a whispered argument. Mem was telling Datt he needed to go find out what The Yankee wanted, but Datt wouldn't move. We heard The Yankee walking up the stairs to the kitchen and walking through the door. I held my breath. He rattled the handle on the water pail, and he kept yelling my father's name. Still, Datt didn't answer. So The Yankee walked to the bottom of the stairs that led to our bedrooms. He opened the door and yelled upstairs. Datt still didn't stir. My fear was too big to swallow. I wondered what would happen now. Mem got up out of bed and walked to the top of the stairs.

She said, "You're waking the children! What do you want?"

"I want some eggs!"

"Come back tomorrow and I will give you the eggs."

"But I'm hungry, and I need some eggs!" he demanded.

Mem stepped down into the darkness of the stairs and said, "I will give you some eggs, and then you need to leave!" I could hear the fear in Mem's voice. She went all the way down to the basement in her bare feet. A few minutes later, she came quickly upstairs, her feet slapping against the wooden steps. Out loud she told Datt, "I gave him some eggs. Now if he doesn't leave, you will have to deal with him. He smells like alcohol."

I thought Mem meant that he smelled like rubbing alcohol, like what she used to clean our cuts and scrapes. I couldn't understand why The Yankee would smell like rubbing alcohol. I didn't know that people could consume another kind of alcohol and become drunk.

The next day, Datt put up two brackets on the inside of the door frame at the bottom of the kitchen stairs. At bedtime he dropped a two-by-four over the brackets to bar anyone from coming in. At first I felt safer, knowing The Yankee could no longer come into our home in the middle of the night. But then I realized I couldn't reach the bar, and it made me feel trapped. Danger lurked in the shadows of our home, and it didn't always come in from the outside.

～

One morning Joey and Lizzie had gotten on the school bus and Mem was just pouring hot water into the dishpans in the sink for me to wash the dishes when her friend Grace Bradley drove in our lane. Mem hurried to finish preparing the dishwater, as Grace made her way to our door. Mem welcomed her in. Grace's face lit up when she saw me. She oohed and aahed about how much I'd grown. I knew what she meant, even though I didn't understand her English words because she motioned with her hands that I had been "this tall" the last time she'd seen me.

I loved Grace Bradley. She had kindness written into every wrinkle of her face, and she paid attention to us children when she visited. I was sorry when Mem and Grace went through the door into the living room. Mem turned around and said, "Lomie, do the dishes now."

Datt got off his rocking chair and headed outside. He didn't like when other people saw he was sitting inside in the middle of the day.

The water was too hot for me to put my hands into, so I played with the soap bubbles and tried to listen to Mem and Grace. I didn't understand English, so I could only catch a word here and there.

During a pause in their conversation, Mem said, "*Lomie, ich heah dich net cha vesha.*—Lomie, I don't hear you washing any dishes."

I picked up a cup and put it into the water. I swished the dishcloth around inside the cup, then dunked the cup into the rinse water and set it into the drainer.

Then I stopped. I thought I heard Grace and Mem disagreeing. I had never heard that before. I listened, but I could not tell what they were saying, only that Mem's voice sounded hurt and defensive. I thought she might even be crying. Things got quiet in the living room, but it was not a comfortable quiet. Then Grace got up and came through the kitchen door. I could tell she was leaving. Mem followed her to the door, but she didn't say, "Come again!" as she usually did. She watched Grace departing with sadness on her face.

"*Vass iss letz*—what's wrong?"

"*Nix.*"

"Are you and Grace mad at each other?"

"She thinks I shouldn't make you work so hard. But without Datt's help..." Mem's voice faded into tears and she went through the door back into the living room.

Seeing and hearing Mem cry made my tummy feel like it had a tight knot in it. I felt sorry for her. To show her I wasn't working too hard, I set about washing the dishes with a will. I didn't dare think about the feeling down deep of being glad that Grace Bradley cared about me and had stuck up for me.

MEM BUYS A BABY AND A HOUSE

[O]ne is born from the mother...so that the image of the woman is the image of the world. ~Joseph Campbell

One night, just weeks after I turned five, Mem sat in the living room, sewing a bonnet as the sun was setting. She stopped every few minutes and closed her eyes and groaned. I knew something was wrong. She wanted to finish sewing the bonnet, so she moved over to the window for more light. She said, "If I faint tonight, someone bring me a glass of water." I looked at the pail on the water stand, and then back at Mem and thought, Shouldn't someone bring Mem water right now, so she *doesn't* faint? I knew what fainting was because Joey had cut his finger when he was cutting carrots once, and he had fallen backward onto the floor. I didn't want that to happen to Mem.

Mem held her middle and said to Datt, as if in secret code, "I think it's time."

Datt immediately jumped to his feet and went quickly next door to the Sakuras. Mr. Sakura drove their red car in our lane, even though they lived right across their lane from our house. Mem leaned on Datt's arm to walk to the car. Every once in a while, she stopped and bent over. When she finally got in the car, Mr. Sakura drove Mem and Datt up Hale Road. Mrs. Sakura came to stay with us children. I wiped the dishes as Joey washed them, and he told me that he thought Mem was going to the hospital to buy a baby.

The next morning when I woke up, Aunt Katie was there. I sat at the corner of the couch and sucked my thumb on my left hand and fingered my navel with my right, which is what I did whenever I was afraid. Aunt Katie demanded in her bossy voice that I should take my thumb out of my mouth, *"Nem dei damma aus dei Maal."* I did. She ordered Lizzie to set the table. Lizzie did.

For the next several days, everyone in the household did what Aunt Katie told them to do. Even Datt obeyed the orders of his youngest sister.

I missed Mem so much. I wanted her to come home and make everything the way it used to be. When she finally did three days later, she brought home a baby, all wrapped in a blanket. Joey was right that she had gone to the hospital to buy a baby. I wondered why—she already had five children without this baby.

Mem sat down on the rocking chair and held the baby. Joey, Lizzie, and Sylvia crowded around to see him. I saw a hand waving out of the blanket, and I wondered if Mem could still take him back to the hospital. Mem looked up and said, "Lomie, do you want to see the new baby? His name is Simon."

I couldn't tell anyone what I was feeling. I stepped up to the rocking chair and cautiously peeked into the blanket. I noticed that the baby had what looked like two earlobes on one ear. I pointed and said, "What's that?"

Mem explained that the baby had extra skin on his ear. The doctor had tied a string around it. In a few days, it would fall off, Mem said. I looked in her face and wondered why she wasn't concerned. That's when I noticed how very tired Mem looked.

I said to Mem, "But we already have a baby."

"We'll need to start calling her Sadie," Mem explained. That is when I first realized that she and Datt called each of us "Baby" until the next one came along.

Pretty soon Mem went to bed and took the baby with her. I couldn't understand why she was home and yet Aunt Katie was still in charge.

Mem and Baby Simon were only at home for a few days when Baby had to go back to the hospital to have a blood transfusion. I now know that it was because of complications with the RH factor. There was a discussion about who would take Baby back to the hospital. Mem wanted to be with her baby, but in the end, Aunt Katie talked her into staying home. Mem went back to bed, and I heard her cry. As usual, the sound of her crying gave me that sinking feeling in my belly.

I said to Lizzie, "I think it's because of that thing on Baby's ear."

"No, that already fell off yesterday."

"You mean his *ear* fell off?"

"No, the thing on his ear! You know the part that had the little black thread around it?"

"Then why does he have to go back to the hospital?" I asked.

"He has the wrong kind of blood or something."

"The wrong kind of *blood*? What can they do about that?"

"They're going to take it out and put new blood in."

"They're going to take his *blood* out? That's worse than his ear falling off! How can they?"

"I don't know, Lomie. That's just what I heard."

That night I had a terrible nightmare. I dreamed that both of Baby Simon's ears had fallen off, and we were looking all over for them. We finally found them up on the hill under a peach tree in the Sakuras' orchard. And then I awoke.

Datt was still at the hospital with the baby. I needed comfort, but I was afraid that if I cried, Aunt Katie would hear me. I got out of bed and tiptoed to Mem's bed. I told her I'd had a bad dream, and she whispered that I could lie down with her, letting me know that I still mattered, even though her little baby was in the hospital. I felt safe there, in the warm bed with Mem. In this little cocoon, I felt like I had before Simon was born and everything went topsy-turvy.

When Datt came home the next morning, he placed Baby Simon in Mem's arms, and then he went to bed and slept for most of the day.

~

When bath night came, Mem sat up on the rocking chair, nursing Baby. Aunt Katie was getting ready to give us baths, banging around in her *schusslich*—clumsy—manner. She slammed the tub on the floor and the handles banged against the tub. I wished Mem would put Baby down and give us baths like usual on Saturday nights. Aunt Katie walked back and forth from the boiler to the tub with her hard, fast footsteps, pouring hot water into the tub. She wasn't anything like Mem. She wasn't as big and soft, she moved faster, and she talked in a voice that sounded angry all the time. She snapped, "Joey, you will need to go do the chores, so the girls can take a bath."

Then I had to take my clothes off and let Aunt Katie give me a bath. When she took me out of the water, she stood me on a crocheted rug to dry me off. Her movements were rough, as though she were scrubbing a cupboard. I had no choice but to let her finish. I so much wanted Mem to put Baby down and hold me in her soft lap, enveloped in a warm towel and her love.

When Aunt Katie started to undo my braids and comb out my hair, I tried not to cry out. When she began braiding it, she pulled my hair away from my eyebrows so tightly that it felt as though she was trying to raise them. When I finally stepped down from the high stool, I hoped Aunt Katie would never braid my hair again. And when she finally went home, I wished she would not return.

Susan Sakura from next door spent a lot of time the summer Simon was born "teaching school" in the barn across the yard from our house. My siblings and I were her students. She was ten years old, and I was five. There at the picnic table, with my bare feet dangling above the dirt floor, she taught me how to write my name, how to color pictures, and how to say my first words in English. I thought I was all ready for school.

I eagerly waited for the bus to arrive on my first morning of school with Joey and Lizzie and neighbors Susan and Brian from across the lane. Mrs. Sakura came out with her camera to take a picture of us. She lined us up near the mailbox, which was just out of sight of our kitchen window. She knew Mem couldn't say yes to taking the picture if she asked permission, so she took it while Mem wasn't looking. This was the secret agreement many Amish had with their English neighbors. If they asked permission to take photos, Amish parents were obligated to say no, but if the picture was taken without their permission, then they couldn't be blamed.

From left: Susan, Lizzie, Brian, Joey, me

When the bus arrived, Lizzie took my hand and helped me up the bus steps. I sat on one of the brown seats next to Lizzie, and we waved to Mem standing just inside the kitchen window, holding Baby Simon and waving back to us. Then, the bus took off up Hale Road with a roar. When I looked back and couldn't see Mem anymore, I felt like an arrow had pierced my chest. As the bus kept going, taking me farther and farther away from Mem, a lump formed in my throat. I tried to hold back my tears, but I couldn't. Lizzie told me there wasn't anything to be afraid of, but the tears wouldn't stop running down my cheeks.

Stepping inside the school was even scarier. Children moved in all directions. Lizzie took my hand and led me to a room, and said this was the kindergarten class. And then she was suddenly gone, while children I didn't know were moving all around me. I stood in the hallway outside the kindergarten classroom and felt all alone. I put my face in my elbow and cried. A woman came and talked to me in English. I couldn't be sure of what she was saying, though I thought she was telling me to come into the room with desks and sit down. I just kept on crying. Then Lizzie was there saying, *"Du muscht annah hukka."* I shook my head, indicating I didn't want to sit down, and I said, *"Ich vill de Mem."* I longed to be with her in the familiar kitchen, making bread, with Sylvia and Sadie playing together on the floor.

Lizzie and the teacher, Mrs. Maloney, kept urging me, and finally I went into the classroom and sat at the desk with my name taped on the top left side. I put my head down in my arms on the desk and kept on crying. Then I heard someone next to me say, "Hi."

When I stopped crying, the voice said, "What's your name?"

I lifted my head and looked at a girl standing by my desk. I wiped my tears with my hands and whispered, "Saloma."

"Mine's Linda," she said. She smiled at me. Through my tears I saw that she had dark hair and brown eyes, like me. Except she wore a blue print dress and a ribbon in her hair that hung down her back. I could never wear such fancy clothes.

Just then the bell rang and all the children sat down at their desks. I thought I had learned English from Susan Sakura, but I couldn't understand what the teacher was saying as she passed out papers. Everyone else opened their desks and took out a box of crayons. I opened my desk and found a brand new box of crayons. I took them out and colored a picture of a little girl picking flowers.

I followed the example of the other children for the rest of the morning. During recess, I played on the swings with my new friend, Linda. I loved the feeling of the wind rushing past my ears and the butterflies in my tummy.

When the children in my class started lining up to get on the bus to go home, I wondered how the bus driver would know where my home was, and I wondered what would happen if she dropped me off at the wrong house. When I saw her driving down the dirt road toward our home, I knew it was going to be okay.

I'm sure I must have burst in the door, breathless with excitement, talking a blue streak. But I didn't say a word about having cried. Only when Lizzie came home later that afternoon did Mem find out. I promised her that I wouldn't cry again.

The next morning at school, I did cry as I stood in that busy hallway outside the kindergarten room. Mem seemed so far away. Lizzie came and told me that I had to sit down. I tried following her, but she said, "You can't come with me, that is the first-grade room!" She disappeared into the crowd of children. Mrs. Maloney caught up to me and gently led me to my desk. She told me, in her kindly manner, to sit down. The third morning when I started to cry, the teacher just led me to my desk and asked me to sit down. By then I was getting more used to school, and I was learning English quickly.

~

My kindergarten class. I'm in the front row to the right. My friend Linda is standing behind the sign in the dark dress.

Kindergarten was not yet mandatory in public school, so it was a choice Mem made to enroll me that year. At the time there wasn't an Amish school in our area. Children from other Amish families also attended public school, though some parents waited until their children were six years old and then sent them to first grade.

Some of the other grades in my school had more than one Amish child in their classes, but I was the only Amish one in my class, so it was English immersion for me. I think now that my kindergarten experience of going into a class with no other Amish children and having to learn a whole new culture helped prepare me for leaving the Amish fifteen years later. I am so grateful for that now. Had I ever told Mem that this experience had prepared me to leave home, she would likely have regretted sending me to kindergarten.

Somehow my parents managed to live in a four-room house with all five of us children until the summer Simon was born. One night at the supper table, Mem brought up the idea of buying an old house from up the road and adding it onto our own. Datt resisted at first, but Mem was determined. She persuaded her father to manage the project.

Not long after that, I was coming home on the kindergarten bus when I thought my eyes were tricking me. There in front of the bus was a flatbed truck with a house on it. Several other kindergarteners got up from their seats and pointed, saying, "Look!"

I saw something moving on the peak of the roof. At first I thought it was the chimney moving, but then I realized Datt was sitting up there. I'm sure my mouth was open in a big O, just like what I saw on the other children. As the bus driver slowed down, I realized she couldn't turn the bus around in the usual way because the truck had stopped in the Sakuras' lane. I got up out of my seat and walked up next to the bus driver and said, "You can turn down there and back up into our lane to turn around!"

She said, "Yes, I can do that," with a chuckle in her voice. It was the same chuckle I'd heard in the voice of other grownups when they seemed amused by what I'd said.

As soon as the bus stopped, I hopped out and ran toward the house with questions bubbling out of me.

"Mem, why is Datt on top of the house?"

"To move the telephone wires out of the way of the chimney."

"But what about him getting shocked?"

"Telephone wires don't shock people, only electric wires do."

I watched the truck backing up toward the house. *Dodde* (Grandpa) directed the driver of the truck. The driver had to make several attempts before he finally got the house lined up the way *Dodde* wanted it.

Then began the long process of unloading the house from the back of the truck. They jacked up the house and pulled the truck out from under it. Now it was ready for the basement to be dug out.

Then came Datt's hard work. He didn't want to spend money on hiring a backhoe to dig out the cellar hole, so he dug it out by hand, one wheelbarrow-full at a time. I still wonder why he left his rocking chair to do this hard work, even though his inertia often required that Mem or Joey do the daily farm chores.

We lived in the right-hand part of this house until the the part with the tall chimney was added on

After Datt dug out the cellar hole, we had a "frolic," or work party, to put up the cellar walls. Uncles and aunts and cousins gathered at our home on that beautiful autumn day. The men set about constructing the cement block walls with *Dodde* in charge, while the women made *middog*, the midday meal. They set up tables out in the yard under the trees, with rows of benches nearby.

When the meal was nearly ready, several of the aunts brought tubs of hot water out and set them on a bench. They added cold water from the hand pump out by the barn and laid out hand towels and bars of soap.

The men lined up and took their turns washing up. The uncles joked with one another about who was (or wasn't) working hard and they jabbed at each other jokingly.

Everyone gathered around for *hendt nunna*, the silent prayer before meals. I was surprised when *Dodde* asked everyone to be silent before we bowed our heads. Normally the father of the family hosting a gathering did that. Datt didn't seem to take charge of anything, but *Dodde* had no problem stepping in to take his place.

The men and young boys went first. They filled their plates with fried chicken, steaming mashed potatoes and gravy, peas, applesauce, baked beans and bacon, homemade bread and butter, and numerous side dishes that the aunts had brought. The desserts would come later.

After the men had filled their plates, mothers filled plates for their little children, and then the women and girls filled their plates.

After *middog*, the men went back to work on the cellar walls, and the women cleaned up after the meal and washed the dishes.

At the end of the day, the cellar walls were done. *Dodde* stood back and surveyed the work as he slowly chewed his tobacco. It must have been a satisfying feeling to work with others to build those walls, all in a day.

A few days later, *Dodde* oversaw the pouring of the concrete floor in the basement.

Next began Mem's hard work. She repaired the plaster and lath walls on the first and second floors, papered them, and painted the woodwork and the floors. Before winter set in, we moved in and had twice the space we'd had before.

I soon learned that even though we had new spaces in our house, it didn't change anything that happened in our house. Datt still sat on his rocking chair and talked to people only he could see. Mem still worked as hard as ever. And I didn't feel any safer in our bigger house than I had in our small cramped one.

~

Mem carried the responsibilities of two parents, and consequently she relied on us children to help around the house and farm. Joey took on a lot of responsibilities, including many jobs that boys didn't traditionally do. On washdays, he and I put the clothes through the wringer, rinsed them, and sent them through the wringer again, letting them fall into a clothes basket for Mem to hang outside. He and I also folded the clothes Mem brought in from the line and put them away. Together, Joey and I tackled just about any job Mem assigned to us. We were a pair of busy bees.

Most of the time Mem and Joey got along well. I don't remember whether she ever punished him, but I remember in vivid detail the whipping he got when he was eight. She'd given him the job of carrying water to the cow, and he kept saying he had done it when he hadn't. When Mem went to milk the cow, she discovered that Bessy was dehydrated. She said Joey deserved a whipping, but she didn't do it herself. She asked Datt to. Datt took the whip off the top of the china cabinet and whipped Joey once or twice. Joey had learned by then that if he cried right away, Datt would stop whipping. And that is what happened. But Mem said, "That's not enough!" Then Datt used two hands and whipped Joey hard until Mem told him to stop. As I stood by helplessly, I felt sorry for Joey.

There were other times when I didn't feel sorry for Joey at all because he could be mean.

One day that autumn, Joey and Brian Sakura had built a bonfire out in the yard between our houses to roast hotdogs and marshmallows. Joey said it was a "boy's club" and shooed my sisters and me away.

A little while later, I was playing in the yard on the other side of the house when Joey called me over. He and Brian were each sitting on a log next to where their bonfire had been, now a pile of gray ashes. Joey pointed into the ashes and said, "Lomie, will you pick up that toy tractor?" I could see the shape of one of his old toys, but there were no tires left, and instead of red, the metal was as gray as the ashes around it.

"No, it's too hot," I said.

"It's not hot. Look, there is no fire left."

I folded my arms and said, "So if it's not hot, why don't you pick it up yourself?"

"Because if you do it, I'll give you a toasted marshmallow," Joey said in his smoothest voice, holding up a bag of marshmallows.

I didn't trust Joey because he had tricked me before. I looked at Brian, sitting on a log. I couldn't tell what he was thinking, but I didn't think he'd allow me to burn my fingers. I could already taste the marshmallow and feel it melting in my mouth. I bent over, and with one finger and thumb, reached for the tractor. Just as they closed over the metal wheel, Brian said, "Don't touch it!"

He was too late. I heard a sizzle as I felt the searing, burning pain. When I dropped the tractor and looked at my finger and thumb, I wondered how it could be that they weren't on fire. I screamed and cried out and ran for the house. Big, white blisters had formed on my thumb and finger by the time I got there.

Mem put my hand in cold water, as I screamed and cried. Brian brought ice cubes from their freezer in a plastic bag. The ice soothed the pain and my sobs soon turned into hiccups and sniffles. Mem made Joey apologize. He sounded like he was sorry, but I didn't know if I believed him, especially not when I found out that he had made a bet with Brian that he could convince me to pick up the tractor. I couldn't understand why Joey could sometimes be a nice big brother, and other times he could be so mean.

DO-BEES AND DON'T-BEES

[T]oxic parents compare one sibling unfavorably with another to make the target child feel that he's not doing enough to gain parental affection.
~Susan Forward

Mem's relationship with Lizzie was a difficult one. It seemed Lizzie had given up trying to please Mem, and yet she needed her approval and love desperately. It was a vicious cycle. Lizzie acted out when she didn't want to do the chores Mem assigned to her. Mem punished. Lizzie acted out some more. Mem punished some more. The punishments were not always whippings, likely because Lizzie fought back. I remember one time Mem asked Datt to "help" her. Lizzie screamed out like a frightened animal as Mem held onto her and Datt whipped her. I was scared and I felt sorry for Lizzie, but at the same time I believed it was her fault that she was getting punished. I thought that if only she wasn't so stubborn, this wouldn't be happening. I vowed to obey so it wouldn't happen to me.

One night, Mem made Lizzie go to her room and stay there while we ate supper. I don't remember if Lizzie was allowed to eat supper that night or if she had to go to bed hungry. I also don't remember why she was being punished. Lizzie used her nightstand to thump the floor in her room, right above our heads. Things became eerily quiet around the table. I looked at Mem, but she was looking into her plate of food and chewing slowly. I wondered what would happen next.

I knew Mem was at her wits' end. She didn't know how to make Lizzie obey her. She assigned the drudge work to Lizzie, such as washing dishes, cleaning the house, and carrying water and wood. She tried shaming Lizzie into doing the work by telling her she was "just like Datt." That, I learned, was the worst insult in our family.

Mem treated me like the eldest daughter even though Lizzie was older than me. When Mem wanted us to learn something new, such as ironing or baking, or if she wanted to ensure that it was done according to her standards, she relied on me. I played out the part of the smart daughter, showing off that I could do more than Lizzie. This caused tensions between Lizzie and me.

Sometimes I didn't want to do all the work Mem assigned to me. I would stomp my foot and pout. At first when I tried to resist all the responsibilities, Mem used shame to get me to conform, which often worked. She laughed at me and said that my lip was sticking out so far a birdie could sit on it. Eventually, she just called it a "birdie-lip."

The only way to please Mem was to follow her every command. If I was in the middle of carrying out one task for her and she wanted me to bring her a glass of water, I had to stop what I was doing, get her water, and then resume what I was doing before. Sometimes I put up resistance, but I soon learned not to do that.

I was four or five years old when Mem began spanking me. These punishments left me bewildered and confused. Most of the time, she was my nurturing and loving mem. I wanted her to protect me from harm, and yet there were times when she was the one harming me.

One night Mem told me to clear the table as she gathered together the plates from supper. I stomped away from her, saying, "But it's not my *turn!*" Before I knew what was happening, Mem grabbed me by my arm, whirled me around, bent me over her knee, and spanked me hard. Then she set me back on my feet and said, "*NA dusht do fleicht da dish op roma!*—NOW maybe you'll clear the table!"

I was so shocked, I could not catch my breath. I cried and sobbed. I saw black for a moment, and I thought I was going to fall over. I grabbed onto the chair next to me. I didn't understand why Mem had hurt me. How could she be the same mem who had taken such good care of me before?

My memory leaves me standing in the kitchen, sobbing. Did Mem just leave me there and walk into the living room? Did I eventually recover and clear the table, or did Lizzie feel sorry for me and clear it for me? I cannot recall.

This may have been the first time Mem spanked me, but it certainly wasn't the last. As soon as she'd grab my arm with such determination, I'd tense up because I knew what was coming. At least I thought I did. Then one day she added another indignity. After she put me over her lap, she pulled up my dress, pulled down my panties, and spanked my bare bottom. I was five years old.

By this time, I had learned that Sylvia was Mem's favorite daughter. It seemed like Sylvia's personality was okay in Mem's eyes, but mine was not. Sylvia was quiet and shy, and I was outgoing. Sylvia was a compliant follower, while I wanted to be a leader. I sometimes tried being quiet and shy like Sylvia by copying what she was doing so Mem would look at me too. But it seemed no matter what I did, I could not get Mem's attention. Within minutes, I would forget trying to be like Sylvia and turn into myself again.

I wonder if Mem saw in Sylvia the attributes she wished she had—docility, conformity, and a desire to please people—while she saw in me an outgoing, rebellious, and determined child? She didn't seem to accept these attributes in herself or in me. Perhaps she had suffered the consequences of trying to be herself. If so, she may have been trying to spare me the heartaches that she had endured. I hope this was her reason. A more disturbing possibility is that she was determined not to permit me to prevail since she herself had not.

One day, Mem decided my sisters and I were not helping her willingly, so she implemented an idea she'd read about in a magazine. She created a "Do-Bee" and "Don't-Bee" chart. Every night she marked the chart for each of us girls. I could be really good for almost a whole day, then make one complaint, and all the good things didn't count because she'd walk up to the chart and write under my name, "Don't-Bee a complainer." Sylvia would get "Do-Bee a Helper." That seemed to be the way of things: Sylvia the good helper, Lomie the bad complainer.

At the end of the week, whoever got the most Do-Bees got a nickel. Sylvia almost invariably got the nickel.

One night, Mem was washing dishes, and Sylvia and I were drying. The gas lantern hissed softly on a hook above our heads. I was determined to keep the "Do-Bee" status I had maintained so far that week. I was ahead of Sylvia for the first time. We were running out of counter space and Sylvia and I were trying to get each other to put the dishes away. Mem looked over and said, "Sylvia, if you do it, I will change your Don't-Bee from yesterday to a Do-Bee." Right away Sylvia started putting the dishes away. I asked, "If I do it, will you change my last Don't-Bee?"

"No, the offer is for Sylvia," Mem said in her definite voice.

I felt so angry that I couldn't hold it in. I slammed a stainless steel bowl onto the counter and said, "That's not *fair!*"

Mem just said in her solid voice, "That's the way it is."

I had never before felt such pressure in my chest. The rage was so strong, I thought I was going to explode. I stomped my feet and said loudly, "But it doesn't even have to do with who is the best helper! You just like Sylvia more than me, no matter *what* I do! I don't care if I get all Don't-Bees from now on!"

I may have said more, but I noticed Mem was wiping her sudsy hands. Then she headed for the china cabinet with determined footsteps. When she didn't threaten and walked as though she meant it, there was no use begging. She grabbed the whip down off the top of the china cabinet and said in that voice that I didn't dare to disobey, "Lomie, come *here!*"

I don't know why I bothered to beg, "Mem, I'm sorry, I didn't mean that, I take it back, please, I won't say anything more..."

Mem had that hard, angry look on her face that she got when Lizzie disobeyed her. I imagined myself running out the door. I knew she could not catch me if I did, but she could send Joey after me. Then my whipping would be worse, so I had no choice. I walked toward her.

Mem grabbed me by the arm and whirled me around, lifted my dress, and snapped that whip across my legs, bringing the stinging pain down on the backs of my thighs. The whip whistled as she brought it down, over and over, until I thought for sure I wouldn't be able to stand the searing pain. I screamed and danced, wondering what would happen when it hurt so much I wouldn't be able to bear it. I thought Mem would never stop. When she finally did, she gave me a push and said, "NOW let's see if you talk back to *me* again!" as she put the whip back up on the china cabinet. I couldn't stand to look at her mean, hard eyes. And then as if the whipping wasn't enough, she said, "Do you think I *like* whipping you? It hurts me as much as it hurts *you!*" I knew this could not be true. It was *her* choice to take the whip off the china cabinet and use it to inflict that pain on me. I ran upstairs, shivering, and lay on my bed. I cried until the quilt under me was wet. I vowed I would never talk back to Mem again because I never wanted to feel that horrible pain again. I felt the welts on the backs of my legs. They stayed hidden under my dress for days, until they gradually turned color, then faded away.

When Mem said that she hurt as much as I did when she whipped me, she made me feel crazy—I thought I was the one who was hurt, and now I felt guilty besides. I thought the whipping was my fault.

After that I did what I was told, but that chart made no difference to me. I paid no more attention to whether Mem wrote Do-Bee or Don't-Bee under my name anymore. She used it a few more days after that, and then she stopped. This was the only time in my young childhood that I remember preserving at least a little of my dignity in a battle of wills with Mem. I was six years old.

One dark night, not long after the Do-Bee chart, my sisters and I sat at the table, eating bread and milk. The oil lamp cast a faint yellow light around the kitchen, and rain drummed on the windowsill outside. The pungent, oily smell of the lamp lingered in the room. Mem was preparing us for bed, and Datt was snoring on his rocking chair in the living room. Joey was upstairs in his room. The floorboards above us creaked as Mem carried Baby Simon to bed. Even though it seemed like a normal night, something wasn't right. I could feel it.

Mem came down the stairs and through the dark living room. When she stepped into the kitchen doorway, she held our sleeping caps in her hand. My eyes were drawn to her hands and I saw her squeeze the caps in her hand as she gasped and cried out. My sisters and I watched helplessly as Mem reached up with both arms as if she were grasping for air. Then she dropped face down onto the floor in the kitchen doorway with a loud THUD. The silence that followed was louder than her fall. We were too shocked to move.

Joey broke the silence as he came bounding down the stairs. Datt awoke, scrambled toward Mem, and kneeled beside her. He called her name and tried rousing her, but she was limp and did not respond. Datt looked up and said to Joey, "Go to the Sakuras and tell them to call an ambulance!" Joey went running out the door and across the yard in the dark rain in his bare feet.

Datt half-carried, half-dragged Mem to the couch. He looked at us and said, "Girls, go to bed!" We fled up the stairs to our beds. I lay on my back, breathing hard, too scared to move or say anything.

When Joey came back from the Sakuras, he came upstairs, stood at his window, and stared outside. We heard strange voices and banging noises downstairs. I wondered what was happening. Then Joey cried out, "I think Mem is dying! They are taking her in a stretcher to the ambulance!" He ran through our room, Mem and Datt's room, and down the stairs.

Until that moment, I didn't have a concept of death. But now it struck me like a whip, and the terror of it caught my breath. I was too frightened to cry. My sisters and I crept to the window as the ambulance drove slowly out our lane, carrying our mother away. I heard the sound of the gravel crunching under the tires of the white station wagon with the red cross on the back. I wondered whether Mem would ever come back.

I stood by the window, frozen with fear. My memory leaves me there. It returns the next morning when I awoke to the sound of Aunt Katie and Grandmother downstairs making breakfast.

When Datt came home later that morning, he looked more tired than I'd ever seen him. He hung his hat on the peg inside the stairway. I came up behind him and asked, "When is Mem coming home with the baby?" I was going by what Joey had said the night Baby Simon was born. Datt walked by me and didn't answer. The sad look in his eyes silenced me. I wondered if Mem was going to come home at all.

Mem did come home several days later, but she did not bring a baby with her. She walked slowly in the door, like every step pained her, and sat down in the rocking chair. I thought maybe Mem had really been sick instead of going to the hospital to buy a baby.

A few days later, Mem stood in the living room, holding a clear pump with a red ball over her breast. She squeezed the ball and milk flowed into the pump. Tears fell quietly down her cheeks. I touched her arm and asked her what was wrong. She looked out toward the horizon at the far end of the field on the other side of the road and shook her head. I wanted so much to make it better, but all I could do was watch her cry.

The mystery of what had happened to Mem was not solved for me until years later when I was fourteen years old. My Aunt Lizzie and my cousins Marie and Maddie had come to visit, and we went to the graveyard on the hillside by Uncle Ervin's farm. I learned Aunt Lizzie had given birth to four stillborn children. They were all lined up in a row, their little gravestones simply saying, "Stillborn daughter (or son) of Albert and Lizzie Kuhns," along with the dates. I found that sad.

Mem walked over to the row of pine trees that was the border between the graveyard and Uncle Ervin's farm. There she knelt by a little gravestone. I walked over and read what it said: "Stillborn Son of Simon S. Miller." I said to Mem, "I didn't know we had one."

"Sure you did," she said. She stood up. "You remember when we had a baby that died, don't you?"

"You mean the time you fainted and went to the hospital and then you didn't come home with a baby?"

"Yes."

"Why didn't you tell us?"

"Grandma didn't think I should."

I stared with incomprehension at the little grave. "But, Mem, why does this gravestone only have Datt's name and not yours?"

"Datt made a mistake. But don't say anything about that."

Mem walked away to talk to Aunt Lizzie. I stood there staring at the little gravestone. So there really was a baby, I thought. Why didn't Mem tell us, even if Grandmother didn't want her to? It would have been so much better to know than to have wondered at such a young age what was happening. And why does she now think I knew? I looked at Mem and Aunt Lizzie talking in the middle of the graveyard, and wished I could understand my own mem.

LONGING FOR A WIDER WORLD

Children learn from what their parents are actually willing to do; not from what they say they do. ~John Bradshaw

When I entered first grade, I was still the only Amish child in my class. There were times when I had to stay on the sidelines. During exercises in the gym, there were certain things I couldn't do because I wasn't allowed to wear gym clothes. I could not go to birthday parties, even when I was invited. And hardest of all was seeing the pretty dresses the other girls in my class wore, while I had to wear a long, plain dress, black shoes and stockings, and a hair covering—*kopp*—over my braided hair every day.

The teacher was the age of my grandmothers. She divided the class into three reading groups—A, B, and C. It was clear that the A group was the "best" one. I was in the B group, and I strived to read well so that I could earn my way into the A group. But then I noticed partway through the year that no child had been moved. I wondered how Mrs. Molzen had known who belonged in which group on the first day of school.

As Christmas approached, I wanted to be included in the play that my class was preparing for. I practiced for the part of one of four children who were "all snug in their beds." We held a blanket up to our chins, closed our eyes, and took "sleeping breaths," as the narrator recited, "The children were nestled all snug in their beds... while visions of sugar plums danced in their heads...." The hardest part was keeping my eyes closed when there were so many people to look at.

I was thrilled to be part of the play, but there was one problem. I wasn't sure I would be allowed to go to it. Whenever I asked Mem, she'd say, "We'll see." I explained to her that the people who were planning the play wanted to know. She still did not give me an answer.

First-grade class photo. I'm sitting to the left of the sign, on the bench.

A huge Christmas tree was put up in the gym. Maybe it was because we couldn't have one at home that I loved it so much. I would stand under that Christmas tree and look up at the lights and the colorful decorations with such awe.

When the Sakuras across the lane put up their tree, I stood inside our dining room window and looked across the yard at the lights sparkling inside their window. I asked Mem, "Why can't *we* have a Christmas tree?"

"Because the Amish don't allow them," Mem said with a sigh.

"Why not?" I persisted.

"It's just the way it is."

I hated when Mem said that. She'd been saying that for as long as I could remember. It was not an answer at all. And yet there was nothing left to say after that because it sounded like there was nothing I could do to change it, so I had to accept it.

The night of the play came, and Mem still was not sure we'd go, but she said that I should be helpful, "and then we'll see." The Sakuras had offered to take us, so getting there was not a problem. I chipped in and helped make supper, set the table, and filled the water glasses. I also helped carry wood for the stove in the living room. We had our family supper as usual. In eager anticipation, I helped do the dishes, and then I ran upstairs to my room and put on my best dress—a light blue one. I called down to Mem, "We're going, aren't we?"

There was a long silence. Mem said, "I don't think so. Datt doesn't think we should."

I felt such a wave of anger rising up inside me. Here Mem had been building up my hopes by getting me to think it had to do with how well I helped with the chores. I had done them all willingly, anticipating that I could go. Now she was saying Datt didn't think we should, which had nothing to do with the chores I'd done.

I begged. "Please, Mem! The teachers are expecting me to play my part! And I'm already dressed and ready to go... can I *please* go?"

"No, I think we better not..."

"Can I go with the Sakuras without you then?" My voice was rising with the realization that Mem wasn't going to let me go.

"No, you should just stay home with us," Mem said with a sigh.

As my eager anticipation dissolved into bitter disappointment, I threw a fit, stomping my feet and screaming and roaring out my rage at the injustice of it all. I yelled, "But you *said...*!" I was gearing up for a full-fledged temper tantrum, but Mem said in that solid voice of hers, "Lomie, if you know what's good for you...!" I could hear the threat of a whipping.

My rage was so big I thought I could not keep it inside me. But then I remembered the whipping Mem gave me over the Do-Bee chart, and knew I did not want that. I dropped onto my bed and cried my angry tears into my pillow.

When my tears and anger were spent, I lay there in silence. Somehow I knew that if Mem had wanted to go, she would have made it happen, and even if she hadn't wanted to go, she could have let me go with the neighbors. Instead, she had tricked me by getting me to do everything she asked without complaint and then said *Datt* didn't think we should go. By using that as an excuse, she didn't have to reveal that she had no intention of going, or of allowing me to go. I realized that Mem was using Datt to say no, and it was just as bad as telling an outright lie.

The night I wasn't allowed to go to the school play, I learned something about how decisions in my family were made, and it wasn't all on Datt.

My longing to be a part of a wider world beyond my home had nowhere to go.

In May, when the dandelions were blooming in the field next to the school playground, a new baby sister arrived at our house. She was like a live baby doll. Mem taught me how to support her neck when I held her. I rocked her to sleep and helped to give her a bath. I gathered together everything we needed—the baby towel, a clean diaper, clean clothes, lotion, shampoo, and powder—before Mem poured hot and cold water into the baby bath in the kitchen sink, stirred it around, and tested the temperature with her elbow. Then Mem took Baby's clothes off, and while she held her in the water, I shampooed her "hair" even though she had hardly any. Mem rinsed her head with warm water from a pitcher she had filled. I watched her dry Baby off and get her dressed. I loved holding Baby after her bath with her fresh, clean baby smell.

I reveled in the approval that I received from Mem and others for taking care of Baby. I heard things like, "Oh, she's so good with the baby. She'll make a good *mother* someday."

As Baby grew, I often carried her around on my hip. I sang nonsensical little chants about changing her diaper as I prepared to change her: "*Annah veetal oh du, Annah veetal oh du!*" I played games with her when she was awake, and as soon as she awoke from a nap, I was right there at her crib to pick her up.

I had my reasons for becoming a little mother to Baby Katherine. I liked that I could get out of some of the other work that had become drudgery, like doing endless dishes and sweeping the floor several times a day. And then one day, the Bascos rewarded me in a new way.

Joe Basco, our most frequent English visitor, used to walk right in both doors without knocking, as if he lived there. He visited as often as several times a week, most of the time by himself, sometimes with his wife, Bertha.

The Bascos brought us used children's shoes, boots, and toys. At the time, I didn't know that they had taken up a collection for the poor Amish family they knew—our family.

One winter day, when Katherine was six months old, the Bascos brought a big box of toys. I had her on my hip and was standing back, watching the others going through the box and pulling out "treasures." Sadie pulled out a Thumbelina doll baby. She loved beautiful dolls as much as I did, and she was already cradling the doll, when Joe Basco went over and took it right out of her arms. He said, "No, that is for Saloma for taking such good care of the baby." I couldn't believe it. I felt so good that someone had noticed. If I felt bad for Sadie, the feeling didn't last long. My indifference fueled the rocky relationship I already had with her.

I loved that doll. She had a soft body that felt like a real baby when I wrapped her up in a blanket. She had a knob on her back that I could wind up so her arms and legs moved. Her eyes closed when I laid her down. I named her Heidi. I enjoyed wrapping her in one of the baby blankets Katherine had outgrown. The doll felt so real that I could imagine what it would be like to hold my own babies someday.

One night we were sitting at the supper table when Baby was about a year old. We were talking, and she was playing in her highchair, next to Mem's right arm. Mem didn't see Baby stand up and hold on to the side of the highchair, but I saw her as she leaned over. I called out, "Mem, the baby!"

Mem's head jerked around, and just as she did, Baby began falling headfirst toward the floor. Mem's arm reached out and snatched Baby by her diaper. Mem's face became white and she was shaking all over, so I went over and picked up Baby.

After Mem caught her breath, she reached for Baby. She looked at me with such gratitude in her eyes and said, "Lomie, it is a *good* thing you said something!" I felt all warm inside. I realized how much Mem loved her children, especially when we were little. I wished I could hold on to that feeling of being as appreciated by Mem as I felt at that moment.

∾

The summer after first grade, Datt was looking for a paying job. Mem had been making ends meet with the money we made from selling eggs year round, and from the maple syrup we made in the spring. She also occasionally made suits for men in the community. But mostly it was Mem's ingenuity of making do with what she had that kept us fed and sheltered.

I don't know whether Datt had the motivation himself to go and look for work, or if Mem or his mother talked him into it. He had been forlorn for so long that it seemed no one could have gotten him motivated to get up off his rocking chair. Nevertheless, he left home and hitchhiked to wherever he was going for his job search every day. Sometimes he walked down the back road to the railroad track and hopped on a freight train and rode it down to Middlefield. One day he came home and said with a big grin that he had accepted a ride on a motorcycle. He may have wished later that he hadn't told anyone because people criticized him for it.

One Sunday afternoon, we were visiting Uncle Sam and his family. He was Datt's youngest brother and the son Grandmother favored most. His family was growing, and they were making plans to move to Wisconsin to a new, stricter Amish settlement.

I was in the living room with the grown-ups at Uncle Sam's house when the topic of Datt's motorcycle ride came up, and Uncle Sam looked at Datt and said, "I'd like to know how you think it's all right to ride on a motorcycle?"

Datt was rocking on a bent hickory rocker. He stopped rocking and looked at Uncle Sam without saying anything for a moment. Then he said, "Well, at least I'm not moving my family out of state." He crossed his feet, pushed off in his rocking chair, and rocked back and forth as

Uncle Sam listed all the reasons why he was making such a decision—concern for his children, better farmland, moving away from the bad influences among the young people in our community—and then he ended with a challenge: "And I want to know when you are going to do the same."

Datt stopped rocking and became silent. Uncle Sam looked at his oldest brother like he knew he'd shamed Datt. I wondered why. In most families the oldest in the family reigned supreme over his or her siblings. I could feel Datt's shame in his downturned face. It seemed like he wished he could crawl into a hole. I knew what that was like.

My cousin Sarah came and asked me to go outside to play with her. Leaving the living room was like leaving in the middle of a story that was still unfolding.

Back then it didn't occur to me to wonder whether Datt got into any trouble with the preachers of the church for his escapade on the motorcycle. As far as I know, there was no rule in the *Ordnung*—the set of church rules—against riding a motorcycle. However, it was unheard of for an Amish person to do so.

Datt looked for work for a long time. Then one afternoon when we were going about our housework, we heard him joyfully chanting at the top of his lungs, "*Ich happ en cho-op! Ich happ en cho-op!*—I have a jo-ob, I have a jo-ob!" We looked out, and he was hopping, skipping, jumping, and swinging his hands above his head as he chanted. It seemed like it took only ten leaps to get from the end of the lane to the front door. Mem looked out the window and said, "Well, what's gotten into *him?*" I could tell she wasn't angry because I saw she was trying to hold back a smile.

Datt had a toothless grin from ear to ear. I had never seen him so jubilant in all my life. He told us he would be working at an orchard. In the spring he would trim trees, and in the fall he would pick fruit.

That job was literally the best thing that ever happened in Datt's life—at least in the time I knew him. He had a way with trees that was uncanny, considering he had so many other deficits. For years he thrived there, working at the orchard through each spring and each fall. He still spent time on his rocker, sometimes with that forlorn look in his dark eyes, but snapping his eyes and whispering to someone not in the room tapered off and became a thing of the past. He was functional most of the time.

As Datt stopped talking to unseen people, he developed a different problem. He had fits of rage in which he would give a sound whipping to one of us, usually Joey. Sometimes Mem asked him to punish one of us, as she did when Joey had lied about bringing water to the cow. Other times Datt gave whippings on his own, as he did one summer day after we had attended church. As we were leaving the home where the church service was held, I could tell Datt was upset by the way he said, "Giddyap!" and slapped the horse's backside. As soon as we were out of hearing distance of others, Datt said, "Joey went swimming on a Sunday!" Mem asked Datt how he knew. Datt reached over and pulled Joey's hat off, revealing a wet rim around the ends of his bowl-cut hair. Mem didn't have much of a reaction, but she agreed that Joey deserved to be punished. Joey tried to defend himself by saying the other boys went swimming too. I had the sinking feeling this wasn't going to help him. And sure enough, as soon as Datt had unhitched and unharnessed the horse, he unleashed a whipping in the barn that had Joey howling in pain. From the house I could hear both the loud smacking sounds of the leather strap across Joey's backside and his terrified reaction to the whipping.

I could not understand why Datt was so upset about Joey swimming on a Sunday. We kept Sunday as our Sabbath, which meant swimming was one of the things forbidden on our day of rest, but there was probably more to it for Datt. The boys would not have had swimming trunks with them, so they must have shed their clothes. Public nakedness was considered immoral in the community. Whatever Datt's reason for the whipping, it seemed out of proportion to the perceived wrongdoing.

I knew Datt's moods mattered, so I watched him closely. I avoided him whenever I saw that dark look on his face, knowing his temper could erupt with little or no warning. I also knew Mem could not be counted on to protect us from Datt's whippings.

SMILING INTO MY FUTURE

We are all meant to shine, as children do. ~Marianne Williamson

*J*entered second grade with more than a little trepidation. I'd heard about the second-grade teacher, Mrs. Takacs. There were all kinds of rumors about her, including that she was really mean. Someone claimed she had stepped on a boy's leg on purpose because he had stuck it out in the aisle. Had I heard then of the mean and cruel teacher called Mrs. Trunchbull from Roald Dahl's book *Matilda*, I would have thought I was getting her for a teacher.

That would have been an apt comparison.

On the first day of school, Mrs. Takacs dictated the rules for her class as we sat at our desks. I don't remember all the rules, but we indeed had to keep our legs out of the aisle, or else she would step on them. I tucked my feet under my desk as I looked at Mrs. Takacs's enormous size. I didn't want her stepping on *my* legs.

Mrs. Takacs's list of what not to do was very long. She even told us we were not allowed to write in cursive. I loved writing in cursive, so I thought I would do it when she wasn't watching. But what happened next made me change my mind. When Mrs. Takacs was done with her list of what not to do, she said, "And for those who do not obey!" She got up from her desk, stomped over to the counter, grabbed the handle of a large paper cutter, and said, "I will stick their heads under here and..." WHOMP! She brought down the handle of that green paper cutter with one swift move of her gigantic arm. In my imagination, I saw a head rolling off the counter, its eyes bulging and tongue hanging out. I was too scared to move. I looked at the other children without moving my head. Tommy was sitting across from me. His mouth was in the shape of an O and his eyes were wide open. He looked as shocked as I felt. My breath came in gasps, and I had the urge to run from the room.

For the rest of the day, I kept looking at the paper cutter. When I got home that afternoon, I cried when I told Mem what Mrs. Takacs had done, and I said I was afraid to go back to school. Mem assured me that Mrs. Takacs would not actually do what she said. I wasn't so sure.

My fear of Mrs. Takacs didn't lessen during the time I was in second grade. I often had the urge to write in cursive, but I didn't dare. So I did it at home instead. I took letters Mem received in the mail and copied the writing in between the lines.

Then one day, I really had the urge to write my spelling words instead of printing them. My pencil seemed to have a life of its own as I wrote out the words. The next day, Mrs. Takacs said my name loudly and startled me. I looked up. She was holding up my spelling paper. "Is this *your* paper?" she demanded. I nodded.

"Come and get it," she said, "and no more *writing!* You know the rules in this class are to *print!* You can do your fancy writing *next* year!" I walked up to her desk and took my paper from her hand. Without looking at her face, I turned toward my desk and looked at the floor on my way back.

One morning at breakfast, the topic of school picture-taking came up. Mem said to us, "Now if they make you take the class picture, that's okay." I perked right up. It felt to me as though Mem had just given us permission.

Later that day, when it was time for our class to go down to the gym to have pictures taken, Mrs. Takacs said, "Saloma, since you are not allowed to have your picture taken, you can just stay in the classroom."

I didn't like the idea of staying in the classroom all by myself. I popped up out of my seat and said, "Oh, but my mother said I could take the class picture!"

Mrs. Takacs didn't pay any attention to me. She was busy getting the boys lined up to go to the gym. I stood in line with the girls and then walked down the hallway to the gym. Several people were directing one child at a time to sit up on a high stool to smile into the camera. A bright light shone through a white screen onto the person whose picture was being taken. My heart started beating fast when it was almost my turn. I wondered if I would get in trouble for doing this. I decided I didn't care because it was worth it to feel just like the other children for once.

When it was my turn, I climbed up onto the high stool and smiled into the lights and camera. I didn't even mind the bright flashes. As I climbed down from the stool, I wondered what Mem would say when she saw my picture.

Many years later, when my husband and I were in Ohio, we visited my little school and asked if they had photos from the years I was attending. They suggested I check my school records being stored in the town of Burton. That's where I found a little tiny photo of myself in the corner of my records. I asked to borrow it and had a professional photographer enlarge the photo and make several copies. It is the only solo childhood photo I have of myself.

One of the things that strikes me still is that I look happy in that photo. During much of my childhood, I felt scared or bewildered. Perhaps when I smiled into the camera, I knew at least on some level, that I was smiling into my future.

ANGELS IN SUMMER CLOUDS

When nature is your teacher, your soul will awaken.
~Johann Wolfgang von Goethe

When school ended in the middle of June, the dreamy summer days began. I loved lying in the grass on the north side of the house, near the garden, and staring up into the blue heavens. Sylvia and I were inseparable in those days. We'd lie there, pointing at white fluffy clouds and saying what they looked like. We'd see things like trees, birds, horses, or lamb's wool, hovering between heaven and earth. Sometimes I saw angels appearing in the clouds and I imagined they were looking down on us as I looked at them. I never pointed those out to Sylvia because it felt too private, and I didn't know how to put words to what I imagined and felt when I looked up into the clouds.

Our vegetable garden was huge. It was a place where we worked and played in the summer. We had to pull weeds, hoe, and water the plants, usually in the morning before the sun got too hot. When we were hungry between meals, we foraged among the tender vegetables. We picked pods of sweet peas, opened them, and popped the peas into our mouths. Green beans were best when they were still skinny and picked fresh from the plants. I'd eat them one after the other, all the way to the stem end. We pulled tiny carrots and washed them with water from the pump out by the barn. I loved munching on their crunchy sweetness. We gave the tops to the rabbits or the chickens. We found the first cucumbers hiding under the leaves of the plants and twisted them from their stems, brushed off the little specks at the end of the puckers on the skin, and ate them whole.

Sylvia and I often played barefoot in the meadow out behind the chicken house, where buttercups, daisies, asters, and black-eyed Susans grew. We walked along the path with our dresses sliding over the tall grass and flowers. Butterflies of all colors flitted about, flying from flower to flower. I often tried to catch one between my hands, but each time I came close, it darted away to land on a nearby flower, where it displayed its beauty by opening and closing its wings. Sometimes we picked flowers and brought them back to the house to put into a jar or glass of water. Sylvia was good at arranging them to look beautiful. If Mem was in a good mood, the flowers would put a smile on her face.

I also liked roaming the woods around our farmette. Sylvia and I had names for sections of the forest around us, such as Sugaring Woods, Spring Woods, Summer Woods and Autumn Woods. We wandered in all directions around our house where we picked flowers, sat and watched bunnies, chipmunks, and squirrels scampering over the forest floor, and listened to the birds singing in the trees.

During our forays into the woods, we often had to walk around large patches of bright green poison ivy. For as long as I could remember, I had known what poison ivy looked like. Mem told the story of how I had gotten poison ivy from head to toe when I was four years old. She said it looked like I'd rolled in it. I was miserable with the itching, so she put me up on the kitchen table several times a day and used warm Epsom salt water to bathe me. When I finally healed, she said she took me out into the woods and showed me the plant I should avoid. I learned the lesson well, though I don't have any memory of the itching, or of her warning me about poison ivy. Only the instinct to stay away from poison ivy remained with me for life.

$\sim$

Every summer we set up a playhouse in the woodshed. A big piece of wood over a log set on its end was our table, and other logs set on end were our chairs. We had an old cupboard with a few dishes and a place to lay down our dolls when they were "sleeping."

We added new things to our playhouse setup whenever we found items on the trash pile down near the golf course. One day we found an old black telephone that we brought into our playhouse. Of course it wasn't hooked up, but that didn't matter. I had many conversations on that dead phone. It didn't matter who was at the other end, but I had all kinds of conversations with her—silly, serious, profound, sad, and happy. She wasn't like my school friends. It was as if I was talking to myself, or someone like me, at the other end of the imaginary phone line.

My sisters and I played well together most of the time. But when Sylvia or Sadie wanted to hold my doll Heidi, we had spats. I soon learned, though, that if we didn't get along, Mem would put us to work, and the errands were never-ending:

"Go take the clothes off the line."

"Bring in a pail of water from the pump out by the barn."

"Go get potatoes from the cellar."

"Bring the potato peels downstairs and dump them into the bucket of pig slop."

"Go to the cellar and get a jar of pears."

"Go fill the lantern before dark."

The list went on and on. Mem was increasingly relying on me as her assistant housekeeper. Sylvia and Sadie would often sneak away to play. I could never get away with that. Likely it was because I wasn't sneaky enough and because Mem watched me more, considering that she relied on me as she did.

As late summer turned into autumn, my sisters and I took a shortcut through the woods, what we called "crosslots," to Forest Road. We'd take a peck basket along to gather hickory nuts from under the shagbark hickory trees. To get to what we called the Autumn Woods, we crossed Forest Road and continued walking west. There was a spring there, next to the tallest sugar maple tree around, which was where we found the brightest autumn leaves. We wanted to preserve their beauty, so we collected them, took them home, and ironed them between two sheets of waxed paper. We also tried melting paraffin and dipping them into the wax. No matter what we did, they were never as vivid as when we first collected them.

∼

When I was going into third grade, I'd been looking forward to having Mrs. Reed for my teacher because she had a reputation for being a good one. But for some reason, Mem and Datt decided Joe and I should go to the Amish school that was being built, and Lizzie and Sylvia would go to the public school. Because I was curious to find out what Amish school was like, I didn't resist this decision.

The new schoolhouse wasn't quite ready in early September, so Joe and I had to wait to go back to school until it was done. Mem made good use of my time as her helper during those weeks. I was itching to go to school, but there was nothing I could do except wait. The first day of school finally came on September 28.

The school was named Meadow Glow. Joe and I walked there and back every day with the Weaver children from up Hale Road. We walked to Olin and Clara Yoder's house, then crosslots through the woods to the school. Those autumn mornings were crisp and cool, with the morning sunlight shining through the colorful leaves on the trees. On our way home, the slanted afternoon light shone through the trees on both sides of the path. The earthy, sweet smell of hickory nuts filled the air.

Ida Yoder was my teacher. She taught first through fourth grades, and Urie Byler, the head teacher, taught fifth through eighth.

The parents and the teachers had decided that all pupils were required to speak English while in school. Most Amish first graders had not yet learned English, so this rule was created to help them learn the language. It was one thing to speak English in public school, but speaking English to other Amish in the community was never done, so I wasn't used to that and neither were the rest of the pupils. The teachers and older pupils reminded us many times before we finally got used to it.

I soon discovered the other third graders could write in cursive because they had been attending Burton School and their teacher had taught it to them. Even though I had learned how to write in cursive on my own, I'd forgotten some of the letters over the summer. When I couldn't remember, I poked Ruth, the girl in front of me, and asked her how to make particular letters. Ruth was not only patient, but she was also good at writing and happy to show me. It was the beginning of our friendship.

Meadow Glow School

I liked the upper-grade teacher, Urie Byler. I'd seen him at Aunt Ada's when we were there to visit at Christmas. My Aunt Ada was married to Urie Byler's son, so he was my cousins' other *Dodde*. Urie paid attention to each of his grandchildren individually. My *Dodde* had so many grandchildren that it must have been hard to know all of us, so I never got to know him very well. I also didn't like that he chewed tobacco and spit brown juice from his mouth when he was outside, or into his "spit box" filled with sawdust next to the rocking chair in his living room.

I thought my cousins were lucky to have two *Doddes*, and if I could have chosen a second one, it would have been Urie Byler. Datt's father had died long before I was born, and his stepfather had left this world as I was entering it.

I liked playing jacks with my friends, Ruth and Nancy. One day, the little red rubber ball hit a jack and rolled across the floor, so I ran after it. As I hurried past Urie's desk, he looked up and said, "Saloma, don't run." He said it in a kind voice, but my face burned with shame. He had never admonished me before.

One day Urie asked me to come to the back of the room during recess. He had a hand drill. He gave me instructions for holding the middle of the handle tight while he set about drilling a hole in the floor with the handle at the top, moving so fast it was hard to hold on. After drilling the hole, he dropped the rope from the fire bell through the floor to the basement. Then he got up and pulled open his desk drawer. He grabbed a handful of Tootsie Rolls and threw them on my lap and said, "Thank you." I really wished he was my grandfather.

On the bright and sunny morning of my ninth birthday, I awoke feeling excited about going to church. I knew people in church wouldn't sing "Happy Birthday" to me because things like that were not done. But I thought maybe if I told a few people, they would at least wish me a happy one.

The church service was held at the homestead of Al and Ada Miller. People gathered in their tool shed, which had been emptied and spread with clean straw. Long straight rows of church benches had been set up, with the men and boys facing the women and girls. I sat next to my sisters and Mem and entertained myself by making a chain out of straw. I had the urge to braid something. I tried to braid strands of straw, but they weren't long enough. I used my bare feet to sweep away the straw to make a bare spot under my feet until Mem looked at me and shook her head. I knew that meant I had to stop.

Church seemed extra long that day, but it finally ended. I ran through the yard and into the house. Ada's spotless house gleamed. A patch of sunlight from the porch window fell onto the hardwood floor and the woven rug in front of her kitchen sink. Women were bustling about, feeding milk soup to their babies. I walked up to one of them and said, "It's my birthday." She looked at me without saying a word, then turned away. I said it again to the woman next to her. She turned away, pretending she hadn't heard me.

I tried again, this time with my friend Ruth's mother who was pouring coffee. "How old are you?" she asked in a voice that sounded uninterested. "Nine," I said, but she had already turned to talk to someone else. Women turned their reproachful eyes on me. I wondered what was wrong with telling people it was my birthday. My face hot, I turned and fled back out to the shed. Olin Clara, who was slim and short with a sprightly spring to her step, was walking plates of bread, baloney, pickles, butter, and bowls of sweetened peanut butter to the long tables that had been set up. She was the person I'd shown my red boots to when I was four years old. When she saw me, she said, "Happy birthday! Aren't you turning nine today?" I nodded and picked up two plates of bread and followed her to the table. I looked at her white organdy cape with two neat pleats in the back and wondered why everyone wasn't as kind as Olin Clara.

A few days later, a birthday card came in the mail from Clara. She had made a bookmark with a drawing of morning glories on a vine around the border with "Happy Birthday, Saloma" in her beautiful handwriting. I was touched that she had made the bookmark for me. I hung it on the corner shelf in my bedroom with other "pretties" that I had gotten as gifts.

The following Sunday afternoon when I was popping corn, Mem asked, "Lomie, how would you like to go and help Olin Clara with her Saturday cleaning?" Mem had a soft expression in her light blue eyes. I was so surprised by what she had just said that I didn't know what to say.

Mem said, "Clara asked me today if I could spare you, and I said yes. She is particular so you would have to do a good job, but I think you can do it."

"Do you think so? Why didn't she ask one of the older girls?" I said, thinking of all the popular girls in the community she could have asked.

"I think she asked for you because she wanted you," Mem said.

I looked forward to Saturday. When it finally came, I started out on the mile-long walk. The shadows were still long, and the dew sparkled on the tips of the blades of grass, points of light under the morning sun. Red-winged blackbirds sang in the fields along the way.

My heart pounded with excitement as I walked up the last hill on the narrow strip of paved road to Olin Clara's house. Her garden on the hillside below the house had neat rows of vegetables coming up in different shades of green, bordered by flowers of all colors. Next to the garden was a bird feeder with chickadees, nuthatches, titmice, and goldfinches darting between it and nearby trees and bushes.

In front of Clara's house was the biggest maple tree I'd ever seen, with its gnarled branches reaching out like twisted arms, spreading their leaves over the yard. Four of us once tried holding hands around it, and we couldn't reach one another.

As I walked along the sidewalk leading to the kitchen door, a tabby cat walked up, rubbed against my leg, and meowed. It arched its back against my hand when I reached down to stroke it. I knocked on the door. The smell of freshly baked cookies and pies wafted through the screen door.

Clara's pleasant voice greeted me. "Come in, Salomie." She was the only person who called me that, combining my Amish name, Lomie, with my English one, Saloma. I decided I liked it.

I stepped into the kitchen. Clara pulled out a chair and said, "Have a seat. I'm sure you're tired after that long walk. Do you like butterscotch chip cookies? Can I get you something to drink? I have lemonade or milk."

"I came to do work. You don't need to feed me first thing," I protested.

Clara nodded and said, "Just sit down," as she patted the back of the chair. I did. And I wasn't sorry. The cookies were warm, sweet, and crumbly. I finished the glass of milk and got up to wash my glass and plate at the kitchen sink with the chrome faucet. It felt like magic for hot or cold water to pour out of the faucet just by turning one of the knobs rather than having to carry and heat water for dishes.

Though this was my first day at Olin Clara's house, it was not the last. I continued to go to her house weekly for several years. I learned her methods of baking pies and cookies. Through her, I also learned to appreciate Mem's bread. I thought every mem in the community could make good bread, but it turned out Mem was the best bread baker of them all. I didn't know that until one day when I brought one of her fresh loaves of bread to Clara. She praised Mem's bread so highly and in such a sincere way that I began to realize Mem's bread was a specialty. When I returned home, I told Mem how much Clara liked her bread. Her face turned pink and she said, "She is just saying so to make you feel good." I saw Mem trying to suppress a smile, so I knew she was pleased.

Olin Clara became like a second mother to me. Most of the time, Mem supported that, but there were times when there were conflicts, especially when I compared our life to hers. One day I asked Mem, "Why can Olin Clara have running water in her house, and we can't, and yet we are all Amish?"

Mem said, "It's not because we're Amish that we don't have running water in the house. It's because we can't afford it." This was my first realization that being poor limited our choices. While I was the only Amish child in public school, I thought it was because I was Amish that I brought my lunch to school while most of the other children bought a hot lunch. It had never occurred to me that the only obstacle to buying my lunch at school was the lack of money in my parents' wallets.

Olin Clara was the best thing that happened to me the summer I turned nine. It seemed the angels were smiling down on me from the heavens. Clara was a bright spot in my childhood, for which I will always be grateful. She may not have been able to keep bad things from happening to me, but like Urie Byler, she let me know she cared, and it made all the difference.

WHY I COULDN'T WRITE POETRY

Poetry is when an emotion has found its thought and the thought has found words. ~Robert Frost

For some reason, my parents decided to send all of us children to public school when I was entering fourth grade. I've learned as an adult that the Amish schools were controversial within our community when they were first being built. Urie Byler was at the forefront of that controversy, advocating for Amish schools because of the problems the parents were having with the public schools. There was a clash of cultures at one of the public schools in particular, where the Amish children were sometimes forced to go to the gym to watch movies, something that was forbidden by the Amish. The parents told their children not to go to the gym when movies were being shown. There were several instances in which the children resisted and were spanked by the school authorities.

I don't know where my parents stood on the Amish school issue. They may have kept us out of the controversy with a wait-and-see attitude and spared themselves from paying the private tuition at the same time. I liked school no matter which one I was attending. Looking back, I'm glad I went to public school that year, and I'm grateful for a teacher who noticed and encouraged my potential for reading, writing, and telling stories.

School was the only place where I could pursue the things I loved to do, which meant learning of all kinds. I especially loved to read and write, but I was careful not to bring home books that my parents wouldn't approve of, or any writing I did in class. These were the things my family didn't know about.

Our teacher, Mrs. Rusnak, was kind most of the time, but once in a while she walked through the aisles past students' desks and said things like, "You haven't learned a thing in arithmetic this year, and *you* haven't done a thing to improve your penmanship!" I cringed as she slammed their papers on their desks, waiting for my turn to find out what I was bad at. That turn never came because she never said anything to me in that tone.

I read many books that year that my parents wouldn't have approved of, Nancy Drew books among them. I made sure the ones I took home were the "safe" ones, such as the Laura Ingalls Wilder books. Mrs. Rusnak allowed me to visit the school library as often as I liked. This was the most freedom I'd ever had to read whatever I wanted.

That year at Christmas, I was given the first book I ever owned. It was a copy of *Heidi*. I treasured that book and read it so many times I knew exactly what would happen next.

My report card shows that I was absent from class thirty-two days during that school year. My siblings and I had both mumps and measles. As one of us started feeling better, another became ill. Mem was overwhelmed with the responsibility of taking care of us, and so she had me stay home to help her, especially on washdays when she didn't have anyone to watch the little ones while she was downstairs running the gas engine for the washing machine.

On my excuse slips from school, Mem would write "stayed home to help." Then the principal of the school challenged Mem for doing this. So she started writing "Ill" on the slips, whether I'd been sick or not. The first time I saw that I said, "But Mem, I wasn't..."

"Don't say anything about it," Mem interrupted. She turned away and started clearing the breakfast table.

One day Mrs. Rusnak told me I needed to go to the principal's office. Usually when pupils were called to the principal's office, it meant they were in trouble. I could not imagine what I'd done wrong. My heart started pounding hard and I could feel my face getting red with shame. Somehow my feet carried me down the quiet hallway to Mr. Franks' office.

I came around the corner and found his door ajar. He saw me and in a kindly voice asked me to take a seat. When I did, he said, "You're probably wondering why I asked you to come here."

I nodded my head as I looked at the books and papers piled high on Mr. Franks' desk. He said, "I want you to know that you didn't do anything wrong."

I tried to keep the tears at the corners of my eyes from spilling out. I waited. Mr. Franks said, "I just have one question for you. Were you sick yesterday?"

Then I realized that I had handed in the excuse slip signed by Mem that morning. So he knew Mem was not telling the truth. And now I was caught between her lie and Mr. Franks' search for the truth. I had earned whippings at home for not telling the truth. Now that Mem had lied, would she whip me for not lying to cover up for her? Deep down I knew that it was wrong to lie. And besides, I didn't like staying home from school. I often cried when I saw the bus going up Hale Road without me.

Mr. Franks waited from across his desk as I tried sorting out the mixed-up feelings roiling inside me. Tears spilled down my cheeks. He handed me a tissue and asked me again whether I had been sick.

I shook my head to indicate I had not. Mr. Franks said, "Okay, you can go back to your classroom now."

I wiped my tears away on the way back to class. I wondered if Mrs. Rusnak and the other children could tell I'd been crying. I decided to go to the bathroom to give myself more time before I had to face them. I still felt ashamed as I slipped back into the classroom and took my seat. I pulled a book out of my desk and opened it, though I couldn't concentrate on reading.

Mrs. Rusnak gave me a letter in a sealed envelope and asked that I give it to my mother. I did. That night I heard Mem talking to Datt in an upset tone of voice, saying she didn't know what to do since she often needed my help at home. Datt didn't have much to say, just "Yes, ah-huh," and agreed with Mem when she said she thought she would be better off sending us to the Amish school the following year since the Amish teachers understood that mothers sometimes needed extra help. I felt bad for Mem, yet I was glad that Mr. Franks and Mrs. Rusnak cared whether I was attending school instead of being a mother's helper.

~

My friend Linda and I are sitting behind the sign in the class picture.

In June, on the last day of school, Mrs. Rusnak asked to have a few minutes with me alone, which she had never done before. I wondered why. When all the other children had left, the classroom suddenly felt big. She came and sat on a desk in front of me and asked if I had ever thought about writing poetry. I said I hadn't. She said she thought it would be a good idea for me to think about. I couldn't tell Mrs. Rusnak that no Amish girls I knew wrote poetry. Mem depended on me to help with all the work that needed to be done. When I got home from school each day, I had to help fill the wood box, clean out the lunch boxes, bake the next day's lunch cookies or cake, fill the lanterns, help Mem make supper, and finally do dishes and sweep the kitchen. And now that school was out, I would have to work every weekday. I couldn't tell her that there was not even one private space in our home —not a room, not a closet, not a drawer, not anything. I also couldn't tell her that I had an older brother who would snoop and scoff at what I wrote.

I simply did not know what to say, so I sat there mute until Mrs. Rusnak said I should go catch my bus. My ears felt hot as my feet carried me quickly toward the bus and up the steps. I didn't know what to think as I looked out the bus window. I wondered why Mrs. Rusnak hadn't mentioned writing poetry to me months before, so she could have helped me get started. I knew there was no chance of writing poetry or anything else at home.

I think now that Mrs. Rusnak meant to plant a seed that would begin to grow at another time. Maybe she trusted that someday I would remember that someone had noticed that I was endowed with a gift and possibly begin to believe in it myself. I will always cherish Mrs. Rusnak's recognition of the bud that might bloom into a flower someday. I had not yet glimpsed a future in which I would believe I had talents, nor could I have imagined having the freedom to develop them.

One day that summer, Mem had plans to go to a quilting. As I carried out a bucket of pig slop and dumped it over the fence into the trough, I wondered who Mem would choose to go with her. I really wanted to go. It was about time for her to leave, so I hurried back to the house. Like my sisters, I had high hopes that she'd pick me. But I also knew she would only pick one of us.

This was a typical moment when Mem had plans to visit someone for the day. We all rallied around her and eagerly did whatever she asked, hoping to be the chosen one. Those who were not chosen inevitably felt intensely jealous of the one who was. She often chose me. I thought she was rewarding me for taking on so many responsibilities, but I never knew for sure how Mem decided which one of us she would take on any given day. It felt like she was picking her favorite daughter of the day.

When I got back to the house, we all gathered around Mem, waiting. She said, "Lomie, you've been working hard lately, so you can come with me today."

Sadie cried, and Lizzie said, "That's not fair, you *never* choose me!" Sylvia was quiet and compliant.

I knew how Lizzie and Sadie felt, but I didn't want to think about that now. I was looking forward to going to the quilting with Mem.

Datt harnessed up old Don, the horse we used for pulling our buggy and for harnessing up with our workhorse, Tops, to work around the farm. Datt pulled the buggy up to the door, and Mem and I climbed up into the front seat. Mem picked up the reins, slapped Don on his backside, and said "Giddyap!" Don started walking slowly out the lane and down the back road. Mem slapped the reins, urging Don into a slow trot. The flaps on my bonnet blew gently in the breeze and the steel-rimmed buggy wheels crunched on the gravel. I looked out over the fields at the green grass of early summer, dotted with wildflowers. The trees had their new green leaves. Mem pointed out a red-headed woodpecker hammering away at a hole in the top of an old beech tree.

After trotting along for a while, Don slowed to a walk again. Mem didn't seem to be in a hurry to get to the quilting, so Don took his time getting us there.

When we arrived, I found a group of girls who were my age. I assumed I was welcome to play with them, just like when a group of my first cousins gathered at my grandparents' home, so I followed along to play kickball in the side yard and go on cart and pony rides. Then I noticed something strange. It seemed whenever I'd look up from playing, the other girls were running off to the barn, or they were gone and I'd have to look for them. One of them picked up a scooter in the yard and said, "Lomie, look, can you do this?" She used one foot to scoot along. I said, "Yes," and she handed me the scooter. I had barely pushed off on the scooter when I heard a whole bunch of bare feet, pounding away toward the barn. I looked back, dropped the scooter, and caught up to them. We walked in front of a whole line of horses tied to the stalls, where our mothers had tied them after unhitching them from the buggies. Sarah and her cousin Lydia walked along saying, "That's your horse, that is Laura's horse," until they stood in front of Don. Sarah said, "Lomie, this is your family's horse."

"How did you know?" I asked.

"Because, it has such big feet," she scoffed. She and the other girls giggled into their hands. I stood staring at Don's feet, while the girls moved away and then disappeared out of sight.

I stopped following the girls then. I didn't understand why they didn't want to play with me. I wished we had a horse like everyone else. Then maybe they wouldn't exclude me.

On the way home, all I could do was watch Don's big hooves. Mem asked if the cat had my tongue.

"Why do we have a horse with such big hooves?" I blurted.

"What do you mean?" Mem asked, chuckling.

I repeated what the girls had said.

Mem explained that Don was an all-purpose horse, and that's why he had bigger hooves than a regular buggy horse.

"So did the other girls not let you play with them?" It was unusual for Mem to convey sympathy for my feelings. I decided to tell her what had happened.

"They kept running away from me. I didn't know why, and then they said that about Don's feet."

"They should not have run away from you," Mem said.

I started to cry. "Why can't we just be like everyone else and have a buggy horse?"

Mem laughed lightly. "I have a lot more to worry about than the size of Don's hooves."

We were both quiet for a moment. "Those girls were going to find something to mock—if not Don's feet, then something else. Girls can be mean to one another sometimes." As I rode alongside Mem in the buggy, it felt good that she understood me. I held on to the feeling and I wished it could always be that way between Mem and me.

∼

Most Amish children referred to their grandmothers by their last names: "Miller *Momme*" and "Yoder *Momme*" or the like. We couldn't do that because both our grandmothers were a "Miller *Momme*." But they could not have been more different from one another. "Mem's *Momme*" loved to have her children and their families come visit—the more the merrier. "Datt's *Momme*" was severe and believed every child's will needed to be broken, and that as soon as children were physically able, they should be willing to work to help the family. She was widowed, and like a dutiful daughter, my Aunt Katie lived with *Momme* and took care of her. The two of them would at times arrive at our house for a day visit. Whenever they did, they brought their very own darkness along with them. Their buggy was black, their clothes were dark, and their severe expressions and attitudes added to the blackness around them.

Mem knew that Grandmother and Aunt Katie didn't approve of store-bought dolls with faces, so whenever we saw them arriving, she would say, "Girls, go hide your dolls!"

One day, I hastily stuffed Heidi behind the couch as they were coming in the door. I forgot about my doll until after they left. When I went to retrieve her and she wasn't there, I asked all my sisters if they had seen her. They claimed they had not played with her. I looked everywhere —out in the playhouse, all through the house, and even in the basement. The doll was nowhere to be found.

The Bascos had given me the doll when I was seven years old, and I still loved to play with Heidi, even though I was now ten. She had a soft body, making her feel like a real baby, and her eyes would close when I laid her down. I missed her, and I wanted to find her. I thought about all the times I had resisted sharing Heidi with my sisters. Now, as I looked high and low for her, I decided I would share her more.

I asked Mem if she knew where my doll was. All she said was, "I told you to hide her when *Momme* and Aunt Katie came." And then she turned back to the stove where she was making supper. It seemed as if she didn't care. I wished she would talk to me the way she had on the way home from the quilting. But I was alone with my fear of what might have happened to Heidi. Finally, at bedtime, when I still hadn't found my doll, I had no choice but go to bed without knowing where she was.

The next day, I was out in the woods near the leaf pile we had played in the autumn before. And there, in a pile of ashes, was the top of Heidi's head. It was the only part that hadn't been burned. I was shocked. I imagined Grandmother finding Heidi behind the couch and slipping the doll under her apron on her way to the outhouse, taking matches with her, and lighting a fire to burn my doll. I hadn't believed that she would actually burn whatever dolls or toys she didn't believe children should have, yet here was the proof, lying in a pile of ashes before me.

Fear clenched my insides as I ran through the woods, not caring where I was going or whether I was running through poison ivy. I wanted to get as far away from what I'd seen as I could. When I was out of breath, I fell to my knees and sobbed and sobbed. I could not bear how afraid I was of my grandmother. I couldn't believe how cruel she was.

When the heaving sobs slowly subsided, I sat on the forest floor and stared off into the woods. Something had changed in me. The colors of summer had faded from my world.

JOE'S RABBITS

Come away, O human child!
To the waters and the wild
With a faery, hand in hand,
For the world's more full of weeping than you can understand.
~William Butler Yeats

I don't know why Mem decided she could do without our help that summer when she had relied on us as she had to ease her work burden. She and Datt decided to hire out my siblings and me to work for John Roberts, who owned a berry farm. Every summer he hired a group of young Amish children to pick berries. He drove his van out to our homes to pick us up. On our first day there, he instructed us how to pick strawberries. He wanted us to pick the berries clean, meaning all the ripe ones were to be picked, yet the ones with white tips were to be left to pick another day. We filled quart baskets and put them together in flats at the end of the rows, where they were picked up and taken to the sorting shed.

There were days when the sun was brutally hot, and there was no getting away from it except during our lunch break. Mr. Roberts usually assigned the berry-sorting to the boys, which meant we girls spent more time out in the hot sun. I thought they were the lucky ones.

I started noticing things I didn't know how to interpret. Mr. Roberts would have several of the boys at a time go upstairs into his living space. The implication was that they were helping him. I didn't wonder what they were helping him with, and I didn't think it was any of my business. But I noticed that sometimes when the boys came back downstairs their faces were flushed red.

Had Mr. Roberts asked girls to come upstairs to his apartment, I probably would have been suspicious. But I had no concept that boys were as vulnerable as girls in certain situations.

Years later, I learned that John Roberts had been molesting Amish boys for years. Some of his victims became fathers to sons they hired out to John Roberts a generation later. My brother Joe was among these fathers.

The summer we worked for John Roberts, something changed in Joey. He ordered us to call him Joe instead of Joey. Summers before, he and I often worked together when Mem gave us work to do, but she learned to separate us that summer. He was meaner than he'd ever been.

Then one day that summer, Joe went missing. He'd been pestering us sisters relentlessly, so Mem sent him out to chop up a pile of wood next to the lane. At age thirteen, Joe still obeyed Mem most of the time. I went about my work of sorting canned goods in the cellar until Mem called us for our midday meal. Joe didn't come. Mem looked out the window and found he was nowhere in sight. She went out and called him, first toward the barn, then louder toward the woods. There was still no answer.

Mem asked Datt if he'd seen Joe, and Datt said the last he'd seen him, he was chopping wood out by the lane.

We ate our meal in silence, with Mem looking out the window every few minutes as if she expected Joe to appear. After eating, Datt hitched up Don to the buggy and drove down Durkee Road to look for Joe. My sisters and I roamed the woods and called for Joe, and Mem sent Lizzie to the neighbors up the road to look for him, but there was no sign of him anywhere. He'd simply vanished.

At suppertime we still didn't have any idea where Joe was. By now, Mem was in tears. At bedtime we were out of ideas about where Joe had gone. Mem sent us to bed, but I couldn't sleep. I wondered if Joe had run away from home. He had previously threatened to when he and Datt had disagreed. He hadn't yet fought back when Datt tried punishing him, but the tension between them was often like a rubber band stretched too thin and ready to snap.

I was lying in my bed, thinking about what could have happened to Joe when I heard Datt running out of the living room, through the kitchen, and down the stairs. Mem was right behind him. Datt said reprovingly, "Joe, where have you been? You had Mem worried!"

Joe cried, "It wasn't my fault." I listened from my bed as he spilled out his story. He was chopping wood when two men in a pickup truck came along and asked him for directions to Forest Road. Joe gave them directions, but they asked him to come with them to show them the way. Joe said they needed to drive him back, and they said they would. But they kept going, right past Forest Road. Joe asked them where they were going, but they wouldn't tell him. They took him to a horse farm several miles away.

"I kept telling them my family would be worried about me, but they wouldn't listen," Joe said through his sobs. "They told me I had to do this first, and then when I finished that, they made me do something else after that."

"Who were these men?" Mem asked.

"Robley is the man's name who owns the horse farm, but I don't know the other man's name."

"Why didn't you come in and tell us you were leaving?"

"Because I thought I was only going up to the corner and back!" Joe sobbed.

"What did these men want, anyway?" Mem asked.

"They said they wanted to see if I would be a good worker on the horse farm. They did offer me a job."

"They did? Why didn't they come and ask us?" Datt asked.

"They said they wanted me to see the farm first to see if I wanted to work there."

"Would you want to work for them?" Mem asked.

"Not after what *they* did!"

"That's what I was thinking!" Mem said.

Several weeks later, a white pickup truck drove in the lane. A man walked to the door and took his hat off as he came into the house. With his hat in his hand, he acted like he was respectfully asking Mem and Datt if they would allow Joe to work at the Robley horse farm. I had to remind myself that this was Joe's kidnapper.

My parents said yes. I felt like there was something terribly wrong with hiring Joe out to his kidnappers, even if the man acted all meek and mild in front of us. I kept thinking that Mem would "wake up" and decide not to let Joe work at the farm. But no help came for Joe—not from Datt and not from Mem either.

Joe worked on the Robley farm for part of the summer. He hated going there and begged not to have to go back. Mem and Datt insisted he stay with it. Then one day, he was dropped off in the middle of the day. He was in tears, and he walked as if he hurt like he did after a whipping from Datt.

Joe never went back to the horse farm after that. What happened to him there was, and still is, left to my imagination.

It was both parents' responsibility to protect Joe from harm. But I had learned early on that I couldn't expect it from Datt because he didn't seem to have parental instincts. However, I expected more from Mem. Most of the time we relied on her to be the responsible parent, but in this and other instances, she seemed to have her motherly instincts all twisted up like a tangled clothesline. Even though she was a capable parent in many other ways, it seems she was incapable of protecting her children.

That summer before any of the bad things happened to Joe, he'd gotten a pair of rabbits—a black one and a white one—that he kept in a wire pen next to the chicken coop. Their droppings looked like raisins in the grass underneath their hut. We used to feed them carrot tops and lettuce leaves from the garden, and pigs' ears leaves from the yard. We liked watching their bunny noses as they munched their food. It was the first time we had rabbits on the farmette. Until then we'd had chickens, roosters, hens with their broods of little chicks, two pigs, a cow, two horses, a dog, and a group of barn cats.

When Sylvia and I played house in the woodshed, we'd pick chamomile from the yard as pretend food. Several afternoons in a row, we noticed that the rabbits were acting hungry, so we fed them. They were eating everything we gave them as if they were famished.

On a Sunday afternoon when we were eating popcorn, I asked Joe why his rabbits were so hungry all the time. "Don't you feed them?"

"Have you been feeding *my* rabbits?" he demanded as if I had been doing something wrong.

"Yes."

"You *stop* feeding them. Those are *my* rabbits!" Joe said emphatically.

I thought about defying Joe, but I knew better than to cross him. So when he demanded that I leave his rabbits alone, I avoided going near the rabbit pen. But even from a distance, I could see that they were getting thin, looking like they were nothing but fur and bones.

Then one afternoon, I was sitting at the dining room table, eating Mem's buttermilk cookies when I heard that the rabbits had died because Joe hadn't fed them. He'd wanted to find out how long it would take to starve them to death. I don't remember who said it, or in what context it was said. What I do remember, quite vividly, is my visceral reaction. I thought I would choke on that buttermilk cookie, and I felt like throwing up. I ran out into the woods where I could cry all by myself. There I sobbed so hard that my insides hurt. My heaving sobs turned into keening wails. It was a sound that didn't seem to come from inside me. Rather, it was the sound of a hurt animal. My sobs would subside, and then they would start all over again. I wished so much that I had fed those rabbits. Now that I knew what Joe had done to them, I wondered what he would do to me if I defied him.

I do not remember anything beyond sitting in the woods and sobbing until I was all emptied out. Did someone in the family come and find me there? Or did I find my way back home on my own? I cannot recall.

The days that followed were one of those times when the colors had all gone out of my world, and I felt nothing. I was going through my days as if I wasn't really me.

Years later, when I had young sons of my own, I wrote about this incident. I was curious what my parents' reactions had been at the time, so I sent Mem my account of what had happened and asked her that question. I wrote that I would be really worried if either of my sons did anything like that. I told her that I didn't remember her or Datt's reaction and asked if it raised red flags for them.

Instead of hearing back from Mem, there were weeks of silence. And then my family and I visited them. By then Mem and Datt were living in a *Doddehaus* on their property, and Joe and his family had moved into the main house. Mem told me that when she read my story, she just cried and cried. Joe kept asking her what the problem was, and she kept denying that there was anything wrong because she didn't want to tell him. Finally he demanded that she tell him what was going on because he knew that something was up. So Mem showed him my letter. Joe apparently told Mem that this had happened a long time ago, that he had been just a schoolboy, that he was sorry for what he'd done, and that "Saloma should have forgotten about it by now."

"So I burned your letter," Mem said in a tone of voice that ended the story. She had reduced it to ashes. It was yet another attempt to silence my voice.

BUSHEL HEAD

You can't go back and change the beginning, but you can start where you are and change the ending. ~Clive Staples Lewis

Mem and Datt decided to send all of us to Amish school in the fall of 1967 when I was ten. Joe was in eighth grade, which meant it was his last year in school. Lizzie was in sixth grade, I was in fifth, Sylvia in third, Sadie in second, and Simon in first. Only Katherine was home with Mem that year.

I had graduated into the upper-grade room. The school was divided down the middle by a heavy canvas curtain with the first through fourth grades on one side and the fifth through eighth grades on the other.

Levi Hershberger, one of the preachers of our church district and the father of several pupils, was our teacher that year. He was a strict teacher, and he often made me uneasy, watching pupils almost as if he expected them to do something wrong, and he was quick to cast judgment. Sometimes I wished I was still in fourth grade on the other side of the curtain, away from his judging eyes.

Since there was another Saloma Miller in fourth grade, I was known as Saloma S., and she was Saloma J. Most Amish children aren't given middle names, so they use the initial of their father's first name. Saloma J. and another friend, Nancy, and I played jacks every day during recess. We would bounce the red rubber ball, pick up jacks, and catch the ball. If we missed, we had to pass the jacks and ball to the next person. We had feuds over whether we had missed or not, or whether there was "interference," giving us the right to do a turn over. Saloma J. had bony hands with long fingers. She would often turn the ball in her fingers and thumb before making a difficult attempt at doing sevens or eights. With quick swipes of her small hands, Nancy usually beat both of us. The three of us were a tight circle, each of us playing to win. No one else asked to play us because they knew one of us would win.

Saloma J.'s desk was to my left. Teacher Levi's son Reuben sat to my right. During lunch one day, I was looking at Reuben and noticing his unruly, thick, curly hair that stuck straight out. Levi had three sons and they all had that kind of hair. Mem called them "Bushel Heads." I nudged Saloma J. and said, "Watch this." Then I nudged Reuben with my foot and said, "Bushel Head." He wasn't looking in my direction, so the contact surprised him. He turned around and with an angry look on his face, he kicked—hard. He missed me and kicked the bottom of my desk chair. The bell rang just then, and he grabbed his lunch box and went downstairs. Saloma and I looked at each other and said, "Wooow!" I felt lucky he had kicked the bottom of my desk and not me, but I guessed he'd probably hurt his foot. I decided never to do that again.

I didn't think about this again until a rainy day when Saloma J. and I were playing a game of carom. We had the carom board set up on a desk and were taking our turns to "shoot" the caroms into the net at the four corners of the board, like a mini pool game.

I didn't notice that Reuben and his friend Peter were leaning over Teacher Levi's desk, talking to him, until the two of them suddenly straightened up and said, "Saloma, you're in trouble!" Both Saloma J. and I said, "Me?" Peter and Reuben said, "No, not you, the other Saloma." I almost sighed with relief that it wasn't me. Then after several more rounds of, "Not you. You!" Reuben said, "Saloma S, you are in trouble!"

"What did I do?" I asked.

"You kicked Reuben!" Peter said.

"No, I didn't!" I said.

"Yes, you did, a couple weeks ago when I was sitting at my desk at lunchtime," Reuben said.

Saloma J. came up to me and whispered, "Do you think he is talking about the time you called him Bushel Head?"

I asked Reuben, "What are you talking about?"

"I was sitting at my desk at lunchtime and you kicked me right in my ankle!"

"I only touched you with my foot," I said.

"No you didn't, you kicked me as hard as you could!" Reuben said.

"No, I did not," I said. I looked at Teacher Levi. He had his head down, looking at something on his desk. He wasn't saying anything. I couldn't tell whether I was really in trouble or not. Then he rang the bell for recess to be over.

At home, I confided in Mem and told her exactly what had happened. She insisted I continue to go to school. She said she believed me and that she thought it would blow over. I should have remembered that Mem had turned the tables on me before. But when I thought she was "sticking up" for me, it felt so good that it was easy to forget.

One afternoon, when I was getting ready to go home, Annie Troyer, who was in the same grade as Reuben, said to me, "You did kick Reuben. I saw you."

"I didn't kick him, I just touched him with my foot," I said.

"You didn't kick him hard, but you still kicked him," Annie said in her quiet way.

I knew Annie was telling the truth. I went home with my feelings all twisted inside me. I was so ornery that night that Mem said, "Pretty soon I will believe Reuben at school." She knew just how to hurt me. I went to bed feeling betrayed by everyone, most especially by myself.

As I lay awake, I wished I could be as honest as Annie. She had spoken the words so matter-of-factly as if speaking the truth came naturally to her. It was part of the carefree way she breezed through life. I wished I could be more like her. I also wished I could go back and undo that moment at lunch recess when I called Reuben Bushel Head, but I knew I couldn't.

Every day Reuben and Peter reminded me of the trouble I was in by bending over and slapping their behinds and chanting, "You're going to get it!" After a while, I didn't want to go to school anymore. Teacher Levi was quiet, giving me no indication whether I was in trouble or not. Then one day something happened that scared me more than getting a whipping.

We'd had a substitute teacher the day before who was a young woman, just out of school herself. The older boys did something that day that landed them in trouble with Teacher Levi the next day. Why the boys got into trouble has always been a mystery to me. I heard they threw checkers out the window, but I still cannot believe that was the offense. Even Teacher Levi wouldn't have reacted as he did just for throwing checkers out the window.

The day after the substitute, Teacher Levi gave all the pupils a stern talking-to about behaving in school. He was looking at the upper-grade boys. Then he put eight of the older boys' names on the chalkboard and told them they had to come down to the furnace room one at a time. "When Allen comes up, then the next person on the list goes down," he said. The list included my brother Joe, and Levi's son, Reuben. One by one the boys came back. Some of them had red faces from crying. Joe was one of them. Reuben came back with defiance in his step. After the last boy had come back to the classroom, Teacher Levi came upstairs. He stood ready to close the canvas curtain that separated the upper grades from the lower grades. All of us looked at him. He said, "If everyone that got a spanking today didn't deserve it, there was probably another time when they did deserve it and didn't get it." Then he paused. "If there is anyone else that deserves it, now is the time to come forward."

Reuben turned around in his seat and pointed at me and said, "You! You!" Teacher Levi stood there for an eternal moment. I didn't breathe and I wished I could disappear. I thought Levi was expecting me to come forward. I knew one thing—I was *not* going to step forward and offer to take a whipping from Teacher Levi. Finally, Levi pulled the curtain and snapped it shut. I realized I'd been holding my breath.

Later, Joe told me Datt's whippings didn't hurt at all compared to Teacher Levi's. He said Levi had used two whips together and had used both arms to whip him.

Peter and Reuben stopped teasing me after that day. I didn't know why Teacher Levi had let my dispute with Reuben go on for so long. I also didn't know why Peter and Reuben stopped teasing me so suddenly, but I guessed that Teacher Levi finally put a stop to it.

I had already felt uncomfortable in Levi's class before this incident, but now for the first time in my life, I was looking forward to the school year ending.

I learned a valuable lesson that year. Even though I was only ten years old, I learned to trust my instincts about people. I was always uneasy around Levi, even when he was preaching in church. I avoided his sons as much as I possibly could. They had a reputation for behaving well around their father, but they were unruly whenever they were not under his supervision.

When Levi and his family moved to Andover, Ohio, to start a new Amish community, it felt like the whole church district took a deep breath.

Several years after they moved, Reuben went out to swim in a pond on a summer day. When he didn't come home, they went to look for him and found he had drowned. I read his father's account of Reuben's death. He described Reuben's days leading up to his drowning, including how he had held the youngest child, still a baby, that morning for the last time. The story Levi wrote made Reuben sound saintly. I felt bad that Reuben had died at such a young age, but I did not trust Levi's story any more than I had trusted him as a teacher. No one said anything about this, but I silently wondered if Reuben had taken his own life.

UNCLE CRISTY

The life of the dead is placed in the memory of the living.
~Marcus Tullius Cicero

ncle Cristy was different from most people I knew. When I was a child, he was bedridden. He used to sit up in his bed in the corner of *Momme* and *Dodde's* living room when we visited. He was twenty-three years younger than Mem—she was the oldest and he was the youngest in the family. When he was a child, Mem treated him more like a son than a brother. She liked to tell stories about her two youngest brothers Joey and Cristy, who were lively little red-heads. One summer day they were playing in the yard with a little lamb that followed Cristy everywhere. Cristy was laughing at how the lamb was dropping little lumps behind itself while it was running. Mem was braiding her sisters' hair on the porch when she had an idea. She told the boys to go to the barn and get baling twine so she could make a little halter for the lamb and tie a child's wheelbarrow backward to the back of the lamb. Then they let the lamb go. It took off across the yard, bleating, and dropping pellets into the wheelbarrow. It was running so fast, the pellets were popping out of the wheelbarrow as fast as they were dropping in.

Everyone watching had to laugh, but no one laughed as hard as Mem and Cristy.

When Cristy was six years old, he had his first epileptic seizure. When he had a second one, Joey confessed that he and Cristy had been playing in the haymow one day and Cristy fell down the hay chute to the floor below. They were afraid they would get punished, so they didn't say anything about Cristy's fall right away.

The family story goes that Cristy had a brain injury, which developed into epilepsy, but I don't know if this was a doctor's diagnosis.

By the time I was aware of Uncle Cristy, he was in his early twenties and had developed a brain tumor. *Momme* devoted her life to taking care of Cristy.

Mem liked to indulge Cristy, so one day when we went to visit, she decided she wanted to bring Cristy a big capon rooster for his birthday. She asked Datt to catch one of the biggest roosters and tie it into a burlap bag. We were going there by taxi, so the rooster was put in the back of the van for the ride to *Momme* and *Dodde's* house.

When we arrived, Mem went in and asked *Momme* if she could bring the rooster inside for Cristy to see.

Momme asked, "But what if he makes a *mess*?"

"Then I will clean it up," Mem said.

With an uncertain look on her face, *Momme* gave in.

Datt brought in the wriggling gunny sack with the rooster in it. He untied the rope while Christy propped himself up on his elbow, laughing.

The big white rooster emerged from the bag, blinking. His claws clicked as he took two steps on *Momme's* shiny hardwood floor and slipped. He blinked some more. Cristy laughed harder. We all stood in a circle, laughing. The rooster eyed us sideways. Then his tail dipped ever so slightly and he splattered a big wet mess, right next to the woven rug by *Dodde's* rocking chair. *Momme* screamed and covered her face with her hands. Mem laughed hard, but as usual, she swallowed her giggles and didn't make a sound. Her big bosom bounced and her face turned beet red. Cristy fell back laughing so hard, I thought he might choke.

Datt took the rooster out to the chicken coop while Mem cleaned up the mess on her hands and knees. She and Christy laughed together until I thought they must surely have sore stomachs.

Later, we heard that *Momme* had relished cooking up that rooster in a stew. Cristy laughed throughout the process.

~

One early morning in February, when I was still in fifth grade, Dan Weaver, our Amish neighbor from the Hale farm, drove in the lane on a tractor. The Weavers farmed by shares, which meant someone else owned the farm they managed. Unlike the Amish farmers who owned their land, the Weavers were allowed to use the electricity, phones, and tractors that belonged to the English owners of the farm. Sometimes the Weavers used the tractor to come down and give us a message.

On that morning, Dan took his hat off when he came into the house. He said in a soft voice, "Crist died." Mem started to cry. Dan said something else that I don't remember, but it dawned on me then. "Ohhh, it's *Uncle* Cristy!" I said out loud. Mem cried harder.

Dan Weaver stayed a few minutes and then left. Mem went into her bedroom and closed the door. We could hear her crying. Joe said, "You only made Mem cry more when you said, 'Oh, it's *Uncle* Cristy!'" He imitated my tone of voice.

"But I didn't know at first. I was thinking out loud."

"I'm just telling you, you made Mem cry." Joe's voice softened just a little, and I wondered if he understood I didn't do it on purpose.

By then I had already learned that making Mem cry was a shameful thing to do.

I wanted time alone, so I went upstairs to my room. I sat at the edge of my bed and thought about Uncle Cristy.

Cristy was the first person in Mem's family to die. He'd just had his twenty-fifth birthday a few weeks earlier. By then only the adults in the family were visiting Cristy at *Momme* and *Dodde's* house. *Momme* had always taken good care of Cristy, but Mem and the aunts and uncles had been taking turns to help her care for him.

Cristy had liked to read, but in the past several years, he couldn't anymore. So *Momme* read to him, even if it meant reading his favorite book over and over. He loved the book *Light From Heaven* and never tired of it. The story was about Joseph, who has a harsh, unyielding father named Bennet, and a mother who tries to do the best she can raising her children with Bennet as her husband. The author portrayed the mother as a saint and the father as a tyrant.

I wondered why this was Cristy's favorite book. According to Mem, *Dodde* was a good father to his twelve children, and yet I sensed something that made me wary of *Dodde*. He gave out candy to us grandchildren, and he seemed nice. But for some reason, I was always afraid he would lose his temper and hurt someone. I don't know why I had this fear because I had never seen him get angry. Still, I kept my distance.

Over his last two years, *Momme* was the only one who could understand Cristy because it took a long time for him to form and pronounce words. When he did try, his words came out garbled.

I heard Lizzie doing dishes down in the kitchen. It was time for me to go downstairs and help her do the morning work.

Three days after his death, Cristy's funeral was held in the home of my grandparents and the attached home of my Aunt Ada and her family. Every room was full of rows of people sitting on backless church benches. Mem, my aunts, my girl cousins, and my sisters and I sat in the same room. Sylvia leaned on my lap and I leaned on her back. We both dozed off while the ministers preached.

After the preachers were done, people filed past the open coffin to see Cristy. Then it was time for the family to gather around to say our final goodbyes. We were all wearing black dresses. My aunts, girl cousins, and sisters were crying and keening. I felt afraid. With so many others crying around me, I couldn't help but cry with them.

Not long after Cristy's funeral, I started having trouble falling asleep at night. I slept in the smallest bedroom in our upstairs, a room with no windows. The darkness was oppressive. As I was lying down to sleep each night, my fears would set in and my mind would go to Uncle Cristy. I had been to other funerals, but Cristy was the first relative to die. At ten years old, I was able to comprehend the finality of death. I was not as afraid of my own death as I was afraid of Mem's. I could not comprehend my life without her.

Mem tried everything to help me sleep. One night I sat on the woodbox outside her bedroom door and asked her questions about dying and death. I wanted to know where Cristy was now. Mem said we hoped he was in heaven, and that she could not imagine someone who had suffered as he had not ending up in heaven. By this time, I had heard many sermons about the alternative to heaven. The preachers had struck fear into my heart by painting vivid pictures of what would happen when the world came to an end. That night I dared to voice my fear of the world ending.

Mem hesitated for a long time before responding. I wondered if she had fallen asleep. Then she said, "I always think that when a person dies, it is the end of the world for that person."

"But that is not what the preachers say. They claim we will all die."

"If that were to happen, I don't think it will happen in our lifetime."

"But the preachers say it could happen any day."

"They have been preaching that ever since I was a little girl. I'm sure there were preachers who were claiming it long before that."

My ten-year-old mind tried to absorb this. All was quiet in the bedroom. I wondered whether Datt was awake. He hadn't said a word, so it was hard for me to know.

After a long moment Mem said, "Why don't you go back to bed and try to get some sleep?"

Back under the blankets in my bed, I let the tears slide quietly down my face and into my pillow. I had not named my deepest fear to Mem. I was so afraid that she might die. It seemed that if I said it out loud, it might really happen. I could not bear the thought. I knew that Datt could not take care of us children, and I thought we might have to go and live with Grandmother and Aunt Katie in Wisconsin. I knew I didn't want that.

Had I been brave enough to name my fear, I would have found out that my sisters had the same one. And maybe Mem would have told me what she told me many years later, that she was afraid that her mother would die when she was young, and that this also manifested itself in lying awake at night.

Months after Cristy's death, Mem said I should go to bed early to see if that would help. It was still light out. I wondered if the darkness intensified my fears, so I was grateful that Mem was concerned enough to send me to bed early.

I hadn't been lying down long before my nightly fears visited me, even in the light. Before long I started crying, quietly at first, but then I couldn't stay quiet. The door opened at the bottom of the stairs, and I wondered who was coming upstairs. To my surprise, Datt's voice called my name, and I answered. He said in a kind and concerned voice, "Stop crying now, and go to sleep." I was shocked. I had no idea that Datt had any concern for me, and I'd never heard such caring in his voice. To my surprise, my tears dried up, and not long after that, I fell asleep.

My insomnia and night fears stopped the night Datt called up the stairs. To this day, I cannot explain why. I have also never been able to understand why his concern soothed my fears when Mem had been trying for months to work through these same fears with me. Perhaps instead of trying to "fix" things, Datt was conveying the message that he heard my pain. Whatever the reason, I was glad I could sleep at night.

THE BURDEN OF SILENCE

There is no greater agony than bearing an untold story inside you.
~Maya Angelou

The summer I turned eleven, I learned that silence is not always golden. Enduring the unthinkable and then being forced into silence about it became a burden I did not wish to carry. And yet I had no choice.

It happened at the blackberry patch. Every year, my family trekked deep into the woods, avoiding patches of poison ivy and barber's itch, to pick the huge blackberries that grew on the tall, thorny bushes at the edge of the woods. We'd haul home buckets of blackberries to can for winter use.

During one summer when we were still little children, Datt hitched up the horses to the farm wagon, and we bounced over ruts and logs to get to the blackberry patch. Mem became frustrated with the crying little ones and with not being able to help much with the picking. That was the last year she accompanied us. After that, she sent us children with Datt as soon as we got old enough to pick. We girls always wore dresses with long sleeves, and we wore kerchiefs on our heads instead of our *koppa.* Those blackberry vines were like long, skinny arms reaching out to dig their brutal thorns into our soft flesh without mercy. Sometimes they grabbed our kerchiefs and wouldn't let go. We had to pull our heads away and wrest the kerchief from the thorns with our hands.

One summer when Sylvia was the youngest of us pickers, she was deep inside one of the thickets when she started to scream in pain. Datt quickly went to her and pulled her out of the bushes. She was being followed by a group of angry yellow jackets. She'd stepped on their nest in the ground. Datt fought them off, and then he tended to her bites by finding mud to plaster over them. Sylvia was visibly comforted by Datt taking care of her. It was a rare moment of Datt being a responsible parent.

As we grew older, Mem sent groups of us to pick blackberries. Several times we got lost on our way there or back, eventually finding our way when one of us discovered a familiar landmark.

The year I turned eleven, Mem decided to put Joe in charge of the group of blackberry pickers. I'd kept my distance from him since his rabbits had died. He seemed to sense that and didn't bother to try to win me over like he used to. That changed the day he was put in charge of blackberry picking. One of his daily tasks was to take our two horses to the back pasture, out beyond our sugarhouse. This day, he invited me to ride a horse to the back pasture with him. He helped me get on the back of our trusty workhorse, Tops. I sat behind him and kept trying to pull my dress down over my bare knees when he said, "Why do you want to cover your legs?"

I made a feeble comment about my dress not being full enough, and he said, "You don't need to be ashamed, I'm just your brother." His voice was smooth as butter, just like that fall day when he was eight and I was five and he had convinced me to burn myself.

Yet Joe's manner was such a break from his usual threatening, controlling, and angry ways that I was once again lured into thinking things were better between us. When we got to the back pasture, Joe led the horses inside the fence and closed the gate. Then he sat down on the ground up against a fence post and took out tobacco and started rolling a cigarette. He smoked rings into the air above him as he continued to chat and talk with an assumed intimacy that made me uneasy. He said, "You know, Lomie, that I admire you." I didn't say anything. He asked, "Do you know what 'admire' means?"

I did know, but it felt like Joe was guiding my thoughts and actions as if I were a puppet on a string he controlled. I said, "Not really."

Joe was in his element as he taught me the meaning of his admiration. The door to him becoming my teacher had been opened, and he stepped right through it. He asked, "May I ask you a question?"

As if he had put the word in my mouth, I said, "Yes."

"Do you know how babies are made?"

Even though I knew Joe wanted me to say no, so he could tell me, I suddenly didn't want to play his game anymore. I said, "Yes." I was curt, hoping he would sense I didn't want to talk about it. But he continued.

"May I ask you another question?"

I didn't answer.

As if he didn't notice my silence he asked, "May I do that to you?"

"No."

"Why not?"

"Because I don't want to have a baby."

Joe went on to assure me that that wouldn't happen and that it would be a good thing "because we love each other." He said that Mem wanted us to go blackberry picking that afternoon, and that I should think about it and let him know then. He warned me not to say anything to Mem about our "plans."

Sharing confidences and secrets in our family was considered an honor to the person who was "let in" on them. It was like a test to see if that person was to be trusted with the secret. I seemed to fail that test every time, so I had the reputation of not being trustworthy. I knew Joe wanted me to feel honored, but I didn't. I felt burdened.

I was stunned into silence all the way home, while Joe chatted as if we were friends and always had been. He seemed to assume all those times he had smacked or beaten me didn't matter. Sometimes it was a hard smack across my face. Other times he'd smack me on one side of my face, and then the other. Then there were incidents when he'd given me a sound beating. Now, walking next to him, I wanted to turn to him and remind him of those times, but instead I walked along in silence.

I pulled inward during our midday meal as I thought about what Joe wanted from me. I decided the best way to deal with it was not to go blackberry picking. I waited for a chance to get Mem by herself. After my sisters and I finished the dishes in the downstairs summer kitchen, I found her in the upstairs kitchen, ripping strips of blue cotton for crocheting a rug from an old dress of hers. She had strips draped over her shoulders.

I asked, "Can I stay home with you this afternoon when the others go blackberry picking?"

Mem looked at me sideways. She paused before asking me, "Why wouldn't you want to go?"

I was caught. I sensed that Mem knew something I didn't. The very thought of telling her what Joe had asked of me made my heart race and my hands clammy. She was watching every move I made. I didn't look at her but smoothed out the fabric on the table. I thought about telling her what Joe wanted me to do, but I didn't have the words. The eerie way she was looking at me didn't help. Finally I said meekly, "I just don't feel like it."

Mem paused, again looking at me from the corner of her eye for a long moment. Then she said, "Well I think you should go."

Even though Mem's words sounded indefinite, I knew, at least on some level, that she'd made up her mind. My fate was sealed. I would have to face Joe. The worst thing was that I didn't think I could keep him from doing *that* to me.

I kept trying to shake the feeling that Mem knew something she wasn't telling me as I walked with the others through the woods to the blackberry patch that afternoon. Did she know what Joe was up to? I kept telling myself there was no way she would allow Joe to do that.

I wished we would get lost in the woods. I wished I could hide until Joe and the others were far ahead of me and then wait in the sugarhouse until I saw them come back. But I knew that Joe would notice if I slipped away. He was perceptive about people—that much I knew. As much as I wanted to avoid Joe, I couldn't.

When we got to the blackberry patch, Joe instructed the others to pick in the main part of the patch, while "Lomie and I will go out that way."

As soon as we were out of hearing distance, Joe asked, "So did you think about what I asked you this morning?"

"Yes."

"And did you come up with an answer?"

"I don't think we should do it."

"Why not?"

"I don't think brothers and sisters are meant to do that. I think that's for married people."

"But you and I love each other, so how can it be a bad thing?"

"You asked me not to tell Mem. If there is nothing wrong with what you are asking, why does it matter whether Mem knows or not?"

"Because she doesn't understand that I need practice for when I get married."

"I just don't feel right about it." I looked at the grass at my feet. I was too afraid to look at Joe. Then his tone of voice changed in an instant. "Look, if you don't want to do it, I will just get my practice somewhere else," he said impatiently.

The feelings inside me were roiling, like the laundry in the wringer washer with the agitator going. If I didn't do this, would Joe take revenge later? He had beaten me up before, and he could do it again. Or what if he *made* me do what he wanted?

As much as I didn't want to do what he asked of me, I was afraid of what he would do if I refused him.

Joe was waiting for my answer during the war of my thoughts and feelings. I was nearly in tears when I asked, "What do you want me to do?"

Afterwards, my body was not my own. Even though my legs carried me toward the house we lived in with those who were my siblings, I felt alienated from my body. The dry stinging pain "down there" would have had me crying out in any other circumstances, but the shame and the alienation kept me quiet and stoic.

When we got home, I went straight to my room and cried into my pillow. I squeezed my eyes shut, trying to resist the feelings of the grass stems under me, of Joe above me trying to figure out why he couldn't get in, then trying harder. The pain so sharp, he might as well have been using a knife. Me crying out, "Ow!" and closing my eyes against the pain and the sun behind him. Finally him saying, "It's not working. Maybe we need to give it up."

But the damage was done. The violence of entering a body too small to be entered had been committed. He had ruptured a place deep inside me that I hadn't even known was there. A handkerchief stained with my blood was discarded into the grass. I had the urge, as I got up from the ground, to scream out my agony toward the heavens—a primal scream of unbearable and unfathomable pain. But I turned that scream inward and held it there.

Mem appeared in the doorway of my room with flour on her apron and pie dough clinging to her hands. She asked, "*Vas iss letz*—what's wrong?"

"Joe bothered me in the blackberry patch," I blurted.

After a long moment of silence she asked, "What do you mean?"

"He, he..." I stammered, and I pointed to where I hurt.

"Well, why did you *let* him?"

Mem's words struck me like a whip. I didn't expect that she could make the hurt go away, but I also didn't expect her to make that hurt go deeper. I got up, pushed past her, and ran to the outhouse. I sat down and sobbed into my hands. I started to pee, and then quickly stopped myself as I cried out in pain. Mem came running and opened the door and asked me what was wrong. I said, "It hurts to pee!"

Mem looked worried. She said, "But you can't stop yourself. It'll make you sick."

My memory cuts out at that moment of Mem standing at the outhouse door. I could see that she was wondering what to do.

For the next several days, I endured the pain, which gradually lessened. Once Mem followed me to the outhouse and asked me in a whispery voice if it still hurt when I peed. I said no. I didn't often lie, but I couldn't bear for Mem to know the truth. I didn't trust her with it. I wanted to tell someone what had happened, but not her.

As the days passed, my urge grew to tell someone what had happened in the blackberry patch. I needed to unburden myself of this terrible secret, and I needed someone to understand how much it hurt. The only person I could think of to tell was Olin Clara. I had been going to her house for two summers, and I looked forward to Saturday when I would see her again. I thought about how hard it was going to be to tell her, and as I tried to think of the right words, my heart pounded hard in my chest. I decided I would just start telling her and hope that the words would come.

Saturday morning came, and I was getting ready to walk the mile to Clara's house when Mem called me into the upstairs kitchen. She said, "I just wanted to make sure you don't talk to Olin Clara about what happened in the blackberry patch."

I was caught, and I didn't know what to say. I was dumbfounded that Mem knew what I intended. And now she wanted to take it away from me. I was speechless.

Mem said, "If you were to tell her, it would spread like wildfire!" She spread out her arms for emphasis and brought them down quickly as if she were a bird attempting to fly. She noticed my silence and said, "If you promise you won't tell, I will let you go see Olin Clara today."

I had barely managed to muster up the courage to tell Clara, and now I felt that courage dissipating into thin air, like steam rising from a teakettle. Not being allowed to see Clara at all was worse than keeping silent about what Joe had done to me in the blackberry patch. Mem was making that choice for me. All this went through my mind before I said, "I wasn't going to tell her anyway." With that, I ran down the stairs and out the door before Mem could change her mind about letting me go.

I learned to bury the memory of what happened in the blackberry patch in the nether reaches of my mind. Mem was complicit in her silence with whatever Joe did. She was teaching me to do the same. Or perhaps it was my own way of surviving.

GREAT-AUNT MANDY'S DEATH

The fear of death follows from the fear of life. ~Mark Twain

*N*ot long after the incident in the blackberry patch, Mem's Aunt Mandy died. On a Sunday afternoon, Mem chose me to go with her to Mandy's viewing. Later I wished she hadn't.

When we walked into the room where Mandy was laid out, it was just Mem, the funeral director (whose name was Rube Miller), and me. I had heard that Mandy had been sick in bed for a while before she died. She was very afraid of spiders, and someone had been mean enough to throw a big plastic one on her bed not long before her death.

I hated spiders too. It was incomprehensible to me that someone could have thrown a spider on her deathbed. I could not even imagine who could be so cruel. That story upset me and I felt sorry for Mandy.

As we walked into the room, I noticed Mandy's pallor, and I was scared of her body. I was clutching my stomach when Rube noticed how I was reacting. He came up to me and took my hand and said, "Have you ever touched someone like this?" and he put my hand on Mandy's yellow, cold, and stiff cheek.

The moment my hand touched her, I felt something like an electric shock in reverse, as if something had just left my body. The gripping fear left my body along with it, but now it was much more scattered. The fear was even bigger than the room we were in. As I slipped out the door, I heard Rube explaining to Mem how sometimes touching the body makes the fear go away.

The next day, a sharp pain shot through my stomach. It felt as though someone had punched me. I cried out and doubled over. And then it left as suddenly as it had come. I straightened up. Mem heard my scream and hurried into the living room. She and Lizzie were getting ready to go to Mandy's funeral. Mem asked what the matter was. I said I'd had a sharp pain in my stomach, but it was gone. Then suddenly the pain came slamming back. I felt like I was going to throw up. It kept coming and going. After Mem and Datt talked about what to do, Datt went and asked the neighbor to take me to the emergency room. They thought I might have appendicitis.

The pain came and went on the way to the emergency room. We were led to an examining room, where we waited for the doctor. I was told to go into the bathroom, change into a gown, and pee into a cup. When I came back to the room where Mem was waiting, I got into the bed with clean white sheets. We waited there for what seemed like a long time.

"It doesn't hurt since I peed," I said after a while.

"I noticed that," Mem said. "If that's all it was, it sure will be an expensive pee."

I felt terrible. I didn't want to cause Mem and Datt more hardships than they already had when it came to money.

When the doctor came in, he uncovered my belly and told me he was going to poke different places, and I should let him know if it hurt. After his examination, he talked to Mem, and I decided I didn't want to listen. After the doctor left the room, Mem said in a conspiratorial whisper, "He thinks you're developing, and you'll get your period soon. Do you know what that means?"

"Yes," I said quickly, so Mem would know I did not want to talk about it. I was too embarrassed.

I didn't get my period for another four years, so the doctor was likely mistaken. I think now that I must have passed a kidney stone that day. It could also be that the pain was psychosomatic, brought on by my terror of touching the corpse the day before. I probably won't ever know for sure what caused that pain, though I will always associate it with what happened in the blackberry patch and with my close-up view of a corpse in the parlor of death.

BURNING BONNETS

The thing worse than rebellion is the thing that causes rebellion.
~Frederick Douglass

The girls in the Amish school found all kinds of reasons to make fun of my sisters and me, from our shortage of school paper to our winter bonnets, to things we didn't even know about.

Mem didn't allow us to take more than thirty sheets of paper to school at a time. She said she didn't want us to waste it. I know Mem had a hard time making ends meet, but buying paper could not have been that expensive. Whenever I ran out at school, she would only give me a thin set of sheets. Then I'd soon run out and have to borrow from someone else. Other children would bring a whole pack of lined paper to school at a time. I wasn't often jealous of the other children, but I used to eye those thick stacks of blank paper and wish I could have a stack like that. Those blank sheets represented possibilities. Each one was a new beginning, like starting with a blank slate.

Having so little paper was difficult for Sylvia as well. She was a born artist, and Mem told the story about how she'd find crayon drawings on the wall in hidden corners, and she always knew who had done them. Sylvia's need to draw could not be suppressed.

Mem also insisted that my sisters and I wear winter bonnets to school. We were the only girls in school who had to wear winter bonnets, which were becoming outmoded within our community. We called them "covered wagons." We also called them "deafs and blinders"—"deafs" because they were so thick that they muted sounds, and "blinders" because they were deep enough to block our peripheral vision.

My sisters and I tried every which way to avoid wearing those winter bonnets, but we could not go against Mem's authority, and we knew it. We had to put up with the wearing of them and the *schpotting* from the school girls.

When I went into seventh grade, Eugene, who was the father of several pupils in our school, became our new teacher. He was a wiser and kindlier teacher than Levi had been. During my two years of being his pupil, I learned how to think for myself.

Meanwhile, the upper-grade girls continued their *schpotting*. I had already learned that they would often pick on us for being "Sim's *maet*" (Simon's daughters). Simon was my father's name, but he was known as Sim for short. It seemed unfair to be mocked for being someone's daughter since there wasn't a whole lot I could do about being one of "Sim's *maet*."

Ruth was my closest friend. Together we survived the onslaught of whispering, staring, and *schpotting*.

Sara Jane was the worst of the *schpotters*. She had made it clear to all of my sisters and me that she hated us. During class time, she stared at me with hatred that turned her eyes into two shiny black coals. If I stared back at her, she would stare me down. She never gave up first. If I stopped staring at her and did my work again, she would make me feel self-conscious by watching every move I made. I thought about telling on her, but I figured if I did, she would really have something to whisper about to her friends.

One day, someone apparently saw my sister Lizzie picking her nose. This girl wrote a nasty little poem and left it on Lizzie's desk. "Fishy fishy in the brook/ Daddy caught it with a hook/ Mama fried it in a pan/ Baby ate it like a man." Lizzie told Teacher Eugene. He asked to keep the note, and Lizzie let him have it. He waited until all the pupils were seated at their desks after recess. Before he pulled the canvas curtain shut between the two classrooms, he explained that he had a note that was left in someone's desk that was meant to hurt. He said he was going to pass that note around until it came back to the writer of the note. He said we didn't need to read it, but asked the person who had written it to put it in his or her desk and keep it.

The classroom got so quiet that we could have heard a pin drop as the note was passed from one person to the next. When it reached the person who had written the note, she hastily grabbed it, put it in her desk, and slammed down the lid. Her face was red with shame.

Eugene only said a few words about the importance of respecting one another, and then he pulled the curtain shut.

What Eugene had effectively done was deflect the shame that was meant for Lizzie back onto the "shamer."

I felt I was in good hands in Eugene's class.

My sisters and I stuck together when other girls made fun of us in school, and we rebelled against Mem when her rules gave the other girls a reason to *schpott*. We particularly hated wearing winter bonnets.

Then one Sunday afternoon, I had a new idea. I was reading *The Young Companion*, a publication by Pathway Publishers in Ontario, Canada with a wide readership in Amish communities. The purpose of the magazine was to appeal to young people with stories that took place within Amish families and contained lessons meant to reinforce our way of life.

The Young Companion had a column that invited young people to send questions to the editors about Amish life. I don't remember what I was reading that Sunday afternoon when a light bulb went off in my mind—I could write to the editors and ask them if it was fair for Mem to require us to wear winter bonnets. Typical for me, I couldn't keep such a good idea to myself, so I blurted it out. Mem tried talking me out of it, saying they wouldn't print it, and I shouldn't bother them. But I persisted. I sat down and wrote the letter, explaining our situation, including that winter bonnets were old-fashioned, and that only Mem and a few other older women in our church wore the winter bonnets, while all other women and girls wore summer bonnets all year round. I also mentioned that the girls at school made fun of us for wearing them. I put my letter in an envelope, addressed it, affixed the stamp, and sealed it. Then just to make sure it got mailed, I walked it to the mailbox and put the flag up.

Some days later I received an envelope from Aylmer, Ontario. I tore it open and read the typewritten note asking me if there was a rule in our church that said we needed to wear winter bonnets. I thought that was odd, but I sent off the answer, that no, it was not.

One afternoon when I came home from school, Mem handed me an envelope from Canada. She'd been true to her rule about not opening mail addressed to anyone else. It was perhaps the only personal boundary she kept during my childhood. The most private space I had was the outhouse, and even that wasn't always because it had two holes. Still, that is where I went to tear open my letter. I found a short, typewritten note inside, explaining that they would not be printing this question because it was too hard to answer, given that it was not a rule in our church. There were some words wishing me the best with my mother, but they rang hollow. There was no handwritten signature, only "The Editors" at the end of the letter. I sat there stunned. I felt like someone had just slapped me in the face for saying something I shouldn't have. I wondered which of "The Editors" had typed that note. I knew their names—Elmo Stoll and David Wagler. Whoever it was obviously didn't want me to know and was hiding behind his position. I crumpled up the letter and tossed it down the hole next to me.

When I went back into the kitchen, Mem looked up with a questioning look on her face. I walked past her and upstairs to my room to be by myself. I had been silenced once again, and this time not by Mem. The "wise" men at Pathway Publishers were concerned about maintaining the Amish way of life and didn't care that we were subjected to the scorn of our classmates all because Mem made us wear winter bonnets.

∽

One day when we came home from school, Mem was out in the sugarhouse boiling sap. She'd left us a note with instructions about the work we should do. Sadie had gone to her friend's house to spend the night, and Lizzie went out to the sugarhouse to help Mem. So Sylvia and I were alone in the house.

For years, Sylvia had been my closest sister. Back when she was in third grade, she made the same transition I'd made two years earlier. Both of us went from second grade in public school with Mrs. Takacs as our teacher to third grade in Amish school, where the other third graders had already learned how to write in cursive. Our Amish teacher had four grades to instruct, so Sylvia and I had to learn to write on our own. I'd asked for help from my friend Ruth. But Sylvia was shy and afraid to ask anyone. She waited until she got home and asked me.

With the lack of paper in our house, Sylvia and I had to be creative about cursive writing. We used the steamed-up windows in the kitchen and dining room like chalkboards. I wrote a letter or word with my finger and Sylvia traced it, then copied it right underneath. We filled up a window that way and then moved on to the next one. By the time we had used the windows in the kitchen and dining room, the first window was steamed up again, so we circled back to it.

Sylvia and I played together, worked together, and slept in the same bed. I often imagined we were twins, even though our ages and personalities were different.

So on this afternoon when we were alone in the house, Sylvia and I complained bitterly about having to wear our winter bonnets. We looked at them on the sideboard in the dining room with their sides flopping into themselves. Sara Jane had been particularly hostile that day, staring at us with her black-coal eyes.

All of a sudden, Sylvia grabbed one of the bonnets and threw it at me. That started a game of tossing it back and forth, and then we tugged at it and one of the flaps tore. We looked at one another in surprise, but we egged each other on. We tore the flaps off both our bonnets, knowing that Mem would just sew the flaps back on. So we took scissors and cut into them. Then we realized that Mem could make us wear our sisters' bonnets as punishment, so we decided to cut all of them up. But now we had to get rid of them. We stirred up the fire in the stove in the living room and threw the pieces into the fire. We poked the fire until all the pieces of the bonnets were burned.

I knew we were in trouble. I said to Sylvia, "You know we're going to get a whipping for this, right?"

"I don't care. I'd rather have the whipping than have to keep wearing those bonnets."

It dawned on me then that Sylvia could say that because I had never seen Mem whip her. If she'd had any idea how much pain I had to endure from Mem's whippings, she'd probably not have said that. But then I had a new thought. What if burning the bonnets with Sylvia was my protection? Since we'd both done it, Mem couldn't very well whip me and not Sylvia. Of course she could say that I was the older one and therefore the one who should be punished. By this time, my role as the family conscience and the fixer of the family's problems had been well established. I often felt overwhelmed by the feeling that I was responsible for things that I had no power to change. Now Sylvia had helped me change something we hadn't thought we could, and I was afraid I might have to stand alone in taking responsibility for it.

The next morning as we were getting ready for school, I asked Mem whether we could wear our summer bonnets. I argued that spring was coming and we didn't need the winter bonnets anymore. Mem was standing at the kitchen sink with her hands in sudsy dishwater. She sighed and said, "No, just wear the winter ones for today. I will get the summer ones out of the cedar chest later."

I felt my heart in my throat. I said, "We can't."

Mem turned around and looked at me with her mouth open. "What do you mean?"

I was too scared to answer. After a long pause Sylvia said, "Because... we burned them."

Mem's mouth opened and closed in shock. She looked at Sylvia and said, "Well, I didn't know you hated them *that* much!"

Had I not been so relieved by her reaction, I would have been tempted to say, "Of course you knew. Why else would I write to the editors at Pathway Publishers?"

After a long pause Mem said, "Go upstairs and get your summer bonnets."

We did. On our way out to the end of the lane to wait for our ride to school, Sylvia and I wanted to dance for joy. Behind us, Lizzie said, "You girls are lucky. You could have gotten me into trouble."

I turned around and looked at Lizzie. "But aren't you glad you never have to wear your deafs and blinders again?"

"Yes, but if *I* had done that..." Lizzie's voice trailed off. She did not need to finish her sentence. I knew what she meant. I'd been saved from punishment only because I'd committed this act of rebellion with Mem's favorite daughter. Had I done it with Lizzie, we would have gotten our whippings then and there.

Then came the day when my relationship with Sylvia changed irrevocably. It was a Sunday in winter, and she and I were getting ready to go out sledding. The slanted light of the afternoon sun was shining on the snow, but it was cold out, so we were pulling on layers of coats and scarves to stay warm. We discussed whether we should go to the little hill in the woods right above our house, or to the long hill down Durkee Road, where the snowmobiles had packed down a trail. We were not allowed to go there alone, so I was trying to convince Sylvia to go to the long hill, and she said she wanted to go to the other one. I was making my case for the longer rides that Durkee Hill would give us. Sylvia was considering when Mem interjected. "Sylvia," she said, "you don't always have to do what Saloma says, you know."

Sylvia immediately decided she was not going with me down Durkee Hill.

I was not happy as Sylvia and I climbed the little hill above our house. After about the sixth "little baby ride," I told Sylvia that I could go down this hill with my eyes closed.

Sylvia tried talking me out of it, saying that it was not a good idea with all the trees around. But I didn't listen. I lay down on my sled, and put my head in my arms. I don't remember if Sylvia pushed my sled to get it going down the hill or not, but I do know that when the sled started moving, I was determined not to look up until my sled had stopped at the bottom of the hill.

I don't remember what made me look up. Maybe it was Sylvia yelling at me, or maybe it was because I hit the weeds on the side of the path. I looked up in time to see the trunk of a beech tree up close, just before my forehead collided with it. I heard a dull *"Thunk!"* inside my head. I got up off the sled, dazed, and walked toward the house as fast as I could. I couldn't walk in a straight line. When I got to the kitchen, I started to take my coats and scarves off. Mem looked at me in alarm and asked, "What happened?" She immediately poured cold water into the basin and dunked a washcloth into it, and told me to put it on my forehead. When I reached up, I found a bump the size of a golf ball on the left side of my forehead.

Mem made sure I didn't fall asleep that afternoon because she was afraid I'd have a concussion. I played Chinese Checkers with my siblings. That night when it was time to fall asleep, I worried that I might not wake up. But when exhaustion took over, I couldn't help it.

Mem may or may not have scolded me for having been so foolish. Maybe she thought I'd learned my lesson, and she would have been right. I never tried a stunt like that again.

What I remember from that day was not only the head injury, but also the sense that it marked the end of my relationship with Sylvia as I had known it. Perhaps Mem wanted Sylvia to be able to form a mind of her own rather than following my lead. But I think she may have misunderstood Sylvia's personality. She was shy and reticent about making decisions for herself, and she seemed to need to follow another's lead. I had the desire to be the leader, which is why we got along so well. When Mem told her she didn't always have to do everything I said, Sylvia seemed to interpret the message as meaning that she *shouldn't* follow my lead.

When Sylvia started resisting my desire to be the "big sister," she and Sadie began spending more time together. Even though Sadie was younger, Sylvia was still the follower. Sadie and I had never gotten along with one another. When Sylvia became buddies with Sadie, I felt intense jealousy.

Without Sylvia as my closest sister, the tension between Mem and me grew, and so did the tension between Sadie and me. Mem used to say,

"The only time you children get along with each other is when you are mad at someone else."

Mem was right. The relationships and alliances in our family were complex and ever-changing. I didn't yet understand that Mem's role might have had something to do with the relations among us siblings. As we developed our personalities, she put us into categories. Joe became her confidant and our father figure. Lizzie became Mem's scullery maid. I became the conscience of the family and the fixer of our problems. Sylvia was the favorite daughter. Sadie was the naughty daughter. Simon was the errand boy. Katherine was the baby of the family.

Mem also instilled in us the drive to stay in her good graces, and even to compete with one another for who was in best standing with her. She usually withheld her approval from at least one of us at any given time, creating fierce rivalry among us. She was like an invisible stage director. We played out our parts on the stage of life without even realizing she was directing us.

YOU DON'T NEED TO BE ASHAMED

I never wonder to see men wicked, but I often wonder to see them not ashamed. ~Jonathan Swift

The summer I turned twelve was stormy, both in terms of weather and what else was happening in my life. The Fourth of July was hot and humid, even for northeastern Ohio. We were picking and canning beans by the bushel. The house was so sultry that we moved benches outside to create a station for snapping beans. The air was so still, not a twig or leaf moved in the trees above us. Mem opened her dress at her chest, and she pulled her skirt above her knees. I had never seen her do that before. It made me feel ashamed and I told her so. She told me to look the other way then.

As the afternoon wore on, it became hard to breathe in the sultry air. Mem said she thought we were going to get a storm. Indeed, it started to get dark, so we moved everything inside. As we were doing so, Joe arrived home from work early. He came running in, saying there were tornado warnings, and we needed to go down to the basement right away.

As usual, we had moved the oilstove and kitchen table and chairs downstairs to the basement for our "summer kitchen." It was our version of air conditioning for the summer.

As the thunder rolled in and the lightning flashed, we all gathered in the summer kitchen. Most of us sat down, but Datt stood by one of the windows, staring outside.

I sat on a chair by myself, feeling claustrophobic in the humid and close basement surrounded by my whole family. My mouth felt like it had sand in it. I realized that the drinking water was upstairs. Almost to myself, I murmured, "I am so thirsty."

Joe retorted, "We're getting a tornado, and all you can think about is how thirsty you are."

"Oh, that's not all I can think about. I can also think about what a mean older brother you are."

"Why didn't you get a drink of water before you came down here?"

"Because I wasn't thirsty then."

"Then you can't be *that* thirsty."

"How do you know how thirsty I am? Don't you think I'm the best judge of that?"

Mem wiped the sweat off her face with her hand and said, "Oh, Joe and Lomie, must you argue...?"

Boooom! A clap of thunder drowned out the rest of Mem's sentence. Then the rain started pouring down on us as if from huge barrels. We didn't see a funnel cloud because of the torrential rain.

The storm raged all around us. The thunder boomed, the rain poured down, and the wind howled. I'd heard that a tornado sounds like a train going by overhead, but it sounded more like an army of furious giants carrying out a battle all around us.

Datt suddenly jumped away from the window and yelled and pointed, "Lightning just hit that tree behind the outhouse!" I looked out, but the rain was lashing against the window too hard for me to see anything.

I had to endure the suffocating basement with my family even though I had the urge to run out of there. There were enough big trees around our house that it would have been dangerous even to go up to the first floor.

When the storm finally passed, we saw that the tree behind the outhouse had been hit and had lost one of its huge branches. There were puddles everywhere and branches lying all around the farm. Our place looked like giants had indeed fought a battle and left destruction in their wake. While we were surveying the damage, the sun came back out. The air was still hot and humid, not refreshing like after most summer storms.

At bedtime it had cooled enough to make sleeping bearable. I willed myself into a deep sleep, as I often did. This was a daily reprieve from my difficult life.

In my dreams, a storm raged like the one we had experienced that afternoon. Then Mem woke me, and I realized another real storm had entered my dream. Mem said we had to go to the basement again because another tornado was hitting. I was dimly aware of everyone else going downstairs, but I willed myself back to sleep. I heard the storm raging, and in the far reaches of my mind, I knew if a tree or large branch were to come through the roof, I could be harmed or killed. But I told myself that if God wanted me to live, then I would survive the storm. I wasn't afraid of being killed. Perhaps there was even a small part of me that wished for it.

Mem came into my room again and urged me to go downstairs. I said I wasn't going to, and pushed my head back into my pillow. She commanded me to go down, but I still refused. She eventually gave up on me. I was already asleep before she left my room.

When I awoke in the morning, I realized I still had my life to live. This realization came with both relief and dread. My family derided me for refusing to go to the basement during the tornado in the night. I didn't respond. I could not have brought myself to join them in the dungeon. I decided that this was better left unsaid.

We found more downed tree limbs that morning. Datt walked around our property and was relieved to find all his big trees still standing. We found out later that we were fortunate. The woods behind Olin and Clara Yoder's house had wide swaths of huge trees that were downed. They had all fallen in the same direction as if they were dominos. Right next to the downed trees were untouched saplings, as if the giants had toppled the timbers with a mighty sweep of an arm.

Forty-two fellow Ohioans lost their lives that day, according to a 2013 story in the *Cleveland Plain Dealer* that deemed the tornado of 1969 a "killer storm," stranding hundreds of vacationers on islands of Lake Erie. More than one hundred boats sank, more than five thousand trees were downed, and a quarter of a million people were left without electricity. To this day, I am surprised that Mem didn't force me to go to the basement the night of the tornado.

~

Tornados were not the only storms that happened that summer. As my pubescent body started to change, I longed for more privacy than I'd had as a child. The lack of privacy and boundaries in my life left me feeling violated and vulnerable.

One day I was pumping water with the hand pump at the kitchen sink when I saw the dark pickup truck coming slowly down the road and turning into our lane. I yelled to my sisters, "Joe Basco is coming. Let's go upstairs and hide!" We scrambled up the stairs and crouched under the window until we heard him walking in the outside door and up the five steps to the kitchen door. As usual, he walked into the kitchen without knocking.

He called out, "Hello!" My sisters, Lizzie, Sylvia, Sadie, and I looked at one another, hardly daring to breathe. My heart was thumping so hard inside my chest that I could hear it in my ears. I was glad Mem had decided to take Katherine with her to visit Mem's sisters for the day. Katherine was too little to hold still for very long.

Joe Basco had been coming to our house for as long as I could remember. He and his wife had brought the toys for Christmas when we were little, including my favorite doll I named Heidi. As I got older, I became uncomfortable around him, and I tried to stay away from him whenever I could. Perhaps I didn't like that he was the only visitor who came into our home without knocking or the way Datt seemed to disappear whenever Joe Basco showed up as if he knew he wasn't welcome in his own home with the intruder around. Maybe I didn't like the feeling of him watching me with his dark, beady eyes. Maybe it was because it didn't seem fitting that he came so often—sometimes three or four times a week. Or maybe it was all of these things put together.

I willed Joe Basco to go away. "Hello, is anyone home?" he called out.

He walked through the kitchen and dining room toward the living room. I pictured his craggy face and his short, stocky figure standing in the living room, looking around. I wondered if he sensed that we were in the house. I didn't know what to do if he decided to stay. I wanted to shrink into my body and disappear.

Joe Basco jiggled his keys and said, "Well, I guess there's no one home." Then he walked down the stairs and out the door to his car at the end of the lane. We peeked out the window and saw him driving away. We decided to stay upstairs until we were sure he wouldn't come back.

I wondered why Mem liked having Joe Basco around. Sometimes he came with his wife, but most often he came by himself. Even though Joe Basco was old enough to be my grandfather and he came often, my sisters and I instinctively wanted to hide whenever he came to visit and we were alone in the house.

A few days later, Mem said to me, "So I hear you were hiding from Joe Basco the other day. You don't need to do that. He's just like family, you know."

How had she known? And why would she say that when he wasn't even Amish? I wondered. I had no idea why Joe Basco made me so uneasy. I only knew that he did.

One night when Joe Basco and Mem were in the living room with the doors partly closed, we heard him asking her for permission to tell her daughters "the facts of life." Mem granted him that permission.

A day or two later, Joe Basco set about doing just that. He showed Sylvia, Sadie, and me a drawing of a nude woman from behind. With one of his stubby old fingers, he traced her waist to the outline of her hip. He said that women had these hips so they could carry a baby. He repeated several times, "Any woman can carry a baby."

The three of us ran upstairs, away from Joe Basco. We kept mocking him, "*Any* woman can carry a baby!" and exploded into giggles.

I didn't understand Mem. Why wouldn't she protect our privacy? It seemed like she didn't understand boundaries. There was not one private space in our home. Even our outhouse had two holes and no lock on the door. In the summertime, we showered in one corner of the basement with a curtain around the drain and a window above, making it possible for my brother Joe to peep at my sisters and me whenever he had the chance. We learned to plaster wet newspaper up against the window to make sure he couldn't see us.

In the winter, we bathed in a galvanized bathtub in the living room, which was even more treacherous because of the many windows. One night Sylvia was getting ready to take a bath. She'd already covered all the windows when Joe asked to go through the room and up the back stairs to his bedroom. So Sylvia left the living room. After he came back down and went outside, she went back into the living room. She noticed that the curtain at the window to the west had been propped open with a broom handle. She kept her clothes on and waited. She heard him outside the window and whisked the curtain back. There was Joe's face, right up to the window. He was standing on a log so he could see in. She yelled, "*Joe!* What are you doing?!"

Joe stepped backward so fast that he almost fell off the log. He fumbled around and said, "I was, ah, just doing something with my dog."

"No you weren't, you were peeping! That's why you wanted to go to your room, so you could make a peephole!"

Joe stormed into the house and said in a voice as innocent as he could muster to anyone who would listen, "Sylvia is accusing me of peeping. Can you believe that?"

Whenever two people disagreed in our family, the person who first told his or her side of the story was believed more readily than the person trying to defend herself. Anyone who believed the first story and then changed her mind when hearing the opposing side was seen as "two-faced."

Joe knew this. And so by bursting in the door, he could get his side of the story told first. Mem and my sisters and I were all in the kitchen. As soon as he started telling his side, Sylvia came from the living room and told us what had actually happened.

Joe said, "See, she's accusing me of peeping."

I was peeling potatoes for supper and turned to Joe and asked, "And *did* you?"

Joe turned on his heel and said, "I am not going to waste my time talking to *you*," and stalked out of the house.

"Good, then don't," I said to his retreating back.

I looked at Mem at the other end of the counter. She wore an impassive expression and didn't look away from the dishes she was stacking.

My sisters and I reinforced one another's resolve to be ever more vigilant about making sure our curtains were in place when we took a bath. Yet I felt exposed, not only because of Joe's penchant for peeping but also because of Mem. Most of the time she was good about not coming in while we were bathing. Once I started developing breasts, I felt deeply self-conscious about my body. I didn't even like exposing myself in front of my sisters, though it couldn't be helped because I shared a room with at least one of them during most of my growing-up years.

One particular Saturday afternoon in late fall, when I was twelve years old, Mem opened the door to the living room just as I had gotten into the tub. I said, "I'm taking a bath." I wrung out the cloth and plastered it on my bare white chest and held it there.

Mem said, "I have to tend the fire," and she busied herself with putting more wood in the stove. That wasn't exactly true because I had seen her tend the fire just before I'd gone into the living room to take my bath. I felt her eyes on me, looking me over. I did not like that feeling. She noticed I was uncomfortable and said, "*Du muscht dich net schäme, ich bin dei Mem.*"

Odd. That was the same line Joe had used the day he violated me. "You don't need to be ashamed. I am just your brother." Now Mem was using the same language. She lingered while I became increasingly uncomfortable as she eyed me. Her presence violated yet another boundary.

Several months after the bathing incident, I stayed home from school with a raging fever. As she usually did when we were sick, Mem let me sleep in her bed during the day so I would be closer to the warmth of the wood stove in the living room and she could watch over me. Our upstairs had no heat and no insulation, so it was as cold or hot as the outdoors. Sometimes we slept in below- freezing temperatures.

I was dimly aware that Joe Basco had come to visit because I heard the two of them talking in the living room as I fell into a feverish sleep.

I awoke when the bedroom door opened and Mem came in. I thought she was checking up on me, and that she would soon go back out into the living room while I continued to sleep. Instead she announced in a loud voice that I should come out into the living room. I could barely lift my head off the pillow, but I looked up and whispered, "But Joe Basco is out there."

"That's okay, come on out. He is just like family, so you don't need to be ashamed."

But Joe Basco was *not* family, and I *was* ashamed. And oh so very sick. I said, "But I just want to sleep," as I lay my head back on the pillow.

"No, come on out. It will do you good to get out of bed," Mem urged. I don't remember if I got up on my own, with her urging, or if she physically pulled me out of bed. But I remember standing next to the bed, shivering in my blue flannel nightgown, with my arms crossed over my chest. My teeth chattered as she put her hand on my shoulder and pulled me out into the living room. It smelled of Vicks camphor oil, and I saw the jar cap that she used to melt Vicks on the top of the stove. I felt my heart sink into my stomach. Joe Basco was standing there, next to the stove, looking at me with an expression in his dark eyes that made me shiver even more.

Mem urged me to take down my nightie and allow Joe Basco to rub my chest with Vicks. I looked at her then, begging her with my eyes not to make me do this. I willed her to come to her senses and protect me.

I stood there, crying and shivering, clutching my nightgown, and trying to cover my chest with my crossed arms. My breasts were just beginning to grow and I did not want them to be touched. But Mem moved in and took down my nightgown herself. All the way down to my waist. She would have let it fall to the floor, except I held it to my waist as tightly as I could. She pushed me up next to Joe Basco. He dunked his fingers in the Vicks and then he rubbed my budding breasts really fast with his stubby old fingers.

I had the feeling I was going to throw up, as Joe Basco's hand left my chest to reach for more Vicks. Then my body did something of its own volition. I pulled up my nightgown, and my feet carried me toward the stairway as fast as they could go. I barely felt my feet hit the cold stairs. I only knew that I *had* to get away from Mem and Joe Basco. I barely heard her calling me to come back. This was one time when the fear of what would happen if I obeyed her was greater than the fear of disobeying. When I got to my bed, I crawled into the middle of it, pulled the covers over myself, and curled into a fetal position. There I cried myself into a delirious sleep.

I did not get out of my bed for days. Most of the time I slept, but when I wasn't sleeping, I stared at the wall, hardly aware of my surroundings. I think someone must have brought me water to drink and food to eat, and I must have used the chamber pot, but I don't clearly remember doing anything except lying in my bed. Mem kept trying to coax me to get up, but I could not have left my bed if I had tried. I had lost all will to do anything. I'd lost my will to live.

Mem finally came up to my room one morning, yanked the covers off me, and said, "You've played hooky long enough. I know there is nothing wrong with you. Today you are going to school!"

"There is nothing wrong with you," is what she said. I looked at her then, and I saw a flicker of recognition on her face. She knew what was really wrong with me, and by then it had nothing to do with the flu. But then her blue eyes turned icy and I saw a warning in them that said, "Don't you dare!" I knew then that I was expected to never speak of the nightmare I'd lived through. I was to keep this secret inside of me for as long as she and I lived, if I knew what was good for me.

Even at school, I felt something had irrevocably changed in me. I wasn't the same girl who used to go to that same school and sit at that same desk. I was sure anyone looking at me could see that I was different. I tried to shake off the feeling, but I felt so ashamed.

Of all the ways Mem wronged me as I was growing up, this is the one I had, and still have, the hardest time understanding. At times I wanted to explain away this violation or tell myself that it hadn't really happened. Was I delirious, and had I imagined her turning into someone other than the mother I knew? But then I would remember the details—the feeling of Joe Basco's hands all over my breasts and his fast breathing. Then I would know that it had happened. I also now know the signs of someone who is sexually aroused. What would have happened had I not run upstairs that day?

I realized I could no longer trust Mem. Her betrayal was final. I now had to rely on my own intuition to protect myself from harm.

Over the years, I wondered what Mem would say if I were to ask her about the incident with Joe Basco. I didn't think I'd have the courage. What would I do if she denied what she'd done? Then I would always wonder if I'd imagined what had happened.

Years later, when I had two grown sons of my own, David and I were visiting Mem in her little house at the home place. Joe and his family had moved into the old family house years before. His wife and daughter were Mem's designated caregivers.

I was sitting on the vinyl couch in Mem's living room, across from her sitting in her recliner. She was battling cancer, so the time for breaking the silence was now or never. She likely guessed what was coming when I said, "Mem, I remember something from my childhood that I have never understood."

She listened while I told her what I remembered about her encouraging Joe Basco to rub my chest with Vicks. I ended by asking her, "Why did you do that?"

Mem looked at me sideways and sheepishly said, "I didn't think you'd mind."

I wanted to scream at her, You didn't think I'd *mind?* I was twelve years old—how could you not understand what a violation that was? How could you be so disengaged from being the mother I needed? Do you think this *justifies* what you and Joe Basco did?

I didn't say any of this. I sat there too overwhelmed with all that was wrong in the few words Mem had spoken. If ever there was a reason for her to apologize and ask for my forgiveness, this was it. But she had never done that before, and she wasn't going to do it now. Even though this violation had taken place thirty-six years earlier, she was still as incapable of offering me a sincere apology as she had ever been. Instead she sat there with a sheepish face. I knew that look. She'd been using that hangdog, poor pitiful me act for as long as I could remember. I was now supposed to feel sorry for *her* instead of the other way around. I was now to take pity on *her* and not press this any further. After all, *she* was dying of cancer.

I still wonder why I didn't unleash my outrage on Mem. At the time I wasn't conscious of all the reasons why I held back as I did. I knew what it was like for my family to gang up on me. To get them on her side, Mem would have told my siblings the story of how I had hurt her feelings. If I'd given voice to my feelings, the fallout might have been severe enough to prevent me from attending Mem's funeral. Maybe I would've been accused of putting Mem in the grave prematurely.

Stories abound of people wanting to unburden themselves of the wrongs they have done by reconciling with their loved ones as death approaches. Not Mem. Ever the martyr, she used her impending death as another way of invoking sympathy. I was supposed to feel that it was cruel to voice my feelings about what happened on that long-ago winter day.

So, I held back the words from spilling out of my mouth. But I didn't want to be sitting there visiting with Mem in her living room any longer. I felt like I was going to throw up.

At that moment, Joe's daughter walked in the door, giving me the perfect excuse to escape.

CIRCLE OF LIFE

Unable are the loved to die, for love is immortality. ~Emily Dickinson

Our family occasionally got together with aunts, uncles, and cousins on my mother's side. When we gathered, there were more than one hundred of us. These gatherings were usually jolly and fun. Then came the Christmas of 1970, when it wasn't jolly and it wasn't fun because Death came knocking on the door to claim one of the Miller clan.

When we were young and we still fit into our buggy, we would travel eight miles by horse and buggy to my grandparents' house. Then as we outgrew the buggy, my parents hired a "taxi" instead.

One Sunday afternoon upon arrival, we entered through *Momme's* kitchen, which was the next best thing to getting an embrace. No one in the community hugged as a way of greeting one another, but *Momme's* kind and welcoming smile was enough. Her kitchen smelled of baked beans and bacon that made my stomach growl.

Momme was a meticulous housekeeper. Her hardwood floors gleamed, and everything was in its place, neat and clean. She kept her sewing machine at the far end of the living room. A white porcelain rooster stood proud and tall on top of the sewing machine, right inside the front windows.

Aunt Saloma's family had arrived before us. I waited eagerly for more cousins my age to join us, when *Dodde* exclaimed, "Here comes Sarah and Dan. Boy is *that* buggy full! The springs are completely flat!" The buggy, pulled by two horses, stopped out by the barn. Several of the menfolk walked out to help Uncle Dan unhitch the horses. Two of the youngest children sat on Aunt Sarah's lap, with another three on the little bench by her feet. Before Aunt Sarah stepped down from the buggy, she handed the babies to her daughters who had climbed from the back. But the number of cousins emerging from the back of the buggy was what had us all standing and staring out the kitchen window with our mouths open. When six of them had emerged, we thought that would be it. But then another cousin stepped down, and another, and then another, until at least a dozen of them had stepped out of the back.

We soon heard how Dan and Sarah had come upon a group of cousins who were walking and decided to pick them up to give them a ride to my grandparents' house. Farther down the road, they'd come to another group and took it as a challenge to fit them in, too. Their buggy had two seats in the back facing one another. Cousins had piled in, two or three deep.

When Uncle Dan came in, he hooked his thumbs in his suspenders and said in his bragging style, "Oh, we had plenty of room! We could have picked up two more!"

Come one, come all—that was the feeling at *Momme* and *Dodde's* house.

The food was always sumptuous, especially on Thanksgiving and Christmas, with my mother and the aunts competing to prepare the tastiest dishes. The men clearly had it easier on those holidays. They would sit in the living room, smoking their pipes and laughing and joking, while the women cooked the meal and we girls set the table. My mouth watered when I saw the platters of turkey, the mounds of mashed potatoes with browned butter running down the sides, *Momme's* homemade dressing, homemade bread and jam, various pickles and relishes, squash, and applesauce. But I was a girl, and so I had to wait for the second seating. The men were called first and they came and sat down at the table. Then the boys came and sat down, according to age—the oldest to the youngest. Most of my cousins had red hair, so there were plenty of curly redheads, with the occasional dark-haired boy, all lined up tight on the benches on both sides of the table. The women took it as a challenge to seat all the men and boys at once, with the group totaling more than forty. When the benches at the main table were full, the rest of the boys sat at a smaller table around the corner in Aunt Ada's living room, and the toddlers and babies were fed by their older sisters or their mothers.

My girl cousins and I waited on the men and boys, bringing more food as they emptied the bowls and platters, and we poured water into their glasses. When they were done eating, the uncles patted their full stomachs and went back to the living room while we cleared the table, washed the dishes, set the table again, brought out the food, and finally sat down to eat. Just as we were beginning to enjoy our meal, the men came sauntering out of the living room, stood over us with their full bellies, and said, "Are you *still* eating?" One of my aunts meekly said, "Next time, maybe you should serve us, and we'll be done first." That brought laughs and guffaws from the men. I wondered how the women could defend themselves so meekly when I had visions of throwing my fork at the men.

After our meal, another mound of dishes had to be washed, dried, and put away. When the relatives got together at my aunts' homes, the women and girls sometimes played a trick on the hostess by taking some of the greasiest pots and pans and hiding them, most often under the aunt's bed. The smell would usually alert the aunt to the trick that had been played on her. As far as I know, they took it all in good humor.

No one played dirty tricks on *Momme*, however. We all knew how generous she was to invite our big families to her house, and so we diligently did the dishes from beginning to end. This was the only time that the girl cousins of all ages interacted. We did them in shifts because not all of us could fit into *Momme's* small kitchen at once.

Uncle Ervin and his wife had the biggest family—fifteen children, including four sets of twins. The eldest were twin daughters, Ella and Elva. When Elva was a young child, she contracted polio, which left her disabled. One of her legs was much shorter than the other, and one of her shoulder blades protruded out of her back in such a way that it looked as if it must hurt. She was shoulder-high to her twin, Ella, which made her look much younger. I noticed, even at a young age, how cheerful Elva was despite her handicaps. She had a heavenly smile that radiated from her whole being, and I marveled at Elva's sunny personality, her contagious laugh, and her sense of humor despite her physical condition. It seemed to me that if anyone had a right to feel sorry for herself and complain about her lot in life, it would have been Elva. Perhaps there were times when she did, but it seemed to me that she maintained her positive outlook and got along well with her siblings. It was clear that her whole family loved and cherished her.

If Thanksgiving was bountiful, Christmas was festive. I enjoyed spending the day with my girl cousins and, of course, the food was plentiful and delicious. When we were finally done with the last batch of dishes, my aunts brought out the Christmas goodies: turtles, popcorn balls, Rice Krispie treats, coconut bars, thumbprint cookies, hickory-nut cookies, two kinds of fudge—maple and vanilla—and homemade chocolate-covered cherries. Even though we didn't have a Christmas tree, we had the candy table at *Momme's* house. At these large family gatherings, there were enough sweets and goodwill for everyone.

Then one year, shortly before Christmas, news reached us that Ella and Elva had been in a car and buggy accident. They were riding home from a young people's gathering on a cold December evening with Ella's boyfriend, Jonas, when a car came up over the brow of a hill unexpectedly and the headlights blinded Jonas' horse. The horse panicked and bolted into the car's path and was hit. The buggy broke apart on impact. Elva and Jonas were thrown to the side of the road, but the horse dragged Ella and the wrecked buggy down the road for quite a way before someone was able to stop it. Jonas escaped without serious injuries, but Ella had deep and terrible scrapes on her hip from being dragged. Elva had a broken leg and was covered with bruises. She was in the hospital with her leg in traction, which Mem explained meant having her leg strung up from wires overhead. A few days later, she contracted pneumonia. Each day the news sounded increasingly grim. I had the feeling Elva was going to die. I wished I could shake that feeling, but it was like an inner knowing I sometimes had. When I noticed pregnant women in the church, I would have a feeling about whether they were having a boy or a girl. Once I was sure my "feeling" was wrong because I thought a mother of four daughters was going to give birth to a son. I wanted to be wrong because I didn't like having this way of knowing that I couldn't explain. When Vincent was born, I realized I couldn't deny my feelings of knowing something deep down. Now the feeling I couldn't shake about Elva troubled me. I wished I could share in her mother's hopes that Elva would pull through.

On Christmas Day, we gathered at my grandparents' home. The relatives were quiet and subdued, and even the food didn't taste as good as usual as we thought about Elva in the hospital, and her mother who wouldn't leave her side. While we were sitting quietly that afternoon, someone brought the news that Elva had died. We sat for a time to try to absorb and comprehend this news, and then each family left for home in silence.

The funeral was held three days later in my uncle's big home. They couldn't fit everyone into one house, so people gathered in two other homes in the neighborhood. Each house had a different preacher officiating. Our family was in Elva's house because we were *freundshaft* —relatives. We sat on backless church benches in straight rows across the kitchen. Girls sat next to their mothers and boys next to their fathers. Everyone wore black. Only the women's head coverings and the men's shirts were white. Where I sat with Mem and my sisters, I could see into the living room where Elva's family sat next to the coffin set up on two kitchen chairs next to the wall. The coffin was closed while the preacher talked about "the sister who now walked with God." He said it was not for us to question why or when God calls us home, and that we needed to accept everything as God's will. Then the preacher went on to say that it was important for everyone to be ready because we could never know when our time would come, and that if we were in good standing with God when we died, we'd have a better chance of making it to heaven. Our Maker had a Book of Life upon which everything we did was recorded. At the end of our lives, if we had done more good things than bad, we would be allowed to enter heaven through the pearly gates.

I was glad the preacher didn't elaborate on the alternative to heaven because it was too horrible for me to fathom. Some preachers had a way of describing hell in such vivid detail, I wondered if they had been there. Perhaps these sermons were the reason why I was terrified of death. The preachers claimed there were only two choices of where our souls could end up when we died—heaven or hell. They also claimed it was very difficult to get to heaven. I knew I was no saint, but I also didn't think I was bad enough to deserve to go to hell. When I was a young child, I didn't have to worry about going to hell. Children were considered innocent and therefore they'd go straight to heaven if they died. But I didn't know when this free ticket expired. I found myself in a precarious position between child and adult and between good and bad. I didn't know where I belonged, so I often felt like a lost soul.

After the second sermon was done, we all knelt in prayer. Then we took our seats, and Rube, the funeral director, opened the coffin. The people from the other two houses filed by to see Elva one last time. The men took off their hats as they came into the house, filed past the coffin, and then left by a different door. It seemed as though the line went on forever.

Elva's sisters cried into their handkerchiefs as we waited solemnly for people to file past. Finally it came time for the relatives to see Elva. I walked behind Lizzie, so I couldn't see Elva at first. When I did, I saw that she had big black and blue marks on her face, neck, and hands. I was afraid of Elva's dead and bruised body in the coffin, of death, and of people crying and keening. So I cried, too. After filing past Elva, we went back to our benches and sat down.

Finally Elva's family went up to the coffin. They formed a circle around her, and the whole family wept and keened. Elva's siblings leaned into the coffin and keened as if they were begging their sister to come back to life. Their sobs were contagious. I tried to hold back my own, but they kept heaving out of my chest. When Rube came forward to close the coffin, Elva's sisters clung to the sides. Finally, the aunts pried their fingers from the coffin, took them by their shoulders, and guided them back to their seats. There they continued to weep as if their hearts were all broken into pieces.

The pallbearers carried Elva out into the cold winter day and slid her coffin into the funeral buggy waiting there. I didn't go with them; only the adults followed the funeral buggy that bore the coffin, drawn by a horse that walked slowly, out to the road, up the hill, and into the graveyard where Elva would be buried, on the knoll above her family's farm.

Later, when we were back home, Mem described how the bitter cold wind made it nearly impossible to hear the group of men singing the lonely farewell hymns as the younger men who were pallbearers lowered the coffin and filled in the grave. The singers used their hats as shields to try to keep their voices from being lost in the wind. I felt a cold shiver go through me, even though we were warming ourselves around our wood stove in the living room. The foreboding feeling that Elva would die had come about. Now her death haunted me, and I couldn't help but empathize with her family's intense grief.

THE UNBEARABLE PAIN OF BEING

No matter what sort of difficulties, how painful experience is, if we lose our hope, that is our real disaster. ~Dalai Lama

By the time I turned thirteen, Mem had trained me well to take on family responsibilities by giving me tasks beyond my development as a young child. It started with me standing on our little bench to reach the sink to do dishes when I was three or four and baking cakes and cookies before I could read the recipes. I also learned to iron clothes with a gas iron when the ironing board was chest high for me. The flame inside the iron was in line with my upper arm as I pushed it, back and forth, over the piece of clothing I was ironing. My face got hot being that close to the gas flame. When I helped Mem with canning, I often burned my fingers, especially as I dipped boiling hot tomato juice into jars. The steam burns hurt the most. I'd walk around with the burned finger in a glass of cool water until I could bear to take it out. One day Mem berated me for being too sensitive to pain. I told her it hurt more for me than it did for her. She laughed and said that it hurt her just as much, it was just that she could bear the pain better. I wondered if there was a difference.

I had become Katherine's second mother when I was seven years old. Mem probably noticed that her youngest was not developing as quickly as other children her age, but I had no concept of that, though I did notice how temperamental and stubborn Katherine was. She was hard for my sisters and me to manage when Mem was out in the sugarhouse. Katherine would decide that she wanted only Mem to change her diaper. She'd kick and scream and cry and flail her arms so that it took both Lizzie and me to do the task. One of us had to hold her down, while the other changed her. This was the only way we knew to deal with it.

It was terribly hard to potty-train Katherine. Mem relied on me to teach Katherine as she developed, but I did not know how to help her learn to use the potty. Once Katherine's diapers didn't fit her any longer, Mem finally managed to train her while we were at school, when Katherine was four years old. Most children were potty trained at two or three years old.

Katherine was still only making baby sounds when she was four. Around that time I suggested that we start calling her by her name, rather than calling her "Baby." I kept saying if we called her Baby, she would act like one. I don't know where I got this idea. Perhaps I heard Grace Bradley or someone else say it. It was hardest to get Datt to change his habit. Katherine was five years old by the time everyone in the family was calling her by her name.

Despite of all this, Mem wouldn't admit that Katherine was handicapped, or what was deemed "retarded" at the time. Mem claimed that she was "just slow," and decided not to send Katherine to kindergarten in public school. She thought the other children would make fun of her. So she waited until Katherine was six and sent her to the first grade in Amish school. I was in eighth grade at the time, and by then I no longer felt like her second mother. She was my youngest sister who had problems getting along with children her age. One day she hurt another child on the playground and the teachers decided they needed to teach her a lesson.

The head teacher, Eugene, called Katherine down to the furnace room with him. My heart sank. At home, Katherine resisted spankings. Mem usually protected her from any punishment at all. I could not imagine this turning out well.

The whole schoolroom became deathly quiet. I could hear Eugene talking to Katherine, and then all of a sudden Katherine gave a blood-curdling scream that raised the hair on the back of my neck. As Eugene began whipping her, the screams became louder. She sounded like a trapped animal.

I sat stone-still at my desk, with my heart pounding hard inside my chest. As I stared at my desk, I sensed that others were looking at me and wondering what I would do. I thought about interrupting Eugene, but I didn't dare. I had always looked up to him as a wise teacher. But deep down in my gut, I knew he was making a mistake this time.

Katherine's screams became more frantic. I could stand it no longer. I bolted out of my seat and ran down to the furnace room where Eugene was holding a thin whip in his hands—those hands that were twisted with arthritis. He turned when I said, "Everyone can hear this."

"Leave us," he said with a grim look on his face. "I'm almost done. She needs to learn her lesson."

As I turned to leave, I saw Katherine's tear-stained face looking at me, her blue eyes begging me for help. But I couldn't, so I turned and fled up the concrete stairs. I could not bear to hear Katherine's screams, and I couldn't go back into the classroom and face the seventy pairs of eyes looking at me, so I ran to the outhouse to be alone. There I sat down and stared at the floor in the semi-darkness, biting my fist. I could not cry. I could not scream. I could not do anything. My mind froze in the helplessness I felt. I knew what I had witnessed was wrong. I could feel it way down deep, and there was nothing I could do to fix it.

Mem was upset that afternoon when she found out that Katherine had been spanked at school. She asked me, "Why didn't you stop it?"

I cried then. I felt like I had failed. Even though I'd tried, I had failed Katherine, and I had failed Mem. How could I tell Mem that I could not handle the responsibilities that she was heaping on my young shoulders? How could I tell her that mothering Katherine was her responsibility and not mine? How could I tell her that I still had some growing up to do myself? Why was she asking me to intervene on Katherine's behalf, even though Mem herself had often whipped me until I couldn't bear the pain? No one had ever intervened then. I couldn't say any of this to Mem because I didn't yet understand it myself. I only knew that my insides felt all mixed up. All I could do was shake my head and cry.

I dreaded the day I would be receiving my eighth-grade diploma. Most other Amish young people were happy to be done with school by the time they were thirteen or fourteen. I felt like the good part of my life was going to come to a complete end. Ever since I'd started kindergarten, I looked forward to September so I could go to school. That would no longer be the case when I received my diploma. Finishing eighth grade meant finishing school for the rest of my life—at least if I stayed Amish. The Amish traditions were deep and wide and strong and would not allow me to continue my education, no matter how much I wanted to.

I officially graduated from eighth grade at the year-end school picnic when Eugene handed us eighth graders our diplomas. My diploma is dated May 1971, but I don't remember anything about that day. I must have been in complete denial. It still seemed to me that I would be going back to school with my siblings when fall came.

After the school picnic, it was time to face the summer work. The chores in our household were never-ending. My sisters and I had to take turns doing the daily "morning work" (cleaning up after breakfast, making beds, and sweeping the floors). Then we'd make the midday meal and supper, wash and dry the dishes, and sweep the floors each time.

Mem was usually busy with a sewing project, canning, gardening, or making meals. By this time, Mem no longer set the table, did dishes, or swept the floor. These were now our jobs.

Mondays and Thursdays were washdays when we carried and heated the water and filled up the wringer washer with hot water. We'd put the clothes through the washer, rinse them in the tubs, send them through the wringer again, and then hang them out on the clothesline. In the afternoons, we'd take the clothes from the lines, fold them, and put them away in their rightful drawers.

Then came hours and hours of ironing. Dozens of dresses had to be ironed, put on hangers, and hung in closets. The Sunday capes and aprons had to be starched before we ironed them, carefully folded, and placed in the Sunday clothes drawer.

There was always work to be done in the garden. In late April, Mem had us help plant the garden, which was as big as a field. By the time the planting was done, there was always weeding, hoeing, and watering to be done. As the vegetables grew, we had to pick them to can for winter use, starting with peas, followed by beans, cucumbers, beets, carrots, peppers, corn, and tomatoes. In late summer, we harvested cabbages and dug up potatoes to store in the basement.

Saturday was our cleaning and baking day. I was glad Mem trusted me with learning new things because I often did the baking, which meant I didn't have to do the cleaning.

Finally, on Sundays, we got a day of rest. Every other week, our church district had a church service in someone's home, which we attended religiously. On the in-between-church Sundays, we spent the day reading and playing games or getting together with other families in the community.

In the spring, we all pitched in to help with making maple syrup, which usually lasted several weeks, starting with hauling in the sap buckets, washing them in the washtubs downstairs, and turning them upside down to build pyramids so they could drain and air out. A day or two later, we stacked them inside one another and Datt hauled them out to the sugarhouse. He usually distributed the buckets with our team of horses, Don and Tops, while we were in school.

Then came tapping time. A team of us followed Datt as he bored holes in the maple trees, being careful not to put too many buckets on one tree. He bored the new holes away from the old ones from previous years to allow the tree to "heal." We came up behind Datt to tap in the spiles (metal spouts), hang the buckets, and put the covers on. I loved roaming the woods and hearing the sound of the first drips of sap inside each bucket: dink, dink, dink.

Mem and Datt prepared the sugarhouse as the sap collected in the buckets. All year, Datt had been cutting and splitting wood for the sugarhouse so it was seasoned and dry when sugaring time came.

As the buckets filled, Datt hitched up the team to the sled when there was snow, or to the wagon when the ground was bare. Then he put the gathering tank on, and away we'd go with our buckets to help him gather. As soon as Datt unloaded the first batch of sap into the storage tank, Mem started boiling it down. I sometimes helped her at night to fire up the arch and "syrup off" when it reached the right thickness, then filter the boiling-hot syrup through the felt filters into the syrup tank. I also helped to change and clean the filters of the mineral sediments (called niter) to prepare them for the next batch of syrup.

During sugaring season, Datt made deliveries to the Maple House in Burton, where they sold our syrup, along with syrup from other farms, to tourists and to Cleveland area residents.

After boiling season was over, we collected the buckets, covers, and spiles and stored them in the sugarhouse for the following year.

Preparing the soil and planting the garden came after sugaring season was over. Gardening season lasted all summer. In late summer we picked blackberries and elderberries. That is when the canning started. I once tried keeping track of how many jars of fruits and vegetables we canned each year, but it was always changing as we added and subtracted from the shelves of jars. When the shelves in the basement were full, there were between 500 and 600 jars of food stored for the winter.

The cycle of work in our house lent daily, weekly, and yearly rhythms to our lives, though at the time I experienced it as drudgery.

Most of the memories of my childhood that live in my mind are of the struggles I lived through. With a little effort, I can recall more pleasant memories. At times Mem could still be the good mother I knew when I was little. As we girls outgrew our playhouse, she taught us the homespun arts of embroidering, sewing, crocheting, quilting, and braiding rugs. Our summer days were often filled with work, but there were afternoons when we gathered in the living room, where it was cooler than anywhere else in the house, and worked on our crafts. This was our recreation. Mem was patient with us as we learned crafts from her. She allowed each of us to choose the project we wanted to work on. If I started embroidering a dresser scarf, I got to work on it to the end. I became meticulous about making my stitches small and even, and I took good care of the embroidery floss that could easily become tangled. Lizzie also enjoyed embroidery work, and she taught herself how to knit. She was the only one among us who enjoyed that craft. Sylvia was artistic, so she enjoyed doing all the handwork, though she gravitated toward those that were more freestyle, rather than having to follow patterns for colors or stitches. Because Sadie was younger, she often played with Simon and Katherine outside while the rest of us stitched.

Mem must not have enjoyed ripping rags for making carpets because some afternoons we had to rip old dresses and shirts into strips before we settled down to do our chosen craft. She would then sew the ends of the strips together, and we'd snip the threads and roll the long fabric strips into a ball for crocheting or weaving the rugs that dotted the floors in every room of our house. Mem crocheted rugs and my Aunt Saloma wove rugs on her loom.

After we learned how to rip the carpet rags, Mem taught us how to sew the strips together on the treadle sewing machine. One day I decided if I was going to rip and sew the fabric strips together, then I wanted the fun of crocheting them too. Perhaps that was what Mem hoped I would do. She taught me how to get the rug started, including how to "increase" by putting two stitches into one hole every so often around the "curve," which made the rug flat instead of cupping the edges. When my rug started cupping, Mem would say, "You'll have to open it and do it over. You know what you need to do to make it lie flat." Eventually I got the hang of it. Most of the time, I followed Mem's guidance on the colors to use in a rug, but sometimes I made my own choices.

Mem also ripped strips of wool fabric from coats and suits, sewed the ends of the strips together, and braided them into rugs. These strips were wider and thicker than the cotton ones we used for crocheting.

I loved the feel and the rhythm of braiding. I had learned to braid three strands of twine together to make a jumprope when I was five or six years old. My sisters and I braided one another's hair as we got older. I used to watch Mem braiding three strands of wool together for her rugs. I longed to braid, so she allowed me to braid without folding in the edges, and then she'd take it out before braiding it properly by folding the edges of each strand in so the braid would look nice and smooth.

Long before Mem taught me how to braid properly, she taught me how to rip the wool into strips. Then I learned how to lay the two ends together to hide the seam on the inside of the braid and sew it together on the machine. When I insisted, Mem taught me how to fold in the edges of the wool fabric and hold it with my fingers as I braided. It took months of trying before Mem deemed my braiding good enough to "keep."

One summer when I was twelve or thirteen, Mem decided she was going to teach us to quilt. She had put together a patchwork quilt with used fabric, and she said she didn't care what the stitches looked like because this one was for us to learn on. I had never gotten used to wearing a thimble. Mem told me I would need to learn how to use one for quilting. I told her I wouldn't because I hated thimbles. She said, "Suit yourself." For several days, I used my middle finger to push the end of the needle up and down through two layers of fabric with batting in between until I wore a hole into my finger. When the needle kept slipping into the hole, I finally had to get used to a thimble. It was one of those times when Mem could easily have repeated what she often said to me, "Oh Lomie, you always have to do things the *hard* way," but this time she didn't. I was allowed more autonomy when I was doing handwork in Mem's living room than in any other arena in my home life. It is no wonder that I still enjoy practicing the homespun arts I learned from Mem.

BATTLE OF WILLS

I had a very dysfunctional family, and a very hard childhood. So I made a world out of words. And it was my salvation. ~Mary Oliver

My friend Ruth had graduated from the eighth grade the same day I did. I was grateful that our mothers allowed us to walk to one another's homes to visit. Ruth had been a constant friend in school when many of the other girls spent time *schpotting*. She wasn't mocked for being the daughter of her parents like my sisters and I were, but she also wasn't included in the inner core of popular girls.

Visiting Ruth that summer was the highlight of my life. It gave me a break from my battle of wills with Mem. Whenever someone was visiting, Mem turned into my good mother.

On the walk up Butternut Road to Ruth's house, I felt like I was being kissed by summer when the sun shone down on me and breezes blew across my cheeks. I passed the beautiful Shanower farm on the hill on the left. On the right, fields of yellow buttercups swayed in the wind. Red-winged blackbirds clung to tall grasses and belted out their summery songs. Little flocks of goldfinches flitted about over the fields, and butterflies of different colors fluttered from flower to flower.

Two of Ruth's sisters were Sylvia's and Sadie's ages, so two or three of us often walked together to their house. Whenever it was time for us to walk home, Ruth and her sisters walked part of the way home with us. When they visited us, we did the same.

One Sunday after church, I went home with Ruth's family to stay for the afternoon. Her family ate popcorn on Sunday afternoons like my family did. So Ruth was popping one popper of corn after another as we visited. She was shaking the popper when she said to me, "I will tell you something if you promise not to be surprised." I had the feeling that she wouldn't tell me unless I promised, so I did. With a smile on her face, Ruth announced that her family was moving to Michigan.

My hand stopped with two kernels of popcorn halfway to my mouth. I'd promised Ruth I wouldn't be surprised, but I couldn't have been more shocked. It struck me that Ruth was happy about it. I felt like crying on the spot. Ruth might have noticed my crestfallen face. She promised she would write often but at that moment, that was no consolation. I realized that the one bright spot in my life was about to move away.

Ruth and her family did move to Michigan later that summer. I wrote to her, and a long time later she responded, but the letter didn't give me much insight into her new life and what it was like. I wrote to her again and didn't hear from her for months. Soon the letters stopped coming. In incremental steps, I had lost my best friend.

After Ruth's family moved, the tensions between Mem and me intensified. They weren't always about whether I would do *what* she said, but *how* I did it. I often wanted to do things differently than she'd taught me. She did not like that. She would say in her solid voice, "When you have a house of *your* own, you can do things *your* way. Until then, you do things *my* way!" I would have to let that be the last word and do it *her* way.

The same summer Ruth moved, Annie Troyer came to our house with a message from her mother to mine. I liked Annie's carefree ways. At school she'd managed to stay out of the circle of mockers because she wasn't clannish and didn't seem to need to have an exclusive friend. She'd graduated from eighth grade the year before I had. Having her at my house that summer day was a rare treat. She stayed a while, and when it was time for her to go home, Mem allowed me to walk partway home with her.

Annie and I walked up Hale Road, talking about school. The name of the French explorer who "discovered" Florida, Ponce de Leon, came up. I don't remember how that developed into what we did next. We linked our arms at the elbow and danced in a circle singing "Ponce de day Leon, Ponce de day Leon, Ponce de day Leon," and then giggled at how silly we were. When I looked into Annie's smiling face, I saw pure delight. It was infectious. For that summer moment, I laughed right along with her. According to the Amish rules, it was wrong to dance, but Annie didn't seem to feel guilty about anything. I wondered what could be wrong with something that felt so delightful.

After we lingered there in the middle of our dirt road, reluctant to leave one another, Annie said she had better get back home before her mother wondered where she was. She walked in the direction of her home, and I walked in the direction of mine. Now and again, we turned around and waved to one another, then continued on our way until she was a small dot on the landscape and I could no longer see her waving.

When there was no one visiting, my battle of wills with Mem would commence. She required both obedience and conformity. Like many other Amish parents, she saw it as her duty to break my will. She varied her punishments to make them more effective.

One summer, Mem forced me to aid in my own punishments by commanding that I go out into the woods to find and bring in a whip she would use to punish me. I soon learned to take my time so her anger would cool down. I chose a stick that looked like it was sturdy, but it would break the first time she whacked me with it. She soon figured that out, so she sent Joe to cut the whips. Since Mem didn't whip him, he took pride in bringing her the ones that stung.

Mem sometimes smacked me across my face so hard I would bite my tongue. The hurt and rage I felt then was almost overwhelming. The assault made my ears ring and left her finger marks on my cheek. I wouldn't have had words for describing this at the time, but now I think of a person's face as representing one's identity. Mem was attacking my identity when she slapped me like that. She also hit me on one shoulder or another—one great big stinging slap. For reasons unclear to me, I hated that almost as much as being slapped in the face. It was painful and humiliating. Perhaps when she hit me on the shoulder, she was diminishing my stature.

Mem had yet another way of breaking me down. She would dissolve into tears, go into her bedroom, close the door, and sob out loud. Then I'd feel so ashamed, especially when my siblings would say, "Lomie why can't you just do what Mem says? Now you've made her cry." Making Mem cry was one of the most shameful things I could do.

When Mem seemed at a loss to know what would make me conform, she threatened me, most commonly with her emphatic, "*Ich tzill die Scheiz aus dich schaffa!*—I'm going to work the *shit* out of you!" With that, she demanded I do a list of the tasks she knew I didn't like.

Of all the chores I had to perform, I hated doing dishes the most. I did everything I could to get out of them. I learned that a long visit to the outhouse usually did the trick because most of the dishes were done when I got back to the kitchen. Then one day that changed. When I came up the stairs, my eyes went directly to the counter to see how many dishes were left. To my dismay, they were all still piled high and the table had not even been cleared. From the living room came Mem's voice, saying that the dishes were all mine and that I had better get busy.

I knew Mem was making me do them alone to show me who was boss. I also knew I had not been doing my duty when I stayed in the outhouse so long. Anger welled up inside my chest as I poured hot water from the teakettle into the dishpan and pumped cold water from the hand pump to cool the boiling water. I knew deep down that I deserved this for all those times I had avoided the dishes, but that only made me angrier. I slammed the dishes into the drainer as my way of expressing my rage.

Mem said in that warning voice of hers, "Lomie, if you know what's good for you..."

Before I could even think about it, I said under my breath, "Yeah, then what?"

Mem got up from her sewing chair and said, "I'll *tell* you what!" She headed toward the kitchen. I looked around as chills of fear crept up the back of my neck. I expected that she would grab the whip from the top of the china cabinet and make me come to her for my punishment. Instead she walked past me to the hand sink. Now I realized what she was up to. She had washed my mouth out with soap before. But this time she came up with a new twist. She grabbed the dirty rag that we'd used to clean eggs from the chicken coop. She rubbed it on the green bar of soap, and turned to me and said, "*Comm du do haeh!*—You come here!"

When I saw what Mem was up to, I stood there crying and shaking my head slowly back and forth in disbelief. There was no use begging, but I did anyway. "Mem, I'm sorry. I'll do the dishes."

"Come *here!*" she demanded.

I had never been able to disobey that voice of Mem's before, and couldn't now. I took a step toward her, crying and begging her with my eyes not to. She grabbed me by my arm, whirled me around, put her arm around my head in a chokehold, grabbed my chin, and said, "Open your *mouth!*" The thought of aiding Mem in this bizarre punishment made my insides roil in fury. But I had no choice. Mem took that chicken-shit rag with soap on it and scrubbed it all over my tongue. The urge to bite down on her fingers was almost unbearable, but my gag reflex saved me. The taste of soap was bad enough, but the taste of it mixed with chicken shit was far worse. When Mem finally let me go, I ran outside and gagged and gagged. I could not gag enough. My rage was so great it caused pressure in my chest. I promised myself I would never defy Mem again, yet at the same time, I wanted to throw a chair through the kitchen window.

In the following days, I could not get rid of the taste in my mouth, even when I was eating. I went through my days without feeling or thinking and did what I was told without resistance. Mem seemed satisfied that she had broken my will. Her ultimate aim seemed to be to annex my will to hers. If I could have turned my "self" off permanently, my relationship with Mem would have been a lot simpler. But eventually my will emerged from my despondency and fought to survive. Then my battle of wills with Mem would commence once again.

One day that summer, Mem decided it was time for me to put my hair up in a bun instead of braiding it. She had me take down my hair and wash it. When it was dry, she showed me how she put up her hair with a string and hairpins. Except she was missing a very key thing—my hair was much thicker and heavier than hers, so the bun she made on the back of my head with the hairpins was not going to hold up—I could feel it. I told her that the only thing holding up my hair bun was my *kopp* and if I were to shake my head, my hair would fall down. Mem didn't believe me. So I shook my head, and my *kopp* fell off, hairpins went flying, and my hair tumbled down my back.

Instead of getting the point, Mem put my hair back up, told me to put my *kopp* back on, smacked my back, and told me to behave myself.

Upstairs, I asked Sylvia to braid my hair for me, and she did. Later, I asked around and found out how other girls were putting up their hair so it would stay. I bought myself big barrettes and used them to clip my hair up. I thought hairpins were for old ladies, and I wasn't there yet.

For reasons I still don't understand, my close relationship with Sylvia had changed the day she and I had disagreed about where we were going sledding and Mem had intervened to tell Sylvia she didn't always need to do as I said. Perhaps Mem thought I was dominating Sylvia. But it seemed like Sylvia had heard the message that there was something wrong with doing anything I said, and she resisted it ever after. She and Sadie began to pal around instead.

My relationship with Sadie was quite clear. It seemed like she just plain hated me. She refused to talk to me, sometimes for weeks on end. It felt like she regretted having me as a sister. So it was out of the question for the three of us to pal around together.

Sometimes Sadie and Sylvia had disagreements. That's when Sylvia and I would get along. Whenever Sylvia was on my side, I hoped we could always be pals, but inevitably she dashed those hopes and returned to siding with Sadie. Sylvia continued to shift loyalties between Sadie and

me. Even though I realized at some point that it didn't have much to do
with what I did, but more to do with whether she was getting along with
Sadie, it felt so good to have her close again that I wouldn't have
considered icing her out as she did me.

In the meantime, Mem continued to heap responsibilities on me.
Often I found myself working while Sylvia and Sadie were out playing. I
resented that they didn't have to work as hard as I did. Mem wouldn't
listen to me when I voiced this injustice. She considered such criticism
backtalk, which often led to more punishments. So I tried changing the
imbalance by bossing Sylvia and Sadie around. They only distanced
themselves more, creating a vicious cycle. Mem allowed the tension
among us to grow with her silence. Sometimes my jealousy and
resentment threatened to boil over.

Then one day they did.

It was a typical Saturday cleaning day. Mem had sent us upstairs to
clean our rooms. When we were done, we were expected to go downstairs
and help clean the rest of the house. I was shaking rugs out my window
when I turned around and saw Sadie's little yellow kitten. I had nearly
dropped the rug on it without knowing it was there. My rage at that
moment was overwhelming. Sadie was playing with her kitten instead of
cleaning her room, which meant that she would still be upstairs dawdling
when I had to go downstairs and clean the rest of the house. The cats
belonged in the barn and were not allowed in the house, but Sadie had
snuck the kitty in anyway. She'd been refusing to talk to me for days, and
there was nothing I could say or do to change that. I was insanely jealous
of the affection she lavished on her pet kittens while shutting me out
completely.

My hair stood on end as I picked up the kitten, walked over to the
window, and unceremoniously dropped it out. As soon as I took my
hand out from under that furry little body, I leaned out the window,
wishing I could take it back. The ground seemed a long way off. My heart
sank as I watched the kitten hit the ground. It lay there for a long
moment, and then I watched as it got up and started walking away while
meowing in pain.

Sylvia immediately went and told Sadie what I'd done. Sadie went
through my room and down the stairs. She wore a grim expression on her

face and refused to look at me. I sat on the edge of my bed and stared at the floor. I was too shocked to move. I'd been outside of myself when I dropped the kitten out the window. I closed my eyes against the regret. I felt all black inside.

I was dimly aware of the bustle downstairs. The kitten was alive, but crying pitifully. I heard people talking about what I'd done, but I was too shocked at myself to feel hurt by their words.

I recall sitting on the edge of my bed, but then I don't remember what happened after that. I must have been going through my day without thinking or feeling because I don't remember anything until later that night when I went to bed. Two rooms away, Sadie tried comforting her kitten, which was crying out in pain. Mem had splinted one of its hind legs, and she allowed Sadie to take the kitten to bed with her. The kitten's cries sounded helpless and pitiful.

Sylvia and I shared a bed. I lay awake for a long time after Sylvia fell asleep. That is when I allowed my tears to flow. So many emotions pushed out through those tears: shock at my violence and the heartless act I had committed, anger for all the injustices in my life, and frustration for not being able to change any aspect of my circumstances. But most of all, there was overwhelming sadness for all the pain I had endured. Through all of that pain, I'd clung to the feeling that I was still a good person. Now I had lost even that. What I had done to the kitten was no better than what Joe had done when he starved his rabbits. I closed my eyes against my cruelty and was engulfed by a great black void inside.

Somehow that long night of my soul did come to an end. When I heard the birds chirping and twittering in the predawn, I finally drifted into sleep.

In the days that followed, whenever Sadie willfully avoided me, I felt I deserved whatever hostility or hatred she aimed my way.

I had felt a sense of hopelessness in my life before. But now I felt I deserved it for being sinful. I worried about dying and going to hell. I tried praying to God to help me be a better person, but it didn't feel like God heard my prayers because I was unworthy.

For weeks I had no energy to do the things being asked of me. I often snuck away to be alone in my room, where I cried, read books, or lay on my bed, staring at the ceiling, wishing I had a different life. I had no idea how to frame what I was experiencing, but I was aware that my absence was intensifying Mem's workload. I am surprised to this day that Mem allowed me to get away from the work she usually assigned to me. Perhaps she knew that something had broken in me, and maybe she preferred this to my rebellion against her.

One day while we were preparing for an upcoming church service that was going to be held in our house, one of the Weaver daughters was helping us clean for the occasion. When she and I were alone, she admonished me for not doing more for Mem. She said something to the effect of not knowing how Mem could survive her difficult life.

As I listened to Anna Marie say all this, I felt a tight knot of guilt in the pit of my stomach. First of all, I felt shame that other people knew I was not doing my part. Mem must have told someone. But then, worse than my shame was my fear that Mem would die, leaving us children with an even more unbearable life. I resolved that I would have to do better, even though I didn't know where the energy was going to come from. I could not live with myself if I felt responsible for Mem's death, so I did what I'd done many times before—I felt Mem's pain to the exclusion of my own. There was no way to bear both, so I put mine aside and focused on how to lighten Mem's burdens. This was what she expected of me. I dragged myself through the daily chores with no hope that my life would ever change for the better.

EXCLUDED FROM SCHOOL

Oppression that is clearly inexorable and invincible does not give rise to revolt but to submission. ~Simone Weil

*A*t summer's end, the door to school learning was slammed shut by my Amish heritage. The traditions would not yield to my desire to return to school, no matter how much I yearned for it. For nine years I had loved attending school. Each grade presented a whole new adventure in the world of learning. Each new book I opened, each new sheet of paper, and each new lesson in school fed my insatiable desire for learning. I had been expelled from school for the rest of my life through no fault of my own, but because I happened to be born Amish.

During my school years, and even that summer, I could not conceive of my life without school learning. When September came, that all changed because now I had to face it. Mem, Lizzie, and I stood at the south window and watched Sylvia, Sadie, and Simon get into old Mr. Yoxall's station wagon on their way to the Amish school. The longing to go with them and experience another year of school, and the knowledge that I couldn't, gave me a sinking feeling in my stomach. A school bus arrived to take Katherine to the public school where she attended special education classes.

Watching my younger siblings return to school came with the stark realization that my life as I'd known it was over. The tears were right behind my eyes. I went up to my room, sat down on the edge of my bed, and had myself a good cry. It was as if part of me had died, yet there was not going to be a funeral for what I'd lost. I had to bear this one on my own. As I sat there staring at the woven rug at my feet, I thought to myself, if I could change this, I would. But that felt as impossible as uprooting one of Datt's big maple trees with my bare hands.

I wished I could tell someone how I felt. But there wasn't anyone who understood. Lizzie was glad she was no longer in school. Ruth had moved to Michigan, so I couldn't talk with her. I didn't know if Olin Clara would understand. Her children had quit school after the eighth grade, like all the other Amish children in the community. Perhaps Annie would understand. I thought about walking to her house and visiting her sometimes. But I could do that only if Mem allowed it. Her first priority was having my help with the household work.

It seemed to me that my boring life was stretching out before me like an empty desert. I knew Mem was happy to have me at home so she could tell me what to do from one minute to the next. She was canning tomatoes, and I hated canning tomatoes.

Mem called me and asked me where I was: "*Wo bischt du?*" I wanted to yell at her, "Where do you think I am!" But I had no choice—I had to go down and pretend everything was all right. So I called down that I was making my bed, which I did while brushing away my tears.

When I got down to the kitchen, Lizzie was washing the dishes. I picked up that hated dishtowel and started drying.

There was nowhere to place my rebellious feelings about not going back to school, so I must have directed them right at Mem. Perhaps she'd also had a hard time leaving school behind, but there was no way for me to know whether Mem would sympathize with me or turn against me. Likely she would have alternated between one and the other. I decided to keep my feelings to myself.

When the "schoolchildren" came home that afternoon, Mem sent

Sylvia and me out to pick tomatoes from the garden. Sylvia loved eating fresh tomatoes. As she stepped between the tomato vines, she ate a tomato like an apple. It was clear she felt at home in the garden. I hated tomatoes, and I didn't like gardening. But that afternoon, I asked Sylvia all kinds of questions about her day in school, and she was glad to answer them. I savored every detail—who was sitting where in the classroom, what the new teacher was like, what textbooks they were using for each subject, and what she did during recess. Sylvia took me back to school in my imagination.

Each afternoon after that, Sylvia and I spent time in the garden together, harvesting tomatoes, peppers, and lima beans. Teacher Ellen was reading a story to the whole school after the noon recess, a chapter each day. As Sylvia told me the story about an Anabaptist woman named Genevieve who had escaped her oppressors back in Europe during the Protestant Reformation, I could imagine being in the classroom. In the story, Genevieve bore a child out in the forest. She found food from plants and managed to tame a wild goat that she milked to sustain herself and her child. There were many more rich details that I don't remember, and I also cannot recall how the story ended. I believe she found her way back to her family and society.

I was grateful to Sylvia for her generosity in sharing her school life with me. I felt as close to her on those autumn afternoons as I had when we were young children. But as all good things come to an end, so did our crisp, clear autumn afternoons in the vegetable garden.

Several weeks after school started for my younger siblings, Datt came home from the orchard and asked Mem if she could spare Lizzie and me to help at the orchard. The owners of the orchard had put out the word that they would like to hire someone to pick up the apples that had dropped from under the apple trees to squeeze for cider. They would pay fifty cents a bushel. Lizzie and I wouldn't be allowed to keep that money, but I liked the idea of working in the orchard better than having to obey Mem's every command.

Mem let us go, so Lizzie and I started our new job the next day. A van driver usually picked up Datt and other Amish men who were also pickers, to transport them to the orchard in Huntington Valley. It felt strange to be the only two girls in a vanload of Amish men, but I soon got over that as I looked at the autumn colors go by. The leaves on the sugar maples were especially bright that year, so the ride was pleasant.

When we arrived at the orchard, the men were dropped off in one part of the orchard, and Datt asked the driver to drive Lizzie and me to a different part. He came with us and showed us how to sort the apples by starting at the base of the tree and selecting the good apples to collect in the wooden crates that had been dropped off for that purpose. Then as we moved out from the base of the tree, we were to throw the rotten apples toward the trunk. In that way, we made our way to the outer branches, all the while picking up the good apples and discarding the rest.

After Datt got us started, he walked to a different section of the orchard to pick apples with the other men. Now it was just Lizzie and me with the apple trees under the clear autumn sky.

After we'd been working for several hours, Datt came and told us it was time for a break. All three of us sat on crates turned upside down and ate our lunches. Then Datt left us again, and Lizzie and I went back to sorting apples and stacking the full crates along the lane where they would get picked up at the end of the day.

Datt left us alone and didn't visit us after several days of sorting apples in the orchard. We were allowed to eat as many apples as we wanted, and if we got tired, we could take a break. Around noon, we had a half-hour to eat our lunch. At the end of the day, we looked at the stacks of crates we had filled and felt like we had accomplished something. On our most fruitful days, we could each fill fifty crates, give or take.

I was used to proving myself better than Lizzie in nearly everything. But out there in the orchard, Lizzie and I were equals. We kept one another going in friendly competition for who could pick up more apples, but for once we did not bicker or argue.

My siblings and I regarded Lizzie as being someone to avoid. She was big and strong and had a temper. She would often lash out physically when she became angry or frustrated. Her tendency was to hit us hard on our backs, over and over, like a threshing machine. I tried fighting back, but she was bigger and stronger. Sylvia usually managed to get away from Lizzie in time. But Sadie and Katherine got the worst of Lizzie's temper.

Out in the orchard, there was no reason to fight. Home, where those tensions brought out the worst in all of us, seemed a long way from our autumn days of sorting apples together.

One day we were in a new section of the orchard when we encountered a snake. We didn't know what to do about it. Our upbringing had us thinking that snakes were evil and needed to be killed, but normally there were menfolk around to do the deed. Neither one of us wanted to kill it, but we did want it to go away so we could do our job. Lizzie had the idea of throwing apples at it. But the snake wouldn't go away. We kept pelting it with rotten apples, but it just curled up tighter and wouldn't move. We realized we'd killed the snake when we poked it with a long stick and it wouldn't move. So we took that stick and carried the snake over to the wood's edge and threw it over into a ravine. It caught on a branch and hung there.

That's when I discovered the magical place. The forest floor down in the ravine was covered with a carpet of newly fallen autumn leaves, and there was a babbling brook down there with a little wooden footbridge over it. It was as if I had opened a fairy tale book and it had become real. I said, "Look down there, isn't that beautiful? I want to take a walk down there when we break for lunch."

Lizzie said, "I don't know if we're allowed to."

"Why wouldn't we be?"

We got back to sorting apples, Lizzie under one apple tree and me under another. We kept debating whether we should or shouldn't take a walk during lunch. We continued the debate when we stopped and ate lunch, each of us sitting on a crate. Finally I said, "I really want to go down there. What could it hurt? I'm going, whether you come or not." I stood up and headed for the pine grove where the path led down into the ravine.

Lizzie followed me, saying the whole way, "I don't know if we should be doing this." But I was determined. I wanted to enter that fairy-tale scene.

Just as I was heading for the footbridge to cross over the brook, Datt's angry voice shattered the tranquility as it boomed through the forest, "Lizzie, Lomie, where are you!"

"Down here!" I called.

"You get back here, right now!" Datt yelled.

Lizzie and I immediately turned around and headed back. Before we even got to the pine grove, we met up with Datt. I could not figure out how he'd covered so much ground so quickly. He shepherded us back to "our place" by walking behind us, really fast. Lizzie kept saying, "I didn't think we should do it." I was too flabbergasted to argue with her.

When we got back to our crates, Datt demanded, "Now you girls get back to work!" He stomped across the field and disappeared.

I wondered why Datt had had such a strong reaction on the day it happened, and I still wonder to this day. Did he think we were disobeying him and trying to avoid work? Did he feel responsible for us and think we might get lost in the woods? Did he have fears I didn't know about?

I also wondered whether Datt was watching us more than we realized. This was the only time we'd ever left the area where we'd been stationed for the day. How else would he have seen that we were gone from our spot unless he was watching us closely?

I never made it back to that place of Beauty. It was the closest I came to entering a magical realm in my young life. It's as if I'd been expelled from the Garden of Eden before I could even enter it.

The first hard frost ended the work at the orchard for Datt, Lizzie, and me. During the days at the orchard, I'd been free of feeling responsible for the never-ending housework and distracted from my desire to continue my school learning. Now all that came back full force, and I dreaded getting out of bed each morning. After breakfast, Mem laid out her plans for what needed to be done, and in what order. She still insisted on governing not only what I did, but how I did it. Whenever she said, "When you have a place of your own, you can do things *your* way. Until then, you do things *my* way," I'd set my jaw and vow that I would, too. I couldn't wait.

Only weeks after the work at the orchard ended, I was rescued once again from being Mem's slave. I was sitting in the living room ripping carpet rags when one of our egg customers, Mrs. Hadlock, came and asked if she could hire me to babysit her three children. She lived over on Forest Road, and she had a potter's studio in her basement. She wanted me to take care of the children from ten in the morning to three in the afternoon each weekday while she made pottery.

Mem said, "What about Lizzie? She is older than Saloma."

Mrs. Hadlock said, "I am asking for Saloma."

Lizzie was right there. She looked stricken. After the time we had spent in the orchard as equals, she must have felt the sting of rejection. This would have reinforced Lizzie's inferiority complex. I don't remember whether I later "rubbed it in" that I was chosen over her, but I cringe at the possibility that I might have.

Mem hesitated and then said, "Okay."

Mrs. Hadlock offered fifty cents an hour, and Mem accepted. It was considerably less than what I'd been making at the orchard, but it made little difference to me. Whatever money I earned went to Mem and Datt anyway. This would get me out of the house and away from Mem determining every move I made.

I started my new job the following Monday. Mrs. Hadlock had a set of twins, Kathy and Paul, followed a year later by their sister, Carol. The twins were potty trained, but little Carol was still in diapers.

I learned their routine. First they watched *Sesame Street* on television, then we took a walk in their orchard or played in the yard. Mrs. Hadlock made lunch and we ate around noon. Then as she went back to her studio, I got the children ready for their naps, making sure the twins went potty, and I changed Carol's diaper.

Then came my favorite part of the day—story time. We settled into the easy chair in the living room with two of them on my lap and another sitting on the arm of the chair. All three of them had "blankies" that they fingered, and each of them sucked fingers or a thumb. I enjoyed the warmth of their little bodies, as they snuggled in to hear stories. I wished someone had read me stories when I was little. Perhaps my longing made this time with the children all the more special. I could have stayed on that chair with the three little ones all afternoon. But eventually one of them fell asleep, and then it was time for them to settle into their beds for a nap. I carried the sleeping one as the other two padded down the hall to their bedroom. I got them settled in and I said, "Have a good nap," as I turned off their light and I left the room.

Then I cleaned up the dishes from lunch and straightened up the playroom before sitting down in the living room to enjoy the quiet. I pulled out my crocheting or whatever handwork I'd brought from home. I felt like it was cheating to have this hour of quiet time when Mrs. Hadlock was paying Mem and Datt for my time. The only sounds in the house came from the studio below. I could tell when Mrs. Hadlock was turning a piece on her wheel or when she was mixing clay. Through a crack in the floor, I could see her cut the clay in two with a blade stretched across the table. Then she smacked first one, then the other half onto the table. There was a pause as she cut it again, and then, *"Smack, smack... pause... smack, smack!"* The rhythm reminded me of what it was like to knead bread dough.

At three o'clock in the afternoon, Mrs. Hadlock drove me home. The children's grandmother lived in an apartment attached to their house, and she watched the children during the time Mrs. Hadlock picked me up or drove me home.

Inevitably Mem had work for me to do upon my return home. I didn't mind because most of the day I didn't have to do exactly as she said. Babysitting for the Hadlocks made my life a whole lot more bearable, and I was grateful for that.

Mem was concerned when I turned fourteen and I hadn't gotten my first period. She would tell me in an anxious, whispery voice that I should come and tell her when I did get it. Then one day in March, three months before I turned fifteen, I felt cramps in my lower abdomen at the Hadlocks. I thought I had eaten something that didn't agree with me. When I returned home, I discovered the reason for the cramps. This, I realized, meant my life as a child was over. The pain of losing my childhood was accentuated by my cramps. I felt tears sliding down my cheeks and dripping onto my dress. This was part of the inevitable march toward the life that awaited me of becoming an Amish wife and mother. Judging by Mem's life, that didn't always go so well.

Mem was in the sugarhouse boiling sap. I dreaded telling her, and yet I had to. I walked past the mud puddles to the sugarhouse door, pushed the sliding door open far enough to get inside, and then pulled the door shut.

Mem seemed surprised to see me. I didn't know how to tell her, so I sat there as the fire crackled in the arch (furnace) and the sap hissed in the pans. I could feel her eyes watching me. She said, "Do you have something to tell me?"

"I have my period," I mumbled, looking at the dirt floor.

"I thought so," Mem said. "Did you find the pads?"

"Yes," I said abruptly as a way to stop her. I didn't want to talk about it anymore. Except I was desperately afraid she would tell Datt or Joe. I said, "I don't want Joe or Datt to know."

Mem eyed me sideways and said, "This is nothing to be ashamed about, you know."

I got up, pushed open the sliding door, and walked out into the darkness. I could not tell Mem that she had no right to tell Datt or Joe and that it was none of their business. I knew she wouldn't listen. She didn't seem to understand that I wouldn't feel ashamed about my period if she were to allow me the privacy I deserved. I wondered, didn't she ever have this need when she was young? As I tromped through the mud I muttered, "Maybe she skipped that part of her life."

PONCE DE DAY LEON

[T]he encounter with death is the great turning-point in the lives of those who live on. ~Dorothy Canfield Fisher

One summer when we were still going to school, Mem seemed to feel like the little old woman who lived in a shoe who had so many daughters she didn't know what to do. So she began sharing us with the Yoder family in the community who were even less fortunate than we were. This family lived in a cramped little home. The mother, Irene, was not a good housekeeper, and so it fell on my sisters and me to help her out.

Two of us walked over to the Yoder house at least once a week in the summer. We were met with a pile of dirty dishes every time. We tackled the daunting and thankless job of washing them, drying them, and putting them away in the cupboards, knowing that the next time we came, the counter would again be piled high with dishes that had dried-out food in them.

We picked up toys strewn all over the house, shook out the rugs, and swept the floors. These were chores that most Amish mothers performed each morning. Irene wasn't one of these mothers, and we knew that the only time these chores got done was when we did them.

I didn't resist helping this family as much as my sisters did because I knew I'd at least get a break from home. Being a slave to someone else was preferable to being a slave to Mem. And at least I had the mile-and-a-half walk between their house and ours under the summer sky, with the birds singing along the way. It turned out that I was sent to this home more often than my sisters, probably because I didn't fight it as much as they did.

By the time we started helping out the Yoder family, I had gained a reputation for being a good babysitter. Many Amish mothers had daughters of their own who would look after the younger ones when needed. However, most young mothers who didn't yet have a child old enough to take care of the younger ones didn't want to take their children to the day-long church services—Council Meeting and Communion Service—that took place in the spring and fall of each year. Inevitably, I was busy taking care of someone's children on those days. I didn't get a choice about whose children I babysat because Mem said yes to whoever asked first, which was how I ended up babysitting for the Yoders on the day of Communion Service.

I started out early that Sunday morning for the half-hour walk. The morning dew sparkled on each blade of grass, bright points of light under the morning sun. A pair of cardinals flew across the road and disappeared into the woods. I heard a woodpecker hammering away, though I couldn't see it. I wondered which kind of woodpecker it was, but it remained hidden from me. I walked past fields, past the first Hale farm, then the second one, on up the hill where Olin and Clara Yoder lived, past the home of the Colliers, who weren't Amish, past more open fields to Burton-Windsor Road. Now I had only a short walk through a neighborhood to the Yoders' house.

I approached the Troyers' home where my friend Annie lived. She and I almost shared a birthday—hers was the day after mine, though she was a year older than me. Remembering the visit from Annie when we'd danced in the middle of the road singing "Ponce de day Leon" brought a smile to my face. I wondered if she had told anyone about the fun we'd had. I hadn't. I held that bright moment close to my heart, safe from the judgment of others.

As I was about to pass the Troyers' home, Annie's mother came out on the porch and called out to me. She asked if I knew if any other *youngie*—youth—would be attending church that day. I said I didn't. She said that Annie didn't want to go. She shook her head and disappeared back into the house. I continued on my way.

Mercifully, the only dishes I had to wash when I got to the Yoders were the ones from their breakfast. I tied the baby to the highchair and the other three girls played on the floor. I finished the dishes quickly, then bundled up the baby and asked the others, "Want to go out and play?"

I said, "Go find your jackets." I wasn't sure they needed them, but there was still a little chill in the air.

Once outside, I sat on the top step in the sunshine with the baby in my lap and watched the girls playing. They had found their little red wagon and the oldest daughter, Esther, pulled the wagon around the yard. The younger ones alternated between riding and pushing.

Then I saw Annie walking toward us. "Hi, Saloma," she said in her clear voice. "Would you like a visitor?"

I loved Annie's voice. It had a melodic quality to it.

"Sure!" I said as I scooted over so she could sit next to me on the steps. With a smile, Annie said, "Nice day to play outside."

"Yes, I thought they'd enjoy it."

We were both quiet for a moment. I asked, "What are you doing today? I see you didn't go to church."

"No... I didn't feel like sitting all day."

"Your mem must not be as insistent as my mem."

"How did you know Mem wanted me to go?"

"She asked me this morning if I knew whether other girls would be going. I told her I didn't know."

"Thanks," Annie said and chuckled.

"But, I really didn't. Mem would have made me go if I wasn't babysitting."

The children went inside, and we followed.

"Have a seat," I said. I sat down at the table and nestled the baby into my left arm. Annie sat in the chair on the other side of the table from me. She asked, "So, how do you like being out of school?"

I had not admitted my feelings to anyone, but I felt like Annie would not judge me. I said, "I miss it."

"I miss school too," Annie said.

"Last fall it just seemed to me that I would get to go back with the others, but then of course I couldn't..." My voice trailed off wistfully. I knew my desire for more education did me no good. Ending education at the eighth grade was "the way of things" and there was no use questioning it.

Annie said, "Maybe you can become a teacher. You'd make a good one."

"But I don't want to be a teacher, I want to be a *pupil*."

"I know what you mean. I wouldn't want to be a teacher either. It would be too much responsibility."

I hesitated, then decided to ask, "Do you wonder what it would be like to go to high school?"

Annie paused before she said, "I've heard it's pretty rough."

"I've heard that too. But I'm sure there are some pupils in high school who focus on learning and getting good grades."

I hadn't been paying close attention to Esther playing near us until a motion caught my eye. She was holding a black umbrella over her head, and just then a cloud moved across the sun and darkened the room. I felt a shudder deep inside me. Esther's mother, Irene, had told me all kinds of eerie things that I only half-believed. However, when Esther raised the umbrella and the cloud covered the sun, it felt as though Death itself had cast its shadow over the house. I said, gesturing with my hand for emphasis, "Esther, put that down! You shouldn't open it in the house!"

Esther looked alarmed and shut the umbrella. I was holding the baby in my left arm. I got up, and with my right arm, I stuck the umbrella on a shelf above the counter where she couldn't reach it. "Now go play with your sisters," I said. She went into the bedroom where the others were playing dolls.

"What did she do? What's wrong with playing with an umbrella?" Annie asked. The sun came back out from behind the clouds and the children laughed. Feeling a little foolish, I told Annie that their mother believed that holding an umbrella over one's head inside the house was a sign that someone in the house would die soon.

Annie laughed and said, "I never heard that before. If it were true, everyone in our house would probably be dead by now."

"I don't believe everything Irene has told me, that's for sure. She's got all kinds of crazy stories."

"Like what?"

"Once she told me about a woman who died and was buried up on a hill. Dogs kept barking above her grave, so finally someone opened it, and they found the woman had flipped over, *inside her coffin!*"

Annie said matter-of-factly, "Oh, I know that one. She'd pulled all her hair out of her head."

"But how could that *be?* Was she not really *dead?* And how could anyone make such a mistake for the three or four days that it took to have a funeral? She would've been lying there in the house, in her coffin, wouldn't she?"

"She must have been."

We were quiet for a long moment before Annie said she needed to go.

I walked out to the porch with her. "Ponce-de-day-leon," I said, and we both laughed.

"We need to see each other more often," she said, and we waved to each other as she walked down the road toward her home.

I had no idea this would be the last time I'd see Annie.

Less than two weeks later, my cousins from Pennsylvania came to stay at our house overnight. Two of them were sleeping with me in the bed I normally shared with Sylvia. We had talked and giggled until late into the night before we finally fell asleep. We were sleeping sideways across the bed so we'd have more room between us, but that meant I couldn't stretch out my legs, which is why I hadn't slept well.

I heard Mem walking slowly up the back stairs to my room. It was the morning of Ascension Day, which most Amish kept as a holy day. Mem hardly ever came upstairs in the morning, and in my half-sleep, I wondered why she wasn't allowing us to wake up naturally, especially on a day when we wouldn't have to work.

Mem said, "Girls, wake up. There is something I must tell you."

I rolled over, knowing that something was wrong.

Mem said, "Annie Troyer died this morning."

Mem might as well have hit me over the head. I was stunned into silence.

Someone asked, "Of what?"

"They don't know. She died in her sleep about three o'clock," Mem said.

I had a sinking feeling in my stomach as I remembered the black umbrella. I wished I had watched Esther more closely. Maybe she wouldn't have opened that umbrella in the house. What if it was not a superstition, but a real sign?

I moved woodenly through the day. People in the community speculated about what Annie had died of. She'd mowed the lawn the day before, and people wondered if she'd worked too hard. But I knew that hard work was not fatal—we all mowed our lawns with a rotary push-mower and nobody had ever died of it before.

I kept thinking of the black umbrella. I wondered, if the umbrella was truly a sign, then why her and not me? It was obvious from her light and carefree ways that Annie had been much happier with her life than I was with mine.

People also talked about the significance of Annie dying on Ascension Day, the day Jesus had risen into heaven in a cloud, forty days after his Resurrection.

The day after Annie died, I walked to the Troyers' home for a viewing with the neighbor girls my age. My legs shook as I followed the others into the house and then into the glassed-in porch right off the living room where Annie's body had been laid out. She was lying on a stretcher, and it seemed like she was just sleeping, except that she was so very pale. She wore a white dress, a white organdy cape and apron, and a white head covering. Usually when a woman died in our community, she was clothed in a black dress, with a white cape and apron. I had never seen anyone in the community wear a white dress for burial before.

As I stood before Annie's body, her death still seemed unreal. I almost expected her to get up and walk away. And yet she just lay there, so white and so still. I was too shocked to cry. My grief and fear got caught in my throat. There before me was proof that I could die at any time, for no reason. That terror gripped and held me with tendrils that felt as though they would choke me.

My memory leaves me here. I know I must have left the room and walked back home with the neighbor girls, but I don't recall what we talked about or anything else about our walk together.

Back home, I asked Mem about Annie's white dress. She explained that some families dress a young girl in white if she was still considered innocent when she died.

"Who decides if they are still innocent?"

"Her mother decided it," Mem said, as though she didn't want me to ask any more questions.

I wondered if Mem had ever thought of me as innocent, and whether she would dress me in white if I died. For as long as I could remember, she had been trying to break me of my rebellious nature, and I was not the compliant daughter she wanted me to be. I was not innocent, and Mem knew that first-hand. She had certainly taken part in stealing my innocence from me.

To make matters more complicated, I didn't have a black dress to wear to the funeral because I'd outgrown it. Mem was altering one that Lizzie had outgrown. But Lizzie was a lot bigger than me. When I tried it on, it was like wearing a black bag. In tears, I begged for a new dress instead.

Instead of saying anything, Mem pedaled away on her treadle sewing machine. Then words seemed to spill out of my mouth on their own. "You don't care about me. At least Annie's family cared about her! I wish I was in *her* place!"

Mem asked in a matter-of-fact voice, "Do you think you'd be ready to die?"

Mem knew just how to name my worst fear. By now I was sobbing, and I said, "It would be better than living in *this* family!"

Lying awake that night, I regretted what I'd said. I felt all black inside. I wouldn't want to be dead and buried, and I thought for sure God would send me to hell for being so rebellious. That thought was too horrible to comprehend. I told myself I shouldn't be fretting about the dress I had to wear to the funeral. I decided I would wear it without any more complaining.

~

The Amish have a tradition of holding a vigil through the night at the home of the deceased while the family sleeps. It dates back to the time of the Reformation in Europe when our Anabaptist ancestors were persecuted by the state and church authorities who would sometimes snatch the bodies of the deceased as a method of depriving loved ones of their grieving rituals. Though the Amish no longer need to guard the bodies of their deceased, the tradition of keeping vigil has endured through the centuries and is still practiced. The community comes together to move the furniture in the home and bring in church benches to accommodate round-the-clock calling hours. The women cook for the family and out-of-town mourners while the men prepare a space in an outbuilding or the house and collect and arrange church benches for the funeral.

The night before Annie's funeral, I was one of five people keeping vigil and so was a minister in the church, Dan Wengerd, who would later be ordained bishop. We talked in hushed tones for several hours. There was a gas lantern hanging from the ceiling in the living room, and through the window in the porch door, I could see that a dim oil lamp was lit on the porch where Annie lay. It felt like she was sleeping in the next room.

By three in the morning, most of the others were dozing or resting quietly on a couch, chair, or bench. I was lying on a bench listening to the clock's rhythmic tick-tock, tick-tock that lulled me into a half-sleep. The clock chimed three, then continued ticking and tocking.

Suddenly, Dan Wengerd gasped aloud from the armchair where he was sitting in the corner of the room. I sat up and looked at him. With terrified eyes, Dan stared at the door to the porch where Annie lay. I looked over there and saw only the curtain in the window of the door, drawn to one side.

"*Was iss letz*—what's wrong?" I asked.

Dan shook his head. "*Nix. Nix.*" But his wild eyes kept staring in the direction of the window in the porch door. I realized it was just after three o'clock, the same time of the night that Annie had died two nights before.

I could not go back to sleep.

Later I heard that Dan Wengerd told his wife that he thought he saw Annie out on the porch, just on the other side of the door. I didn't know what to think because I'd never heard of the concept of roaming spirits. They didn't exist in the minds of anyone in the community, and not in mine. It made me wonder if Annie was really dead.

It didn't help that I didn't know what Annie had died of. Her parents had had an autopsy done. A report in the newspaper about her death cited the outcome of the autopsy—that the muscles around Annie's heart had simply stopped functioning. I stared at the words on the page and wanted to scream, Doesn't that happen for everyone who dies? Why can't you give us more of an answer?

Annie's funeral service was held in the haymow of the barn across the field from the Troyers' home. Loose straw had been spread on the floor for people to kneel on. The line of people streaming up the hay ramp seemed unending. Rows and rows of women and young girls in their black dresses and their white *koppa* sat on one side of the hayloft. On the other side of the aisle sat rows and rows of men and young boys in their dark suits. I wondered how many neighboring church districts had loaned their benches for the hundreds of people attending the funeral.

I started counting people but stopped myself when I remembered that I'd heard it was a bad omen to count people attending a funeral. I wasn't taking any chances. I saw Esther and her sisters sitting with their mother a few rows ahead of me. I wondered whether Esther had told her mother about the umbrella, or if she'd forgotten. I hoped she had forgotten, and I wished I could.

The preachers reminded us that we don't know when the time of our death will come, and therefore we should be prepared at all times. I knew I wasn't ready, which made me wonder if I would go to hell if I died.

They also talked about the "sister" who was now walking with God and how we shouldn't question why we lose someone like this because God has His reasons. They said God planned our whole lives before we were born, even how and when we die. It made me wonder if it was true. If so, why would the black umbrella even matter?

After two ministers had each preached a sermon, everyone kneeled in the straw. I wanted to pray, but I couldn't. I wondered how I could stop myself from questioning why Annie had died and I also wondered what God's reasons might be.

The bishop read the prayer, then everyone stood up. The Amish funeral director, Rube Miller, directed rows of people to file past Annie to pay their last respects. Annie's casket was set up on four chairs in the outer part of the hayloft, just above the ramp. People filed past on both sides of Annie and walked down into the lawn below the ramp. When I walked past Annie, I smelled the varnish from her casket, and through my tears, I saw her still, white form. I could not accept her death.

Annie's funeral was eerily quiet. I held in the sobs that wanted to heave from my chest because it seemed as though that was what everyone around me was doing.

As usual, the immediate family came last. I thought they would linger around the casket, crying and clinging to their last glimpses of their sister and daughter as was usually done. Annie's two sisters did cry, but Annie's mother barely shed any tears. She walked down the ramp with a straight spine, next to her husband Will. The usual flow of tears became constricted in my throat, and all I could do was swallow my grief. Mem didn't like it when people keened and cried at funerals as they had at Elva's. She called it "making a fuss." Now I wondered if there was a good reason for crying—so that we could release our grief and our fear of death.

When I returned home after the funeral, I was exhausted. Mem allowed me to go to bed early, and I went right to sleep.

That night I had my first nightmare about Annie's death. I dreamed that someone realized they'd made a mistake, so they dug up her grave. They worked at night in a circle of light from a lantern. When they opened the casket, Annie got up, brushed the dirt from her white dress, and nonchalantly walked away.

I awoke and sat straight up. I struggled to breathe. The image of Annie getting up in the circle of lantern light haunted me. Again, I asked myself, *What if she wasn't really dead?* Then I remembered hearing the description of what they do during an autopsy. There could be no mistake. Annie was dead, and that was all there was to it. The grief and the fear of Annie's death overwhelmed me. It would have been a release to sob out my grief, but like a stoic Amish girl, I only cried softly in the dense darkness of my room so as not to wake my family.

The nightmare became a recurring one. I was aware even in my dream of having dreamed it before. Then I would try to wake up, but it was difficult to shed the terror. Finally, I'd wake up gasping for breath as though I had been the one who was buried alive. I sat up in the darkness and made sure I could still breathe.

I wondered where Annie was when I lay awake on those dark nights. I knew a good and just God would not send Annie to hell. I thought she had a much better chance of making it to heaven than I would have if I'd died. I remembered how she had spoken the truth to me about my conflict with Reuben when I was in fifth grade. She'd spoken it simply, as if it came naturally to her. It made me wonder why being good came so easily for her, while it was so hard for me.

I'd often still be awake to hear the long, lonesome whistle of the late-night train. I'd feel so alone with my foreboding thoughts.

My dreams of Annie lasted for years. As time went on, they occurred less frequently before finally ceasing.

Six years after Annie's death, I lived with her family while teaching school, and her mother told me that Annie had been born with a congenital heart defect. Her heart hadn't been growing and developing with the rest of her body and this was never detected. With this kind of heart problem, she had zero chance of living beyond her adolescence without a heart transplant. Annie had lived as long as she could with the heart she had.

When I think of Annie now, I still remember what a free spirit she was. Though I have a hard time evoking her face this many years later, I still remember her clear singing voice, especially during the Christmas program at our school one year when she had led each stanza of the carol, "While Shepherds Watched their Flocks by Night." One of the verses begins with, "'Fear not,' said he..." I can still hear Annie singing those first two words before the rest of us joined in. When I remember this so clearly, it's as if she is still singing, "Fear not."

I hope that Annie passed from this world to the next without ever having known fear. I like to think that when Annie's spirit appeared in the doorway to Dan Wengerd the night before her funeral, she was peering back into the world she was leaving—just one last glance.

I also like to think that when Annie showed up in my dreams, she was trying to reassure me that her soul had found its rightful place and that she was at peace.

I imagine Annie dancing in joy and delight with the angels, singing "Ponce de day Leon."

UNBROKEN

Strength does not come from physical capacity. It comes from an
indomitable will. ~Mahatma Gandhi

One summer day when I was fifteen, I insisted on sewing my own
dress. Mem reluctantly agreed. She and I had disagreed on how
to make my dresses. I thought she made them too baggy, so I altered the
pattern to make my dresses more form-fitting. I also wanted to sew the
pleats in such a way that I could wear my dress without an apron, like
many of the other young girls did. These were called "side-closing"
dresses. I didn't know how, so I asked Mem. She said it didn't matter,
since I wouldn't be making my dress that way anyway. She insisted I
needed to wait until I was seventeen.

I don't know why I thought I might get away with defying Mem, but
I tried being sneaky. I figured out how to make a side-closing dress myself.
I kept pinning the pleats this way, then that, until I figured it out. Instead
of having a seam down the front of the skirt of my dress, the pattern of
the pleats made the dress look more elegant. I was proud and pleased with
the way it looked on me, as I pinned the dress in front of the mirror. I

turned this way and that, amazed at how much it looked like I was wearing an apron already. I thought about occasionally wearing my dress without an apron. The preachers didn't approve, but other girls got away with wearing dresses without an apron because their mothers allowed them to. Whenever Mem had a chance to be stricter than other mothers, she took it. I should have known this would be no exception.

Mem insisted on pinning up the hem of my dress so she could decide the length of it. I wanted it shorter and she wanted it longer. I stood on top of Mem's sewing chair so she wouldn't have to bend over. I made sure I had the apron on, so she wouldn't see the way I had made the dress. She had several straight pins pinched between her lips as she made her way from the back to the front. I held one side of the apron up so she could pin my dress. All of a sudden, she jerked up my apron. By the look on her face, I knew I was in trouble. Before I could react, she punched me in the stomach and sent me flying off the chair and onto the floor. My heart was beating fast as I caught a glimpse of Mem's angry face. She still held the pins in her mouth. She took them out and said, "You know better! Now go take off that dress and give it to me! You are too independent for your own good!"

I did and then went upstairs. I lay on my bed and listened to Mem pumping the treadle sewing machine. She made even the sewing machine sound angry. I felt too helpless and humiliated by Mem's fist in my gut to care about the dress or anything else.

When Mem was done, she had not only moved the seam to the front, she'd also taken a four-inch strip of extra material and sewn it in, so there were two seams in the front—one right in the middle, and the other off to one side. She put no pleats in the front, so when I wore it without an apron it was downright ugly. It felt like she had made the dress as ugly as she could, just to show me she was boss.

After getting punched off the sewing chair, I dreaded sewing on the machine. I sewed only when I had to make my dresses so that Mem wouldn't make them for me. For years, even after I left home for good, I would get a backache just from the stress of sitting down at a sewing machine.

Mem's will had overpowered mine again, which added to the feeling that I couldn't change anything about my life—not even how I sewed my own dresses.

~

One day that autumn when I was fifteen, I found myself home with Mem and Datt during the midday meal. Mem was warming up leftovers from the night before. Normally she was a good cook, often making do with the ingredients she had. It seemed to me that she could make something out of nothing. But this time she had combined ingredients in what she called "goulash" that did not taste good. When she was warming it up for our *middog*, I told her I didn't like it. She said, "It's what we're having," and turned to the stove to stir the pot.

I was famished, but I didn't want to eat what she was making. I said, "But Mem, it tastes like pig slop." I knew I was being disrespectful, and I could feel Mem's silent seething.

I asked, "Can I make myself *rivel* soup?"

Mem reluctantly allowed me to make a bowl of *rivel* soup for myself, but she said I shouldn't make any for her or Datt. This was a soup made by bringing milk to a boil and then dropping in *rivels* made from egg and flour and cooking it until it was done.

Rivel soup rarely came out as good as it did that day. It had thickened the right amount, and it was seasoned just right with salt and pepper. It was steaming under my nose and making my mouth water as we bowed our heads for silent prayer. After a long moment, Datt reached for his water glass, signaling the end of the mealtime prayer.

Just as I raised my spoon to my mouth with my first bite, Datt pointed to Mem's dish and asked, "What's that?"

"Leftovers from last night," Mem said.

"What's that?" Datt said, pointing to my bowl.

"*Rivel* soup," Mem said.

"I'd rather have *that*," Datt said, indicating my bowl of soup.

Before I could respond, Mem unceremoniously reached over and took my bowl of soup and set it down in front of Datt. Then she took Datt's empty plate and set it down in front of me as if to say, There, take that! Datt immediately started eating the *rivel* soup.

I was shocked. I could not believe what had just happened, so it took a minute for the anger to rise. When it did, it rose inside me like a dragon. I thought about grabbing that bowl of soup away from Datt and pouring it over Mem's head. I could imagine it spilling down over her *kopp*. I had never felt so much rage pushing out of my chest. I got up to make myself another bowl of soup, but I was too angry to contain myself. I slammed cupboard doors and rattled the pots and pans. It wasn't enough. The pressure in my chest just kept building. I had visions of picking up my chair and throwing it through the window.

Mem said in her low, solid voice, "Lomie, if you know what's good for you..."

I heard the threat in Mem's voice. With that threat came memories of all the times she had whipped me until I danced in pain and the time when she had washed out my mouth with soap and a rag with chicken manure on it. I remembered times when she asked Datt for "help" when she couldn't get me to give in to her, and the times when she allowed Joe to brutalize me. She would do anything to make me give in to her will.

With the rage building inside my chest, I did know what was good for me. I could not stay in the same house with Mem and Datt for one more minute. If I did, I was in danger of them turning on me, so I grabbed my coat off the hook by the door and stomped outside. I took the path through the woods toward Forest Road. I didn't even think about where I was going. I only knew I needed to get as far away from the house as I could. Angry tears spilled down my cheeks.

I stepped over the little creek in the pasture and kept going. "I'd rather have that, indeed!" I muttered to myself. I was just as angry with Mem as I was with Datt. "So *that* is why she didn't want me to make enough *rivel* soup for Datt and her," I muttered to myself. "She had no intention of allowing me to have my own soup, but she let me think so, just so she could take it away from me."

I wished I dared to run away from home. I imagined walking out to Forest Road and then up to Route 322 and hitchhiking to anywhere, just to get away. But when I got to the field by Forest Road, I lost my courage. Instead I sat in the grass under a maple tree. It was still a little damp from the morning rain we'd had, but I didn't care. Then I realized how hungry

I was. I had gnawing pangs in my stomach. But I decided I wasn't going to let hunger get in the way of at least making Mem *think* I had run away.

After sitting under the tree and chewing on grass stems, I stretched out in the tall grass and looked up into the kaleidoscope of autumn colors as the leaves shimmered in the branches above me. I heard a car approaching on the dirt road and then the sound of the tires changed as the car hit the pavement at the township line. While I could hear the car going by, I didn't feel so alone. I listened as the sound of the tires on the pavement became fainter and then died away.

A bee buzzed in the air above me. A pair of cardinals called to one another in the woods. A woodpecker drummed on the trunk of a tree in the distance, and blue jays called from deep in the woods.

I dozed off. My mind hovered in that space between wakefulness and dreaming, and between consciousness and unconsciousness. In this in-between place, I promised myself that I would one day leave home and go far away. I did not yet know when, how, or where I would go, but I would not always be living this unbearable life. If I left my family, I would have to leave the community altogether. Yet I was determined that I would.

Time was suspended as I lay there under the tree. I awoke when a soft rain began to fall. I had no idea how long I had been lying there. It could have been an hour, or it could have been many. I stayed on the ground and looked at the raindrops falling. I had never looked at raindrops from the vantage point of lying on the ground before. I had the impulse to close my eyes, but I made myself keep them open so I could watch the raindrops falling straight down on me.

The rain didn't last. When dusk began to gather, I thought about going home, but I just did not have the energy to get up and walk there. Then I heard someone calling my name—distantly at first, but then the voice became clearer. It was Joe. Of course, Mem had sent Joe to find me. He was her enforcer. I did not want him to find me, so I kept myself lying still. But Joe had his German shepherd dog, Spike, with him. I heard the dog coming through the grass. He wagged his tail as he came toward me. I knew I'd been found, so I sat up.

"Didn't you hear me calling you?" Joe demanded when he saw me.

"No, I was sleeping."

"Then what woke you up?"

"Spike stuck his nose in my face," I said.

"And you didn't hear me calling?" he asked insistently. Joe liked to catch us siblings in a lie so he could "teach us a lesson." I knew what his lessons were like. I had learned them the hard way. Like the day he broke my glasses.

Back when Joe had gotten his first horse and buggy at seventeen, and he started going out with the young people and dating, his moods were lethal on Monday mornings. One Monday, he wasn't even out of bed when the taxi arrived to take him to work, so they left without him. This meant he was home for the day. I should have known better than to say anything to him.

Joe slept on the couch in the living room all that morning. When the rest of us were about to eat *middog*, Mem told Joe several times that *middog* was ready. He grunted and stayed on the couch, so the rest of us ate and Mem retreated back to her sewing while we girls did the dishes. Mem assigned each of us tasks for the afternoon. Mine was to sweep the basement floor. I was in the middle of doing that when I heard Joe's footsteps going out into the kitchen above me. Then I heard him demanding, "What's for *middog?*"

The words flew out of my mouth before I could take them back. "If you weren't such a sleepy-head you would *know* what was for *middog!*"

There was no hesitation in Joe's steps as he headed for the kitchen door and down the stairs. I thought about running through the basement and out the other door, but I knew that Joe would overtake me, and my beating would be worse. I called out "Mem, help me!"

Silence. Except for Joe's determined footsteps coming down the stairs. He came down and stood before me. He struck me across my face on one side, then the other side. My glasses fell to the basement floor. I screamed out my rage as I picked them up. "You broke my glasses! Now you can buy me new ones!"

Joe had just started going up the stairs. He turned around, stepped back down into the basement, and smacked me over and over: my face, my head, my shoulders, my back. I thought his blows would never stop landing. I screamed out my rage and helplessness. When he finally stopped and went back upstairs, I felt faint. I was sobbing so hard I couldn't catch my breath.

Mem hadn't even gotten up from her sewing chair.

Now that Joe had found me in the field by Forest Road, the memory of his beating from more than a year ago was still fresh in my mind. He kept demanding to know whether I'd heard him calling, but I was determined to hold my ground. I knew he didn't believe me when I said I hadn't. This time he could not prove anything unless I admitted to it. I was bound and determined he wouldn't find out. I would look him in the eye and lie to his face if I had to. But I knew I would be paying for my defiance one way or another.

"We need to go home. Mem is worried about you," Joe said.

I felt like making a retort about Mem, but I kept my silence. I got up and started walking toward home. Joe walked next to me. We were walking past our trash pile when he said, "You should be thanking me for finding you."

"Yeah, and what if I'm not thankful, then what?" I muttered under my breath. Before I was done with my retort, I felt the prickles of fear rising up my scalp.

Joe stepped in front of me and smacked me hard, right across my face. My ear was ringing and my face stung.

Spike turned around and gave a warning growl.

Joe said, "It's okay, Spike," then turned back at me with his face glowering.

Spike's growl became more menacing, but I was not afraid of him. Joe and I both knew he was protecting me. Spike came over and stepped between Joe and me.

All of a sudden, Joe turned on his heel and started walking toward home, faster than I'd ever seen him. Spike stayed with me and wagged his tail. I reached down and patted his back. I said, "Good boy, Spike." He walked by my side all the way home. Spike, with his animal sense, had protected me in a way no person ever had.

The lantern light hurt my eyes when I entered the kitchen. Mem looked at me but didn't say anything. I didn't say anything either. I retreated to my room and went to bed without supper. I was famished, but I could not face Mem that night. Something had broken between us, and I needed time to myself more than I needed to eat.

Up until the day of the *rivel* soup, I could usually count on eating the food that was on my plate. Then that boundary was also broken. It was as if Mem was giving me the message that she was going to break my will, no matter what measures she had to take to do it. But as I was lying in that field next to Forest Road, I vowed to myself that one day I would leave, and that I would take my will with me. Maybe it would be bent, but it would not be broken.

DREAB DAYS

When sorrows come, they come not single spies, but in battalions.
~William Shakespeare

I don't remember my sixteenth birthday. Perhaps it was a day like any other, or maybe we had cake and ice cream to celebrate, even though I didn't feel my birthday was worth celebrating. My life was like the weather in our part of Ohio—gray and drab—what we called *dreab*, for days in a row, leaving my spirit yearning for sunshine to light up my colorless world. *Dreab* is how I describe my joyless life at the time.

I had sustained many losses by the time I turned sixteen. I keenly felt the loss of my childhood and the assurance that I would go to heaven if I died. I often felt plagued by doubts of any goodness in myself, and I lived in fear that I would go to hell if I died. After Elva and Annie died, I was well aware that Death did not always discern between the old and the young.

The loss of my schooling was another struggle. I never stopped craving more formal education, even though I knew it was not to be, at least not so long as I remained Amish.

I had lost my innocence, or rather it was stolen from me, when I was molested by my brother Joe, and later by Mem and Joe Basco. I was still holding these terrible secrets inside me.

As I began getting more cleaning jobs, I slowly drifted away from my earlier Saturday ritual of walking to Olin Clara's house in the morning to spend the day with her and then walking home in the afternoon. I felt the loss of being with someone who believed in me. Now I had no one to talk to who understood me. I also missed Ruth and Annie. Each of them had left a hole in my life that I wasn't able to fill. Certainly not my sisters: most of the time, Sylvia and Sadie pitted themselves solidly against me. They mocked me relentlessly by sarcastically repeating things I said. They mimicked the way I walked and the way I waved to people. They seemed to have taken lessons from the girls at school about how to hurt most with *schpotting*. Though I tried not to show it, their mocking only fed my feelings of self-consciousness and self-loathing.

The overall effect of these losses was a sustained sense of isolation and loneliness. Even though I was surrounded by family and community, I felt like I was marooned on a distant island.

Despite most of my active memories of my teens being wrought with conflicts, violence, and fear, there were days when I enjoyed life. One day, when my sisters and I were walking home through the Sugaring Woods after tapping trees, we heard a shrill *"wheeee-whooo"* whistle from the tops of the trees. Sylvia said, "That is the chickadee's mating call." I wondered how she knew so much about birds and nature. That whistle, promising spring was on its way, became forever associated with my memory of walking home with my sisters that late winter day with the slanted afternoon sunlight shining through the bare branches of the tall maples, beeches, and oaks of the Sugaring Woods.

When the earth would spring forth with new growth and blooms, we visited the Spring Woods to find trilliums, spring beauties, may apples, ferns, and many other varieties of flora. We'd also take note of the birds around us. My favorites were the red-headed woodpeckers and rose-breasted grosbeaks.

In late summer we picked elderberries along the path that cut crosslots to Forest Road. In autumn we foraged for hickory nuts deeper in the woods under the stand of shagbark hickory trees. The scampering of squirrels on the forest floor made us aware that we were competing for the sweet nuts encased in their light, hard shells. After collecting the nuts in a peck basket, we let them sit in the cool entrance on a shelf for several months before cracking them with a press in the basement or hammering them on a stone. Then we spent painstaking hours picking the nuts from the shells and storing the sweet nutmeats in jars for the winter. I don't remember that we ever bought nuts at a grocery store when I was growing up.

I still had my favorite spot in the Autumn Woods by the tall maple next to the spring. As I grew older, I found it to be a place of solitude and contemplation. I listened to the sounds of the water bubbling, the birds singing in the trees, and the squirrels and chipmunks scurrying about, gathering their stores for the winter. Sometimes I carried a book with me and sat there to read for hours. I read and reread the books from home, such as *Heidi*, *Paula the Waldensian*, *Light from Heaven*, and occasionally I read books my siblings brought home from the school library. I especially enjoyed discovering the *Anne of Green Gables* series. I dreamed of going to Prince Edward Island, and I imagined that if I had known Anne, she and I would have been "kindred spirits."

Whenever I was upset and needed to get away from my family, I made sure to go to a different part of the woods. I wanted to keep that place under the giant maple by the bubbling water in the Autumn Woods as my happy place.

I babysat for Mrs. Hadlock's three children until I was sixteen. One afternoon I stayed longer than usual. The children were taking turns on the rocking horse in the living room where the television was. A Western came on, and before I knew it, there was a man in a corral trying to get away from an assailant with a knife by jumping from one fence to another, dodging the man slashing at his legs.

I felt my heart beating fast in my chest, but I couldn't take my eyes away from the television. I was thinking, "Why doesn't the cameraman help that man out? Why don't they take the knife away from the guy going after him?" And here I was, watching and powerless to do anything about it.

I knew that there were pretend things on television. The children watched Sesame Street daily. But these were real people, and this was a real place, I reasoned. It must have happened. I was still struggling with what I'd seen when I returned home that afternoon. I needed to tell someone about it, but certainly not Mem. I wasn't supposed to be watching television, and she'd tell me so. I didn't feel close to Lizzie. Sylvia and Sadie were clearly against me, no matter what I did.

I like to believe that after all that had happened between Joe and me, I never trusted him again for anything. But it was more complicated than that. I yearned for healthier relations between us, and I longed for an older brother I could talk to. So I told him what I'd seen. He said, "Oh, that's all make-believe."

"But I saw what they were doing! Why didn't the cameraman stop the man with the knife?"

Joe laughed. "Those are called actors. They get paid to act that all out. You don't have to worry, no one got hurt."

"I don't think I will ever watch television again. That was awful!"

"Don't worry, you'll get used to it," Joe said, dismissing the topic.

I wondered how Joe knew. Did he watch television, and if so, when and where?

As I was lying awake that night, I tried erasing from my mind the images and drama I'd witnessed. But the scenario of being overtaken by a powerful person—who may as well have been carrying a knife—with the intention to harm, was all too real. I didn't know if I *wanted* to get used to watching violence, even if it was make-believe. Then I thought to myself, why would anyone pretend such things, anyway?

I finally fell asleep and dreamed again what I'd dreamed many times before, ever since I was a small child. I was running, and with each step I took, I floated smoothly through the air, just above the earth. I could make each step carry me as far as I wanted before landing softly, then pushing off for another "flight." I was running through the garden toward the neighbors' peach trees up on the hill with my hair flowing out behind me, and a white gown billowing around me. I felt as free as a bird with its wings stretched out, floating along on summer breezes. I recognized the dream and thought, "I have often dreamed this was happening, but *this* time, it is *really* happening." The euphoria was tangible.

Then quick as a wink, I knew I was in danger. I looked behind me and saw that Joe was pursuing me. I told myself, "If I keep running like this, he can't catch me." I kept floating along, out of his reach. Then I looked behind me and fear caught the breath in my throat. My steps landed heavily, and I knew Joe was going to catch me. Just before he caught me, but after the panic had set in, I startled myself awake. I sat up in bed and struggled to breathe.

Sylvia awoke and wanted to know what was wrong. "It was just a dream," I said. I lay my head back on my pillow, crossed my arms over my chest, and curled up to slow my heartbeat and calm myself down.

Mrs. Hadlock hired me to clean her mother's house when I was sixteen. It was my first cleaning job, which led to another. I soon figured out that getting cleaning jobs was my ticket to avoiding the tensions in my own home, so I filled six days a week with jobs that took me to the suburbs of Cleveland. The people I worked for gave me rides back and forth to their homes. Some of them carpooled with their neighbors who picked up several of us Amish women and distributed us to the homes where we cleaned.

Several of the homes I cleaned had five bathrooms and as many bedrooms. I had a regimen in each home that I followed weekly. Whenever I was alone, I turned on the radio and listened to country western or bluegrass music. When I was in the living room all by myself, I watched soap operas. Joe was right—I did get used to the idea that people were acting out their roles. But he was wrong about something else. I never did get used to watching violence on television. It was all too real. So whenever I started to feel my breath coming in gasps, I turned off the television.

I started out earning twelve dollars a day, and eventually fifteen dollars a day. I handed all the money over to my parents. Mem gave me three dollars a week for allowance at first, and later five dollars a week. I was allowed to keep the money my clients gave me for my birthdays and Christmas. I kept depositing that money into my bank account, along with as much of my allowance as I could. Though it wasn't a conscious thought, I knew that if I ever decided to leave, the money would be there.

No matter how much my siblings and I made and handed over to our parents, our lifestyle did not improve. It seemed we were always poor. My sisters and I said it was like working to earn money that got dropped into a black pit, never to be seen again. We claimed we could do better with managing money than our parents. Mem, of course, blamed this on Datt. But we wondered among ourselves why she gave him the money. Why didn't she manage it?

I often wonder why I didn't keep some of the money I earned before giving the rest to Mem. I wanted to think of myself as an honest person, and I couldn't have it both ways. So I conscientiously handed over my money, even though I knew it would end up in the black pit. I often felt like I was walking in place with the monotony of one week blending into the next. Nothing changed except for what happened in the soap operas I watched on television. My life continued, but there was nowhere for it to go.

Even though I worked outside our home six days a week, I had to do more work when I returned home. Mem still relied on me to get things done, and my sisters still resented me bossing them.

One evening Katherine and I were the ones assigned to do the dishes. She was not doing her part, and I demanded she clear the table. She balked. I slapped her on the shoulder. She immediately began to cry. Mem said to her, "Come in here and let Lomie do the dishes if that's how she's going to be."

Katherine immediately stopped crying and did as Mem suggested, which left me to do the dishes all by myself. There was a mountain of them that night.

My temper boiled up. I had visions of taking the biggest cast iron frying pan we had and throwing it through the window. Expressing my anger had never worked out well before, and yet my anger needed a relief valve. I slammed cupboard doors and still pressure built up inside of me.

I was so beside myself with anger that I didn't think about leaving the house and stomping off my anger outside. How I wished later that I had. Instead, I raged about the kitchen.

Mem got up from her sewing chair and came out of the living room saying, "Lomie, you are *not* too old for a whipping!" She reached above the china cabinet and took down a hickory switch.

Instead of feeling fear as she came at me, my anger intensified. I headed for the door to get away from her, but she cracked the whip right across my back. I turned around and looked Mem right in the face. I thought about grabbing the whip out of her hands and using it to hit her back. Instead, I grabbed it from her and broke it with my bare hands as I looked her right in the eye. The wood broke in long splinters, with the bark still hanging on. I broke it into four or five sections.

I saw a flicker of recognition in Mem's eyes that showed she knew I was not afraid of her. That recognition changed to determination as her blue eyes turned icy. She called out, "*Datt, ich brach dei hilf!*—Dad, I need your help!"

Datt got up from his rocking chair and came bounding out of the living room. He grabbed the whip with the splinters and used both hands to ram the jagged ends into my shoulder. The pain was excruciating, which only intensified my anger and panic. Without thinking about it, my left arm swung around and hit Datt over his head. He landed on the floor behind the door. I saw my handprint outlined on the top of his bald head.

Now I was trapped. Datt was behind the door, so I couldn't get out. I ran upstairs, with Datt behind me. My room was at the north end of the house, which meant I had to go through the three other rooms to get there. I knew my way through there in the dark, but I wasn't sure Datt did. I opened up the first door, then I had an idea. I would close the door, sneak into the closet, and hope Datt would go into the other room, then I could escape by going back down the stairs and outside.

Datt was too smart for that. He figured out that I hadn't gone through to the next room. I crouched in the far corner of the closet, but Datt found me by feel. I cowered on the floor with him pounding on me until Mem came up the stairs with a gas lantern in hand and shepherded Datt out of the closet and down the stairs. She said, "That is the last time

I will ask *you* for help!" I wished Mem would hold to her declaration, but somehow I didn't think she would. I was as afraid of her punishments as I was of Datt coming after me. She and Joe were both calculating in deciding how severely they had to beat me to make me give in to their will. Datt, on the other hand, was as out of control as a wild bull coming at me. Because I wouldn't allow Mem to whip me into submission, she'd decided to unleash Datt. There was no escaping the wrath of both of them at the same time.

I picked myself up from the floor of the closet, went into my room, and lit an oil lamp. My dress had been ripped at the shoulder where the whip had poked through, and the wound was raw and oozing blood. I was shaking uncontrollably.

I lay down on the bed and just stared at the ceiling in the dim light of the oil lamp. I must have been in shock. I couldn't cry. I was too numb to feel the pain. Something inside me had simply gone dead.

This is where my memory of this incident ends. I know someone must have helped me to clean and bandage my shoulder, but I don't recall any of what happened after that. I don't even remember what my shoulder looked or felt like during the healing process.

For weeks, perhaps months, I merely existed. I did only what was required to survive.

RUMSPRINGA

You shall know the truth, and it will make you odd. ~Flannery O'Connor

Sixteen was the age when many of the young people in the community began going to "singings," or youth gatherings, which marked the beginning of their *rumspringa*—dating—years. Joe, like other young men, received his first horse and buggy from our parents for the occasion. I didn't think it was fair that boys got a horse and buggy, and girls got nothing. I was told that the girls got their weddings paid for by their parents, but I said that the boys got weddings, too. Men had many more privileges than women in our community, and that was all there was to it.

The *youngie*—youth—sowed their wild oats as the parents looked the other way. In my community at the time when I was young, this meant that many of the men bought and drank copious amounts of beer and smoked cigarettes. Some of them owned a radio or boom box, which they kept out of the sight and hearing of their parents. The young women dressed in fancier clothes—form-fitting, shorter dresses, and they wore smaller *koppa* when they joined the *youngie*.

I was expected to join the *youngie* now that I was sixteen, but I wasn't ready. I felt isolated from everyone, even other young women. I also knew I would have to rely on Joe to take me to the singings. He was taking Lizzie to the singings, and it didn't sound like fun. She had to clean his buggy every week before Joe would consent to take her. Then if he decided to date someone, he left Lizzie at the singing to find her own way home. Other brothers would normally find a way home for their sisters.

Soon after I turned seventeen, I was invited to my second cousins' home to spend the night. Mary was my age, and we had known one another since we were young children when her family lived several miles away from us. Our families had occasionally walked crosslots through the woods to visit one another. Then her family moved to Donley Road, just up the hill from my grandparents' home. If my family went to visit my grandparents on a Sunday, I'd often walk up the hill to visit Mary and her family.

An invitation to spend the night at Mary's home seemed to come out of nowhere. I wonder now whether someone—Mem and Joe come to mind—prompted the invitation because they were worried I hadn't shown any interest in *rumspringa*. If I didn't date and find a marriage partner, I wouldn't be following the "proper" order of things. Once trapped in a marriage with children not far behind, Amish women are much less likely to leave the community than if they stay single.

As I was getting ready to go to Mary's, I realized I didn't have an appropriate nightgown. My flannel one was faded and worn, and I felt embarrassed. Mem gave me a nightgown that was big enough for her. Two of me could have fit into it. My heart sank as I put it in my bag, along with my faded nightgown.

At Mary's house, I visited and laughed with her and her sisters. She came from a family of fifteen children and she was the third oldest, like myself. When it came time to go to bed, I confessed that I was embarrassed to wear either one of the nightgowns I'd brought with me. She asked to see them. I felt embarrassed as I showed them to her. She said quietly, "I'll ask my sisters for a nightdress you can wear," and she disappeared into another room. She came back with one that was made just like the dresses we wore every day, except that it had buttons instead of pins and it was light lavender, a color we weren't normally allowed to wear. It fit, and I looked at myself in the mirror. I felt glamorous in it.

It took me only days after my visit to Mary's house to buy light green material and make myself a nightdress.

Mary invited me to her home more than once, along with several other *youngie*. In this small group, I was taught how to "play party," which would have been considered a square dance anywhere else, except that this was a form of walking rather than dancing. There was no music as we grouped into pairs in the upstairs of Mary's home and walked forward and back, forward and back, did a do-si-do around the person next to us, and then swung our partners. Each of the four couples did this in unison.

Then one Sunday night while I was at Mary's house, the group decided they were going to attend the singing at a home on Burton-Windsor Road. They urged me to go with them. I was curious, so I decided I would.

The singing started the way the parents wanted with the *youngie* gathering in the house after supper to sing from the German hymnals. Someone announced the page number of a song and then led the song. When one song ended, there was a quiet pause before someone announced another page number. The women whispered to one another and the men teased and elbowed one another. There was tension in the air as we wondered who would be dating whom that night.

The *youngie* drifted in and out of the house. I stayed with my group and we sang until the singing ended. Then I found myself in the dark outside, heading for the barn with the others. The young men had hung a lantern from above, and there was country music coming from a boom box.

A whispering group of young women got together a group of eight to get started with "playing party." The young men were on one side of the barn, with the women on the other. I couldn't help but feel that the men were deciding who they were going to take home for a date.

Mary and her friends, Laura and Lucy, decided to get another ring of party playing started, and they asked me to join them, so I did. It was more fun with music, but I didn't like the feeling of being watched by so many people.

Someone cut in to dance with my partner, so I stood on the sidelines. Mary's older sister Ada motioned for me to go outside with her. There, next to the hedgerow in the dark, she asked, "Is it all right for Gid tonight?"

"What?"

"Gid is asking you for a date," she explained.

"Oh."

"I have to give him an answer."

I was flabbergasted. I thought no one would ask me for a date. I thought to myself, This might be the only time I get asked. I said "yes" with my heart pounding hard inside my chest.

I certainly did not find Gid attractive. He was one of the *youngie* who visited Mary's house on weekends. He and Laura had dated before, and I could tell she liked him, so I was wondering why he'd asked me instead of her. I took it as a compliment.

Ada came back and whispered to me, "Do you know what to do?"

I thought she was asking me if I knew about bed courtship. I thought I did, so I said, "Yes."

A little while later, Ada came and told me Gid was ready to go. She motioned to the buggy waiting in the lane. I stepped up into the buggy and sat next to Gid. He slapped the horse on the rump and took off out the lane and headed west toward my home. Our conversation was stilted. We talked about this having been my first singing, and about other things, but there was an uncomfortable silence that gathered between our topics.

When we finally drove in our lane, I told Gid how to find my room. With a flashlight to light his way, Gid started unhitching his horse to put him in the barn. I hurried in and changed into my new nightdress. I was glad Sylvia had decided to sleep in Sadie's room that night. I waited with the oil lamp lit until he came into the room. He took off his hat, his shirt, and his shoes and socks and got into bed. I lay down next to him. I wondered whether I should blow out the lamp, or keep it on. I was lying there, tense, wondering what would come next. I thought, "He knows this is my first date, so surely he will tell me what to do." He didn't. I could see the awkward silence between us in the lamplight, and I didn't know what to do. So I did nothing.

After a long silence, Gid picked up one hand and laid it on my stomach. I didn't know what he was doing, but I was thinking, "I have to let him do this since he brought me home." After a long moment, Gid got up from the bed and put his shirt and shoes back on, picked up his flashlight, and left. I thought that was odd. Normally dates lasted until the early hours of the morning when the young man left for home.

The following Sunday, I was sitting on a buggy at the singing with Laura. She said, "I heard you had Gid last weekend."

"Yes," I said. I felt strange talking to Laura about it since she'd dated Gid as well.

"I thought that was funny," Laura said as she giggled into her hand.

"What, that I would have a date?"

"No, that you didn't know..." Laura giggled again.

"Know what?" I asked.

"Oh, you still don't know? Then I'll have to tell you. You're supposed to *schmunzle.*" Laura said this while holding her hand over her mouth as if she were letting me in on a secret.

So much dawned on me at that moment. Laura, who had dated Gid before me, was telling me that I was "supposed to" hug and kiss him. How did she know I hadn't? I certainly hadn't told anyone, so that meant he had. Did he tell Laura directly, or did she hear it in a roundabout way? Either way, it was humiliating. I wondered how many other people knew.

Rumspringa was so confusing. A couple was "supposed to" go to bed and *schmunzle*, yet they were not allowed to have sex. We were meant to find a marriage partner and settle down into Amish life, but it didn't seem to matter whether two people had feelings for one another. The turmoil inside was too much for me. I stepped down from the buggy and left Laura sitting there by herself. I didn't want to know any more. I was thinking to myself, "*You* hug and kiss him then."

I headed for the dark shadows where I could be alone. I found myself shaking with humiliation and anger. I realized that even if I could do it over, I couldn't have *schmunzled* with Gid. I just didn't have it in me. I decided I'd rather feel the shame of not knowing than to have kissed and hugged Gid when I hadn't felt like it.

Laura and Gid had a date that night. Several weeks later, they started going steady.

≈

One night at a singing, I was asked for a date for the following Saturday night at a "party." This was a youth gathering without the pretense of being a singing, and therefore not sanctioned by the parents. These "parties" took place when a young man in a rebellious stage announced to other youth that he was going to have a party at his parents' place on a given night.

I was in a fix. I wanted to say yes to the date, but I was only allowed to go out on Sunday nights. I decided to say yes and figure out how I was going to manage to sneak away. I was told to meet him in Middlefield near the grocery store.

I told one of the Weaver girls up the road that I was planning on going to Middlefield on Saturday night. She asked to share the "taxi." I called Mrs. Hadlock, who had become a taxi driver after I babysat her three children. I asked that she not tell my parents.

Mrs. Hadlock drove Sara Mae and me to Middlefield on Saturday night. When it was time for her to drop us off, she made us promise that we would stay out of trouble. I made the promise, but I had no idea what I was getting myself into. I also had no idea where Sara Mae was going. I didn't think she went with the young people, but I paid no attention to where she was going. I had to find my date.

Before long, a young woman came along, asked if I was Lomie, and led me to a buggy. She was dating my cousin, and this was to be a double date. It was a cold night, so I was glad for the extra body in the buggy.

After what seemed like a long time, my cousin and another young man came to the buggy, untied the horse, piled into the buggy, and we headed out of town. I sat next to the stranger, who I realized was my date, while the young woman I'd just met sat on my lap, and my cousin drove the buggy.

When we got to the house where my date lived, it turned out it wasn't much of a party. There were four couples who sat together in a room and talked and drank beer. Then at some point the other couples left, with only my date and myself left in the room. He blew out the oil lamp, and we went to bed together.

I didn't like him. I allowed him to kiss and hug me, but then his roving hands started grabbing at my breasts. I kept pushing his hand away, but it kept coming back. Finally I stopped kissing him and said, "*Do net!*—Don't!"

His hand stopped in midair. Quick as could be, he turned his back and didn't touch me. I knew he was showing his disapproval, but I didn't care. I thought to myself, "Yay, that worked!" I turned my back and fell asleep.

The young man with roving hands was out of bed the next morning when I awoke. I didn't know what to expect. I got dressed and went downstairs. The parents were gone, and the young people sat about the living room, already drinking beer. I wasn't offered breakfast.

Later, when I was sitting out in a buggy, I realized I had snuck out the night before, and all for this? What a disappointment! I started with one beer on my empty stomach. One of the other women kept handing me beers, and I kept drinking them. I don't remember much about that afternoon, except when I got sick. The person who had given me the beers helped me to the outhouse because I couldn't walk on my own. There she stood and kept saying, "Stick your finger down your throat!" After I did, I made myself vomit several times.

Somehow I became sober enough to call a taxi and go home. I went straight to my room, knowing I wasn't getting away with this. Sure enough, I heard Mem lumbering up the stairs and through the three other rooms. She let herself into my room without knocking. She just stood there and looked at me reprovingly.

I became defensive immediately, saying I was asked for a date, and other young people go to parties... Mem interrupted and asked me to promise her that I would not sneak away on Saturday nights again.

I couldn't promise her. This date hadn't turned out well, but what if I was asked for a different one, and I wanted that date? And yet this one had been such a disaster. Out of sheer frustration, I broke into tears. I said, "But Mem, all the other young women are allowed to go out on Saturday nights. It's not fair!"

Before I knew what was happening, Datt came bounding into my room and started pounding on me. I curled up, using my hands and arms as shields against his blows. Mem said, "*Datt, shtopp sell!*—Dad, stop that!" She pulled him away and shepherded him downstairs. On their way, I heard her say, "That is the last time I will let *you* listen in!"

I may as well have promised Mem I wouldn't go out on Saturday nights anymore because I never did it again.

The dates after that were disasters. One of the dates had such stinky feet I could barely breathe. Another had a way of kissing that made me want to gag. Nearly all of them had roving hands. But I had the cure for that: words. They all reacted like the first man to whom I'd said, "*Do net.*" Every one of them turned their backs and ignored me after that.

I was sure I was gaining the reputation of being frigid. Some women had the label of being "loose." But I was determined not to get pregnant before I was married.

I had to come up with boundaries all on my own. I later learned that other mothers advised their daughters on what they shouldn't allow a young man to do, like "nothing below the waist." Mem never even tried talking with me about anything of the sort. It seemed she was clueless about any kind of personal boundaries.

I decided I hated bed courtship. It was absolutely *verboten* to talk about it with anyone outside the community. I used to wonder why it was forbidden to *talk* about bed courtship but not to actually *do* it. If there was nothing wrong with it, then we shouldn't be embarrassed about it, and if there was, then it should be changed, I reasoned.

The last thing I wanted to do was to go before the elders in my community and admit that I had "sinned." It would feel invasive and humiliating to admit this in the presence of four men. And it would give the bishop and his wife another reason to look down their noses at one of *Sim's maet.*

But more than all this, I wanted to wait for the person I wished to share my life with. Such intimacy with another person needed to mean something. Yet I felt trapped in the Amish dating system that left little chance for me to find and cultivate such a relationship.

BOOK OF JOE

It has always been a mystery to me how men can feel themselves honoured by the humiliation of their fellow beings. ~Mahatma Gandhi

My relationship with Joe did not improve once I started going to the singings. By then, Joe had found a steady girlfriend, Emma, who had two sisters around my age, Ada and Ella. Most Sunday afternoons Joe drove me to Emma's house, and then Ada, Ella, and I would find our way to the singings. If it was within walking distance, we'd walk. Otherwise we'd hire a taxi to take us there.

In exchange for rides to Emma's house, I had to wash and polish Joe's buggy every week. He was extra bossy with me, and I had to put up with his paternal attitude without talking back if I knew what was good for me.

Mem assumed a "hands-off" attitude during my dating years. I worked six days a week, and on Sunday afternoons I was out with other youth. Thus, I gained more distance from Mem than I'd ever had before.

Mem and Joe continued to carry on their conspiratorial relationship. It was the two of them against Datt. Frequently, Datt and Joe had clashes out in the barn that resulted in physical fights. The first one had happened some years before when Joe decided he wasn't going to take another beating from Datt. When he stood up to Datt, their tussle in the house became scary as the two of them tumbled up against the dining room chairs and table. I just wanted them to stop before one of them seriously hurt the other. Mem called for Datt to stop, but the two of them were locked in battle. I don't remember how the fight ended, but I remember feeling relieved when it was finally over. I had no idea that this was only the first of many such battles between the two of them. One day it even happened at a church service.

After the first prayer, the deacon always read scripture in German while the congregants stood. It was acceptable for someone to take a break during the reading. The young men usually went to the barn together. Datt told Joe he should not go out with the other young men. Joe ignored him and did what he wanted.

During one Sunday scripture reading at church, Datt picked up his hat from under the bench and went outside soon after the young men had gone out, which was unusual. Later I found out that Datt had confronted Joe out in the barn, and the two of them had had another fight. I also heard that the bishop's son looked at the other young men and said, "Should we be doing something about this?"

Joe hitched his horse to the buggy and left for home instead of going back into the church service.

Our family thought the fights were a result of a personality clash between Joe and Datt. We all looked forward to Joe marrying Emma and leaving home. We thought this would solve the problem. I didn't understand what fueled the tensions between them, nor did I anticipate that Datt would turn his violence on my sisters and me when Joe left home.

Mem and Joe had been sharing confidences ever since I could remember. I used to wonder what they talked about when they were alone together. Then one day when I was ten and Joe was thirteen, I heard part of one of their conversations. The two of them were in Mem's rug room together, and I was lying on my bed in the next room. Joe was telling Mem how an English person had come to our school that day. The visitor had been granted permission by Teacher Levi to give the pupils a set of questions that pertained to our families. Joe said, "I didn't even know how to answer some of those questions."

Mem asked, "Like what?"

"They asked how often we go into a grocery store with our parents. There was a choice of answers, but none of the choices included 'never.' I realized I'd never been in a grocery store with you and Datt."

I didn't move a muscle. I wanted to know how Joe had answered that question because I had gotten stuck on it myself. I also wanted to hear Mem's response. But I felt like a sneak and I didn't want to get caught.

Joe said, "I've been to a grocery store with Datt, but you've never been there. Why don't you ever go grocery shopping with him?"

"Oh well, I decided to leave that to Datt after *Momme* went through the groceries I'd bought one day and told me I should be doing without this and without that."

"Was that Datt's mem?"

"Yes." After a pause, Mem added, "*My* mem would never do that."

Joe asked, "So why did you listen to *Momme?*" All of a sudden, Joe's footsteps came toward my room. He pulled the curtain between my room and the rug room aside and said in a solid voice, "Lomie, go downstairs!"

I shot up from my bed and headed down the back stairs. I heard Mem say, "I didn't know she was over there."

"I thought she might be," Joe said as if he had just averted a major betrayal of their intimacy.

It wasn't new for Mem and Joe to have these intimate moments together. And yet the summer I was turning eighteen, it seemed they were spending even more time with each other without anyone else around. I decided I didn't want to know why.

One Saturday evening, Mem gave Joe a haircut, leaving a pile of dark hair on the linoleum floor. Joe commanded that I clean up the hair. I bit my tongue as I swept the hair together into a pile. I turned around to pick up the dustpan, and when I turned to sweep the hair into the dustpan, I realized Joe had kicked it all over the kitchen floor. He stood there leering at me. I looked at him in shock. Joe said, "Clean it up!" I couldn't believe he was so blatant about making me do whatever he commanded.

I dropped the broom and dustpan and walked away.

Mem called me back. I protested, "But Mem, did you see...?"

"Oh, come on, can't you take a joke?" Joe laughed.

"The joke is that you get to clean it up," I retorted.

Somehow Mem and Joe together convinced me I had to go back and clean up the hair. I don't remember if they threatened me or if I was afraid Joe would take his revenge later. But I was not happy about it. I looked Joe right in the face. "Does Emma know what you're like? Because if she doesn't, she has a right to know."

"Yeah, how will you tell her? I won't be taking you to her house if that is what you plan to do."

"I don't need to see her. I can write," I said with determination. I finished sweeping up that cursed hair, and then I retreated to my room. I was already drafting the letter to Emma in my head.

The next morning, Mem made sure no one was within hearing distance when she said to me, "You aren't really going to write to Emma, are you?"

"Why not? Don't you think she has a right to know the truth?"

"That would just cause trouble between the two of them. Stay out of it," Mem said with authority. I heard a threat in her tone of voice.

I ditched the idea of writing to Emma. I reasoned that Joe getting married was a good thing because he would be leaving home and making my life easier. Yet I couldn't help feeling sorry for Emma.

One Saturday afternoon, only weeks after the hair incident, I found out why Mem and Joe had been conspiring. Joe and Emma's upcoming wedding was going to be announced in Emma's church district the next day. They were to be married eleven days later.

It was common for young couples in the community to keep their wedding plans a secret until eleven days before the wedding took place. However, at least the immediate families normally knew about the wedding plans. Not Joe. He'd only told Mem in his family. He must have told Emma's sisters to keep it from me because I had been visiting them nearly every Sunday for months. They would have been preparing for the wedding well in advance, so they clearly knew. It seemed Joe was sending a message that we were not to be trusted with secrets—all except for Mem.

It was common in my community for the groom to stay with the bride's family to help with wedding preparations between the Sunday when the wedding plans were announced and the wedding day, usually a week and a half later on a Thursday.

Joe ordered me to pack his suitcase. I was so glad that he was leaving home that I didn't protest.

After church the next day, Joe and Emma came driving in the lane in Joe's buggy. They stayed in the buggy and asked Mem to send me out. They wanted to know if I would be one of their *neva-hucka*—literally a "sit-besider," the equivalent of a best man and maid of honor. Customarily, they get to choose a partner.

When Joe asked me, I was taken aback, but I was also excited. Being a *neva-hucka* for a sibling was the only time a young woman had a choice for a partner. They would date the night before and the night of the wedding. I thought about the honor of the position and the chance, finally, to choose who I wanted to date. I went down my mental list of who I might ask. But then I remembered that Lizzie was the one in line for the position and she would be hurt if she wasn't asked. Aloud I asked, "Isn't the next older one in the family usually asked to be the *neva-hucka*?"

"Well, if you don't want to, that's fine. We can ask someone else," Joe said.

"I'll do it."

"We were thinking you would have Emma's cousin, Albert, for a partner." Joe said. Emma sat wordlessly by his side.

My excitement melted. "Well, I don't know him. Doesn't the *neva-hucka* normally get to choose?"

"Ada's partner is going to be our Cousin Andy. I thought it would be nice if we invited Emma's cousin on our side." Joe paused and then asked, "Why—is there someone you wanted to ask?"

This felt like a trap. Why would Joe have me reveal who I'd invite if he'd already made that choice for me? I assessed quickly that even if I did reveal my heart's desire, I would still have to settle for Albert because Joe said so.

Aloud I said, "It sounds like you've already made that choice." I looked at the buggy wheel instead of Joe's face. "I'll have to think about it. Yesterday morning I didn't even know you were making plans to get married, and I didn't know you wanted me to be *neva-hucka* until now."

"You don't have to if you don't want to. Most people would jump at the chance," Joe said.

"I said I will do it, so I will."

"With Albert?"

"Yes," I said. I wanted to retort, "Since you aren't giving me that choice." But I didn't. Even though Joe was leaving home and getting married, he still had power over me. I hated it.

"Here is a sample of the material for your dress," Emma said, speaking for the first time. She handed me a square of royal blue polyester fabric. "You can buy it at Spector's store."

Typically, the bride paid for the dresses of the women *neva-hucka*. It dawned on me that Emma was expecting me to buy my own fabric. And I'd need a new *kopp* for the occasion, along with a new cape and apron. I wondered if Emma was already taking a page out of the "book of Joe."

Mem surprised me and paid for the organdy material for my cape and apron, and for the new organdy *kopp* made by my Aunt Saloma. Likely she used the money I'd earned cleaning houses to pay for these items. Of course it was better than having it end up down the deep pit that my sisters and I had joked about.

~

The night before the wedding, Joe sent a message to me that I should get to Emma's house for supper. Traditionally, Albert would have come to pick me up, but Joe said he lived too far away. This meant I had to pay for a taxi to take me there.

I arrived at Emma's house just before suppertime. I was still taking off my bonnet and shawl when Joe came onto the porch. He had dark stubble on his face. Now that he was getting married, he had to grow a married man's beard. Ever since he'd joined church, he'd been growing a little beard, low on his chin.

As a greeting, Joe said, "You're a little early, but you can help out."

"I got word that I should find my way here, but I didn't know what time," I said.

"Just so you know," Joe said, lowering his voice. "Albert is really shy, so don't embarrass him by talking too much. And Ada is going to need a lot of help. Be sure you do your part." He leered at me and went inside.

Joe had just "put me in my place." Not only had he decided who my partner was going to be, but now Joe was telling me how to act around him. And he had made sure that I would step into second place behind Ada. She was a little older than me, so she had already assumed that role whenever we were together.

Ada came out on the porch and said, "Lomie, come on in. You don't have to stay out here by yourself."

I pulled myself together after Joe's shaming session. "What can I help you with?"

"We're just putting supper on the table." I followed Ada into the lantern-lit kitchen.

Cousin Andy was there, and so was a young man of slight build with blond hair. His eyes expressed how much he didn't want to be there. He sat with his hands in his lap as though he felt helpless. He sat so quietly that I wondered if he thought people wouldn't notice him if he didn't move—like a bird sitting in a tree and knowing someone was around. I also wondered how he was going to survive the next day when more than two hundred people would notice him.

After the meal was finished and the dishes were done, I was shown which bedroom I was to sleep in. Albert was already sitting on the edge of the bed. I had changed into my nightdress, so I got in on the side of the bed closest to the wall. Albert blew out the lamp and got into bed.

We were lying in bed in the dark for a long time without a word. As a way of making conversation I said, "Tomorrow will be a different day for all of us." Albert was quiet for so long that it dawned on me he was not going to respond. I wondered what to say or do next. Ada had whispered to me just before I came into the room with Albert that this was his first date. Should I initiate *schmunzling*, or would that be too forward? Maybe he felt the way I had on my first date.

Albert was lying on his stomach. I put my arm across his back. I could feel him tense up.

I moved away. I was still wondering what I should do next when I heard his breathing deepen, and I knew he'd fallen asleep. There was one thing left for me to do, and that was to fall asleep myself. Lying alone in the dense darkness, I thought about how much I had looked forward to this chance to have my "day in the sun" at Joe's wedding. Now it felt more like it would be my day in the shadows. My disappointment was as heavy as the darkness in the room. After what seemed like a long time, I fell asleep.

~

Albert was not in bed when I awoke in the morning. I got up, got dressed, and went down for breakfast. I hardly noticed that the October morning had dawned bright and sunny.

After breakfast, Emma, Ada, and I dressed in our bright blue dresses and crisp capes and aprons. We wore our black *koppa* for the church service. Right after the service, we would be changing into our white *koppa*. Emma wore her black *kopp* for the last time that morning for her wedding service. That afternoon, she would stop wearing the black one and start wearing a married woman's white *kopp*.

When we were dressed, we joined the three men of the wedding party in a basement room, right next to the washhouse. Through a small window, we could see people arriving by horse and buggy.

We sat there for what seemed like a long time. When the slow German chant began out in the barn, Joe led the way, followed by Emma, then Andy, Ada, and Albert. I was the last to follow. We filed in and stood in front of the chairs provided for us. Then we all sat down in unison. The bishops and ministers got up and shook hands with people and filed out to have a ministers' meeting in an upstairs room of the house. After a few minutes, Joe and Emma stood up, and Emma followed Joe meekly into the house to receive their marriage instructions from the elders.

The singing continued. The second song was the *Loblied,* as it was in every church service. It took twenty minutes to sing through the four stanzas.

A third hymn was announced. Near the end, Joe and Emma came back and sat down again. A few moments later, the elders returned and joined in singing the last verse of the hymn.

After the German hymn books were closed and stashed under the benches, the first preacher stood up. He was one of the ministers in Emma's church district. It sounded much like a sermon at church, except he focused on marriage and how a woman should be submissive to her husband. I cringed. He did not need to encourage Joe to dominate Emma.

Dan Wengerd had been ordained in our church district the year before. He stood up to preach the second sermon. I could tell he was nervous by the long pauses, the repeated clearing of his throat, and his jerky movements. This was Bishop Dan's first time officiating at a wedding.

Normally the second sermon is longer than the first, but not this time. Dan was moving toward the end of his sermon quickly. The cooks and table waiters arrived to watch Joe and Emma exchange their vows. Dan called Joe and Emma to step up before him.

Joe and Emma looked as nervous as Dan. I wondered if it was catching. I was hoping Dan wouldn't mess this up because I wanted to be sure Joe was really married. I listened as they repeated their pledges after Bishop Dan, and then I watched as Dan joined their hands and pronounced them man and wife.

Emma seemed as submissive as a woman could be as she walked in step behind Joe toward her seat.

The cooks and table waiters left to return to their work in the kitchen. The congregation knelt, and Bishop Dan read a long prayer. I couldn't help but feel relieved that Joe would be out of our house. I looked at Emma kneeling beside me, her face unreadable, and I felt an ache of sympathy. She was now at the mercy of Joe and bound to him in ways no one had been before. I hoped God would have mercy on her.

We stood for a scripture reading, then sat down for the parting hymn that sounded lively and joyful. When the last notes died away, the six of us stood in unison and filed out first.

Emma, Ada, and I went upstairs and exchanged our black *koppa* for our white ones. Emma was subdued and asked Ada where she had put this or that. It seemed impossible that Emma could focus on such small details right after she'd made such a huge change in her life.

Several minutes later, we sat at the bridal corner, or *eck,* in the living room, with our respective partners. It felt like Albert wasn't present, even though he was sitting right next to me. Men filed in and sat on one side of the table, the women on the other. When the bishop gave the signal, everyone bowed their heads for silent prayer. Then the table waiters brought out big platters and bowls of food. They brought the choicest pieces of chicken to the *eck* table, along with bowls of mashed potatoes, gravy, stuffing, coleslaw, fresh garden peas, applesauce, and bread with butter and jam.

Lizzie and Ella had the most honored positions of being *eck* table waiters. Both of them were flushed red from the warmth of the day and the efforts they were exerting to get things just right. Joe managed to get a dig in under his breath, something about Ella doing most of the work. Lizzie's face became a deeper red. I felt like saying out loud, "Lizzie, don't let Joe shame you, you're doing a great job." But I stayed mum, just like Albert beside me.

Sarah, Susan, and Emma's youngest sister, Katie, were the next most honored table waiters at the tables that extended out from the *eck*.

After the main dishes came the desserts: strawberry tapioca pudding, graham cracker pudding, and all kinds of pies—apple, cherry, blueberry, and strawberry. The six of us at the *eck* table had a special strawberry pie that had a whipped cream topping and had been chilled in the icebox.

Halfway through dessert, the men who were married to the cooks came around to collect money for the cooks and table waiters. They took saucepans with coins in them and shook them vigorously, making a mighty racket. The more coins that were tossed into the pans, the louder they became.

After the meal, Joe and Emma went outside under the shade tree to visit with wedding guests. Ada and I gathered all the presents into one of the upstairs bedrooms. A group of men sat around the now-empty tables in the living room to sing the German chants. The sound of the spirited hymns drifted upstairs.

Joe went off to the barn with the menfolk to give out cigars. Emma went upstairs to her bedroom to unwrap presents. There were fancy dishes and glass bowls, bowls of plastic and stainless steel, platters, pitchers, glasses, flatware, dishpans, a drainer, pots and pans, bath towels, dish towels, sheets, tablecloths, an ironing board and gas iron, gas lanterns, and every imaginable household item. Ada and I took turns recording in Emma's wedding album who gave which gifts.

Groups of women and girls came and went to watch the unwrapping of the gifts. The room became stuffy, and I could smell cigar smoke drifting up from below. While Ada was recording, I took a break and sat out in the cool shade of the maple tree in the front yard.

As I sat under the tree's expansive shading branches of autumn colors, I closed my eyes and listened to the sounds of singing, talking, laughter, and the horses grazing in the field nearby. I could hear them munching grass and switching their tails and stomping the ground to shoo the flies away. Occasionally, a car went by on the road. I could smell meatloaf baking, along with something sweet—probably date pudding for the evening meal. Enveloped by the very air of Amish around me, I longed to be able to give in, to accept that the life that I had been born into was the one meant for me. I imagined that sometime in the next five years, I would be in Emma's place, unwrapping wedding gifts, and my new husband would be out in the barn being congratulated by other community members. We would go home to a place of our own, and children would soon follow.

I was brought out of my reverie when my Aunt Sarah said in a chiding way, "What are you doing out here by yourself?" She sat down on a bench near me. A group of women joined us. Aunts and cousins came by and visited in between their duties in the kitchen. Lizzie and Ella sat for a while. They looked exhausted. Sylvia and Sadie were inside, setting up their table.

I went back upstairs and helped with the gifts. It was late afternoon when we finished. The crowd had thinned out by then. Some people went home for chore time with plans to return for the evening festivities. Others left for the day.

Around the time when the married folks were eating their supper, the youngie began arriving. They gathered in upstairs bedrooms, with the girls in one room and the boys in another.

Joe began lining up young folks to go down for the supper meal. Traditionally, the young people paired up to eat together for the evening meal at weddings. Sometimes the young men resisted and had to be pushed into line. Joe used to be one of them. Now he was in charge of lining them up—boy, girl, boy, girl. He wasn't giving any thought to who ended up with whom. A few of the young men went back into the bedroom. Joe told them if they didn't want to eat, then they could just stay in the bedroom. That seemed to work, and the boys allowed themselves to be nudged into line.

Finally, when the *youngie* were lined up to go downstairs, Joe took the lead, and everyone followed. We took our place at the *eck* table, and the *youngie* spread out, sitting at the tables in the living room first, then filling tables in other rooms. This time the cooks' husbands brought the food: meatloaf, noodles, several kinds of slaw, corn relish, pickles, applesauce, vanilla pudding, date pudding, and more fruit pies. The money rattlers came back and collected more money.

After supper was over, the young men carried lanterns out to the barn. Someone turned on a tape player and the "party playing" began. Joe and Emma danced together for the last time. Once their wedding day was over, it was forbidden for married couples to dance. When one joined the church, one was expected to obey the *Ordnung*. But the elders did not enforce all the rules until the *youngie* got married. Dancing or "party playing" was considered a courtship ritual. Once a couple was married, their *rumspringa* days were over. Marriage was considered the last step to becoming an adult and a full member of the church. They were now expected to uphold the church rules.

I danced with Ada, but my heart wasn't in it. I didn't even feel like myself. I didn't see Albert anywhere.

Well after midnight, the lanterns were taken from the barn, a signal for the *youngie* to go home. Dates often took place on the night of weddings. Couples climbed into buggies and drove away.

Joe took me to the side of the barn. I knew he wasn't setting me up for a date because I already had mine. He said, "You can sleep in the same room you were in last night, but Albert decided he wanted to sleep alone. I thought I'd let you know."

Before I could respond, Joe walked across the yard toward the house, leaving me standing there. I watched his retreating back disappear into the darkness, the light of the lantern he was carrying casting moving shadows that crisscrossed the yard with each step he took.

I felt so rejected and alone, I almost cried. I wondered if that was what Joe wanted me to do. He had used his wedding to "bring me down a notch," as he often phrased it—as if a woman might get too confident without a male in her life reminding her of her position as second to a man.

I went to bed feeling more alone than ever. Even the darkness in the room was oppressive. I lay awake for a long time before I drifted into sleep and had dreams that were as bewildering as the day had been. I awoke with the feeling of them, yet I didn't remember their content. I heard others moving about and knew it was my duty to help clean up. I forced my body out of bed. Did Emma's sisters and parents know I had slept alone? It was just like Joe to leave that to my imagination.

Joe and Emma were in the kitchen among the dirty dishes left from the night before.

Albert looked like he wanted to disappear down a hole. I decided I was done feeling sorry for him.

We ate breakfast, and then it was time to do the dishes that were piled high on the counter and the tables in the kitchen. I had never seen so many dirty dishes in my life. Emma's mother set up wash and rinse water on three tables for each of us couples. I wondered when the tradition started of men washing the dishes after a wedding. I hadn't seen Joe doing dishes since he was about twelve years old.

Albert went through the motions of drying dishes, but he didn't seem to know how to do the job. I could have dried three glasses in the time he dried one. I wondered why Joe hadn't excused him from doing dishes with me after what had happened the night before. I wished I had the nerve to ask Albert why he had said yes to becoming a *neva-hucka* at all. I wanted to ask him if he thought being shy was worse than feeling rejected. I also wanted to tell him that I wouldn't have chosen him, but Joe and Emma hadn't given me a choice. I wanted to ask him if he had any idea how much he had spoiled my day with his shyness, and if he knew that he might as well not have come to the wedding at all?

When I finished washing the mountain of dishes, I called a taxi from the phone booth down the road and went home. Mem mercifully allowed me to go to bed and sleep. When I got up for supper, she warned me that I wouldn't be able to sleep that night, but I did. Sleep helped soften the memories of the disappointment, hurt, and humiliation of Joe's wedding.

BAPTISM BY EXPECTATION

If the path before you is clear, you're probably on someone else's.
~Joseph Campbell

Our family, like most other Amish families in our community, owned a copy of *The Martyr's Mirror*, which chronicles the struggles of our martyred Anabaptist ancestors. They rebelled against the Roman Catholic and state authorities that required infant baptism, reasoning that a believers' baptism was the only valid one and infants could not make that choice.

The elders in our community admonished us regularly about how our ancestors' faith had been tested and because they had suffered to keep their faith, we should be grateful to have the freedom to follow in their footsteps. But I didn't always feel grateful. Yes, our ancestors had suffered. But hadn't they struggled for the right to make their own choices by wrenching their rights away from the authorities? It seemed to me that part of this freedom was having the choice *not* to become baptized. I didn't feel I had that choice. The expectations and the instilled beliefs were so strong and irrevocable that our parents might as well have made that choice for us when we were babies. Indeed, it seemed they had —only nineteen or twenty years later.

Women in our community were expected to "follow the church"(join the church and become baptized) anytime between the ages of seventeen and twenty. Men had more leeway, but they were expected to join the church by the time they were twenty-one or twenty-two. The expectation to follow the church weighed heavier than state law because the elders of the church had more authority over me than did secular law enforcement.

I first started feeling pressured the summer I was turning nineteen. At first it was just a question, "Are you going to follow the church this summer?" My ambiguous answers conveyed my uncertainty. Then I began getting hints that "maybe it's time."

Olin Clara asked me one day if I had any plans to become a member of the church. She said she would love for me to be a fellow member. While I felt her sincerity, her suggestion only made me more uncertain. I wondered if I would be doing it for the right reasons. If so, I should be eager to follow the church without others prompting me.

Then one Sunday, Joe and Emma invited us to their home for a midday meal. I was quieter than usual that day, observing the family dynamics. Datt was meek and mild, sitting with slumped shoulders in his green Sunday shirt. It was hard to tell that there had been such tensions and trouble between Datt and Joe in years past. Joe and Emma seemed happy together, living in the basement of Emma's brother's home. I wondered whether Joe was still calling people who lived in basements "groundhogs." Then I caught myself feeling jealous of Joe. He had left home, and now he and Emma were expecting their first baby while I was still feeling stuck in our parents' home. After Joe had left, Datt had turned his violent outbursts toward my sisters and me. I wanted to be free of violence too. And I hoped I would someday have babies of my own.

Joe and I ended up in their kitchen alone while the others went out to look at the garden. Even at the time, I felt this was orchestrated. Mem never said a word to me directly about following the church, but I felt she was behind the urgings from others. He asked, "Are things any better at home?"

I shrugged, knowing better than to answer that. Joe looked at me from under his hooded eyelids in the way he did when he wanted to pretend we were good buddies.

"Are you going to follow the church this summer?"

"I don't know yet. I'm thinking about it."

"I think that would really help."

I shrugged again. "Maybe it would help. But what if it doesn't?"

"Then at least you'd be doing the right thing," Joe said, as he walked out the door to join the others.

My feelings roiled inside me. Joining the church would mean going along with the Amish ways without question. I longed to be more content with the life I'd been born into, and I wanted to feel like I belonged. On the other hand, if I joined and later left the Amish, I would be shunned for the rest of my life. I wouldn't be shunned if I wasn't a baptized member. When I caught myself thinking this, I doubted myself even more. Why was I thinking about joining a church that I secretly had thoughts about leaving altogether? Standing there in Joe's kitchen, I knew I didn't have a choice. I told myself I might as well get it over with.

The Sunday morning of decision time dawned bright and sunny. I pinned my organdy cape over my dress, crossing the two front pieces as I had always done before. Then to see what I looked like, I pinned the two front parts of the cape straight down the middle, the way I would if I were going to follow the church. I turned this way and that and realized the way I had been pinning my cape looked too girlish. In the same way that I had gone from wearing girls' dresses to women's dresses when I was an adolescent, this was part of growing up. If I didn't join the church this summer, the pressure would increase for the following summer. So I pinned my cape the new way and walked up the road to the Weavers' house. Two of their daughters were also joining, and they were just finishing pinning their capes into place. Together we walked to the home where the church service was being held. The earth was coming alive and the birds were singing sweetly that May morning as we walked along. I hoped it was a sign that I was doing the right thing.

There were five of us who were following the church—the bishop's son Noah, and four of us young women. As the singing started, the elders left to meet in an upstairs bedroom. Several moments later, Noah got up from his bench, and we followed in order by age. Sara Mae was one day older than me, so I followed her. I was followed by her sister, Elizabeth, and another young woman, Wilma.

We sat down on a bench that faced the elders. The bishop talked to us about the step we were about to take and quoting verses from the Bible in German to emphasize his points. Then the ministers and deacon each took turns talking to us. We listened until the bishop told us we should go back to the service.

After several Sunday sessions, I realized that instruction meant that we got our personal preaching session. I was hoping that the preachers were going to explain the Amish ways, but there was no chance of that.

I thought we would be following this boring pattern all summer until one Sunday morning when we had just sat down in front of the elders and Bishop Dan began by saying that "a brother" had brought to his attention that one among us was still "playing party," and this brother thought this should stop before baptism. "So..." Dan shuffled his feet nervously, "If that person can promise it will stop, we can continue."

An awkward silence followed. Then Dan looked at me. I was confused. Normally, we all had to acknowledge the promises we were making, starting with Noah. I looked at Noah and said, "Me?"

Dan said, "Well, aah... you.. you should probably all make the promise, so Noah, why don't you start?" Five yeses followed, including mine because I didn't know that I had a choice. My thoughts crowded each other out. I knew the "brother" who had come to the bishop was my father. He'd been telling me I shouldn't be dancing at the singings, but I'd ignored him. Usually he had tradition on his side, but this time it was on mine. Other youth danced, church members included. Datt had no say about it, so I danced whenever I wanted to. It was the most fun I had at singings, and I didn't want to stop. But now that I'd made a promise, I thought I had to. I didn't hear a word the preachers were saying.

Back in the church service, I still couldn't concentrate. I wondered if I could still back out of baptism. Some young people had started instructions for baptism and then dropped out, saying they weren't ready. But I knew that the pressure would be intense, and I didn't want that either. As soon as the service was over, I walked home. I usually stayed for midday communal meal, but I was in no mood for that. I wanted to be alone.

Back home, I ate a big bowlful of popcorn and three pieces of pie, then went to the woods to throw it all up. I first heard of the technique of "purging" from my sisters. I thought it was a gross idea and told myself I'd never do that. Then one day I'd eaten too much at the place where I worked, and I had the urge to try. It was not easy, but after I turned in circles until I was dizzy, I tried again. This was the beginning. I told myself I was doing it to keep myself from gaining weight. I didn't know this addiction had the name bulimia. I also didn't realize it was a way for me to part with my feelings. It was as if I kept swallowing down the Amish dogma, my anger, and the feeling that I was trapped, only to reject these feelings, time and again. In this vicious cycle, everything remained unchanged, including the fact that the day of my baptism was fast approaching.

The church was like a person guiding me by my elbow down a long corridor. There was light enough to see ahead, but behind me there was darkness, and this moved as I moved. Deciding not to be baptized would have been like turning abruptly away from the elbow guiding me and running into the dark abyss. According to the preachers, those who turned away from the church also turned away from God. This could lead to being cast into a fiery abyss to be trapped there forever. I could not allow myself to imagine that horror.

For some reason, Joe came to visit the night before my baptism. His presence only intensified my conflict. I was scheduled to go to the deacon's house that evening. The five of us who were about to be baptized the next day were to meet there with the elders of the church to discuss the "Articles of Faith."

Instead of breaking down and crying under all the pressure I felt, I lashed out. I scolded Simon for being slow with carrying in water for baths. Even as I grumbled about little things, I knew I was being crabby, and yet I couldn't stop myself.

Joe said, "If this is what Lomie is like the night before she is supposed to be baptized, maybe she isn't ready."

"Yeah, well maybe you can go and explain that to the bishop then," I snapped.

Mem didn't say a word. She'd never once given me a word of

encouragement that whole summer I was taking this big step into adulthood and the church. It was as if she didn't care, and yet I felt she'd been behind those who had pressured me to join the church. Now I sensed she'd asked Joe to come visit as reinforcement to ensure that I followed through with my baptism.

After taking my bath, I got dressed in my new black baptismal dress and walked to the Weavers' house where I met Sara Mae and Elizabeth. Together we walked to the deacon's house.

Weeks earlier, we had each chosen one of the articles of faith from the little German book *Christianpflicht*. These articles had been written by our European ancestors and handed down through the generations. They were written in high German, different from our unwritten Pennsylvania German dialect, which made it nearly a foreign language to us.

I chose the sixth article, about leaving sin behind and turning toward the good. As much as I doubted I was doing the right thing in joining church, I still wanted to believe it would be a time of transformation. I liked the hope in the article I was going to read, about how in transforming our lives, we use our ears to hear, our hearts to understand, and our willingness to do good. This is what I wanted for my life, though I didn't know the path. The article ended with the beautiful concept that when our lives are transformed, we are sowing eternal seeds. Through God, we are born anew. I read and reread my article until I understood most of it.

Once we were gathered as a group, Bishop Dan explained that these articles are important in the church *Ordnung*. He said each of us would read our article and he would explain the meaning of it. Noah read his article and Dan explained it, then Sara Mae read hers and again Dan explained it. Now it was my turn. I was a bit nervous, but I had studied my article so that I was able to read it with some understanding. When I finished, there was a moment of silence. Dan started to explain the article. He shuffled his feet and said, "Well it means... ahh... just the way you read it." He hesitated a long moment before he said, "Elizabeth, why don't you read your article?"

Dan's remarks felt like a rebuke, like I'd spoiled his chance to explain its meaning. Was I not supposed to understand what I was reading? It was another riddle of Amish life. I didn't know what to think. Being a part of the community didn't seem to be about understanding or finding my way in it. Rather, it was about walking in the same footsteps many had trod before me. It seemed best to leave any understanding to the ordained.

~

The baptismal service was held at the bishop's daughter's homestead in a tool shed. The cement floor was cracked, rough, and dirty. During the service I kept thinking about the five of us who were going to be baptized, kneeling on that floor with our best Sunday clothes on. Why hadn't they spread straw on the floor, as people usually did in sheds or barns where they hosted church services? Then I closed my eyes and tried to put such improper thoughts out of my mind.

The service followed the same pattern as a normal church service. The five of us followed the elders into the house for our last meeting as the rest of the congregation sang a slow German chant. The preachers reminded us of the importance of the step we were about to take. It made me squirm. I already knew that. I still didn't know whether I was doing the right thing. I wanted so much to just give up my own will and go along with whatever was expected of me. I wanted to accept my life as an Amish person and be content with it, but it wasn't coming naturally.

Along with the other four who were about to be baptized, I gave the prescribed answer to whatever the bishop asked until it was time for them to dismiss us. I took my place in line to reenter the service. We joined in singing the German chant.

The preachers rejoined the service as the song was ending. One of the ministers, John Detweiler, got up to preach the first sermon. He talked about how the angels in heaven were rejoicing to see young people turning toward God on this day. I hoped he was right. I had never felt so queasy before. I told myself if I had the right motivations, I should be feeling joyful and sure of myself.

After the sermon, we all knelt by our benches for silent prayer. I tried praying for courage, but my mind was blank. Then the congregation stood for the scripture reading by the deacon, before sitting down for the second sermon, preached by Bishop Dan. I was on edge all during the sermon because I knew what was coming.

Then came the moment when Bishop Dan asked everyone to stand. He invited those of us who wished to be baptized in the name of the Lord to come forward and kneel before him. I wondered if I still had a choice. What would happen if I didn't follow the others? Guilt for my thoughts burned in my mind as I fell into place in the middle of the line.

Then I found myself kneeling on that rough, dirty, and cracked cement floor in my black dress with people standing all around me wearing their black clothing and solemn faces. My turn had come to repeat the vows that I would stay in the Amish church for the rest of my life, and yes, I believed that Jesus Christ was my Savior. Kate, a woman in the church, had come forward to assist with the baptism of the women. She untied my covering and took it off my head. As I repeated the words Bishop Dan said, I tried to blink back the tears. Then he cupped his hands over my head and the deacon poured water into them. Bishop Dan said, "I baptize you in the name of the Father, the Son, and the Holy Ghost, Amen," and poured the water from his hands onto my head. My tears were one with the holy water that dripped down over my face.

Kate replaced my head covering, offered me a hand to get up, and we exchanged the holy kiss—a handshake and a kiss on one another's cheeks. This was my formal acceptance into the church.

When all five of us had been baptized and welcomed into the church with a holy kiss, Bishop Dan asked us to take our seats. I had hoped I would feel like a new person as it had been described to me when someone accepts baptism. Instead, I felt trapped. The tears kept coming, even though I tried wiping them away.

Trying to stop my tears from sliding down my cheeks is the last thing I remember about the day of my baptism. But I remember well a conversation with Sylvia the next day when she asked me why I was crying at my baptism.

"A lot of people cry at their baptisms," I said.

"Were they happy tears?"

"Of course," I said, trying to convince myself.

"They didn't look happy."

I got up and left the room because I knew Sylvia spoke the truth.

~

Ordnungs Gma—Council Meeting—was held two weeks after baptismal services. This church service is even longer than usual and takes place in the spring and fall of each year when the bishop reviews the rules of the *Ordnung*. Regular church services lasted three hours, but Council Meeting lasted until after the midday meal. When I took my place in line to go into the church service, the thought of the long day ahead filled me with dread.

I felt a certain sense of relief that my baptism was behind me. Now there was no purpose left to question it. I was a member of the church and I couldn't take it back. It took me only a few days to realize that I hadn't lost any freedom because there wasn't any to lose. Except now I had obligations like having to sit through long church services. I braced myself for a long, boring day.

Several hours into the service, a small group of older women and a small group of older men left the service to go have their midday meal. When they returned to their seats, another group of women and men left. My stomach was growling by the time our turn came around, but worse than that, I was getting antsy from so much sitting. Thankfully, we stood at a table to eat instead of sitting. I ate slowly and tried to draw out our break. The other women urged me along by saying it was time to go back to the service.

The preachers had started with the Adam and Eve story at the beginning of the service, and then moved through the Bible, telling the well-known stories. They went through the Old Testament in that way.

Soon after we rejoined the service, the bishop began reviewing the rules of the *Ordnung*. First he went through what was not allowed for farm machinery and other modern conveniences. Then he stated the rules about men's clothing: wear suspenders, no zippers or snaps on their pants, buttons on their shirts, black shoes (unless they were for work, then wear shoes as plain as possible), wear their hair so it would cover half their ears, and wear their beards untrimmed.

Bishop Dan then addressed the rules for the women. They should wear their dresses in the right pattern and proper length—halfway between the knee and the ankle. They should wear a cape and apron, bonnets in the summer, and shawls in winter when they left home. They should wear black shoes and socks, and cutting their hair is prohibited. They should wear their hair combed back under their *koppa*, which should cover most of their hair. Mothers should wear pins in their dresses instead of buttons, and they are responsible to dress their children according to the *Ordnung* as well. Dan shuffled his feet and said, "Now, if there is anything that I missed, it doesn't mean it's allowed. Just because I haven't mentioned it doesn't excuse people from not obeying the *Ordnung*."

Church was supposed to fill me with spiritual nourishment, but instead I felt spiritually emptied. I chided myself for feeling this way, even while I dreaded Communion Service, two weeks away. That service would be even longer.

I felt I had to keep the promise I'd made to the preachers that said I would quit "playing party," yet I longed to get out there and dance like the other *youngie*. Singings were boring after that, and I was tempted to ignore the promise I'd made. But I saw myself as an honest person, and so I refrained—at least until one of the bishop's daughters got married.

On the night of Emma's wedding, a lantern hung high in the rafters and music played out in the barn while the *youngie* played party. All of the bishop's sons and daughters who were of *rumspringa* age were playing party, including Noah, who had made the same promise I had. That is when I realized that Bishop Dan had no intention of holding us to the promise. He'd only wished to satisfy Datt. I lost all respect for Bishop Dan with this realization. I thought he was a hypocrite and a coward. I joined in with playing party, and I never looked back.

Gross Gma—Communion Service—began much as *Ordnungs Gma* had, except this time the preachers focused on the stories of the New Testament. Several preachers came from other districts, and they took turns preaching while church members ate their midday meal in shifts—

one table for the women, another for the men. Lunch was the usual fare of baloney sandwiches with sweet peanut butter and pickles, and cookies and coffee for dessert.

When Bishop Dan finally got up to preach, I knew we were on the home stretch. He told the story of the Last Supper, and in a reverent tone described the significance of taking Communion, stressing that we needed to all be right with one another and with God. If anyone wasn't right with God, they should confess their sin before partaking in Communion.

While Dan was preaching, the deacon left the service. He returned with round loaves of bread wrapped in linen cloth and placed them on a table, along with a jug and an enamel cup.

Bishop Dan asked us all to rise. Then he talked about the bread. "First, in the spring, the ground is prepared. Then the seed is sown. The weeds are plucked from the fields as the wheat grows. When the grain ripens, it is cut. When the right time comes, the wheat is separated from the straw, and the grain is ground. Then it goes through the wives' hands and is kneaded into bread. As each individual grain gives up its individuality to become one loaf, so must we give up our individuality to become part of the community."

After that I couldn't concentrate on what Bishop Dan was saying. I was thinking about the concept of giving up one's individuality to become part of the community. Was I willing, or more significantly, was I even able to do that? These were individual grains to start with. Don't we need to be individuals first before we can come together as a community? I imagined the grains being ground on a grindstone. I wanted to be one of the grains that would fall by the wayside to escape being ground up.

I wondered if I was the only one in the whole congregation who had these thoughts and feelings. If others did have them, they seemed to be able to hide them better than I could. My feelings had a way of finding their way out.

I chided myself for having wayward thoughts at my first Communion and forced myself to concentrate on the service.

Bishop Dan repeated Jesus' words, "This is my body. When you eat of it, remember me." I watched the bishop, two ministers, and the deacon exchange Communion bread. Then the deacon followed Bishop

Dan with thick slices of bread as they walked up to the oldest man in the congregation, Al Mullet. Dan broke off a small piece and handed it to Al, who ate the bread, bowed, and sat down. The bishop moved down the line, giving all the men Communion bread. Noah, the bishop's son, who had become a member of the church with us, was the last man to receive Communion bread. Then Dan and the deacon walked to Al Mullet's wife, Ada, and served her bread. He started with the older women and worked his way to us young women.

The order in which the bishop offered Communion bread reinforced every person's place in the community. Gender was most important, then age. Those of us women who had been baptized four weeks earlier would be the last to partake in eating our bread. I was the third to the last to eat my Communion bread. I ate my bread, bowed, and sat down.

Bishop Dan had us all rise again to receive the wine. He described the process grapes go through to become wine, focusing on how the individual grapes give up their identity to make wine.

Then he and the deacon passed the cup around. As I saw Datt drink from it, I realized I had to drink from the same cup. Purple drips trickled down the side of the white cup. The bishop had admonished the congregation, saying no one should shy away from drinking from the cup just because others had drunk from it. I was thinking to myself, "Easy for you to say. You get the first drink." I chided myself for having such thoughts and told myself I should accept this like anyone else. But when it was my turn to drink from the cup, I turned it around and drank from just above the handle, the only place that hadn't been touched by others' lips.

After Communion came foot washing. The ministers and deacon carried in four buckets of warm water and towels. Bishop Dan said we shouldn't think about whose feet we wash because we were all the same in the eyes of the Lord.

Two tubs were put into one room, and two into another. Four older men went into one room, and four older women into the other. As the first four came out of the room, four other women went in. Soon it was time for us younger ones to take our turn. We took off our shoes and socks ahead of time. Elizabeth Weaver and I were paired up. I held my foot over the little tub and she splashed water over it, then dried it with the damp towel that half the other women had used. Then she did my other foot, and we exchanged places. I washed her feet, then we exchanged the holy kiss.

We put our shoes and socks back on. My feet were still damp, and my socks stuck to my skin. I reminded myself it didn't matter because it was the humility of the ritual that counted.

As we passed through the doorway, the deacon sat there, holding a navy blue cloth bag. We all put money in the bag, our contribution to the church fund that would help out families in need. In the washhouse, we gathered our shawls and bonnets and prepared for the walk home. Communion Service was considered a serious time and we were all expected to leave in silence.

At home, I lay on my bed and stared at the ceiling. Now that I'd had my first Communion, leaving would be considered a grave sin and I would be shunned. This was the time I was supposed to be sure I'd done the right thing by joining the church, but I felt as queasy as ever. Regardless of my doubts, I was now a member of the church and that could not be undone.

THE COLOR OF SHAME

If the structures of the human mind remain unchanged, we will always end up re-creating the same world, the same evils, the same dysfunction.
~Eckhart Tolle

*L*izzie turned twenty-one around the time I was baptized, which meant she was now "of age." She surprised us by moving in with her friend Amanda, whom she had befriended at the singings. Lizzie was going to pay rent to live with Amanda and her family.

During a visit home, Lizzie told us that she'd found out that Amanda's father had dated Mem when they were young. Lizzie felt she had found her "rightful" sister, or the sister she would have had if Mem and Amanda's father had gotten married. Lizzie had imagined herself adopted ever since she was old enough to understand the concept. It was her way of accounting for feeling like an outsider in her own family.

I felt guilty that I hadn't been a better sister to Lizzie. I had done my part in the family's rejection of her ever since we were little and Mem had treated me as the eldest daughter. Even though I felt guilty for my treatment of Lizzie, I also felt jealous that she had found her way out of our troubled home.

Datt now focused his attention on the rest of us. Sadie and I were the ones who took the brunt of his rage. He and Mem perceived Sylvia as the good daughter, even though she did many of the things Sadie and I had gotten into trouble for.

Datt began lecturing us every night about the importance of *uffgeva* —submission. He quoted Bible verses in German, which we didn't understand. Then his monologue became jumbled and ceased to make sense. But we didn't dare walk away, lest we trigger a violent outburst. Datt followed up his lectures with all of us kneeling while he read lengthy German prayers from the little black prayer book he kept in his desk.

Sylvia and Sadie had borrowed a book from the library and taught themselves sign language so they could communicate with one another privately. One night, Datt had his back turned to the two of them. They took this opportunity to use their sign language. Datt had been reading prayers for what seemed like an eternity. I had to endure both Datt's use of prayer to bring us to our knees and Sylvia's and Sadie's antics.

After this had been going on for some time, Mem suddenly got up from her knees and said, "Datt, the girls are not listening, so you may as well stop!" Datt turned around and took a seat in the rocking chair he'd been kneeling by. He looked shocked. Mem dismissed Simon, Katherine, and me from the living room because we hadn't been part of the perceived dissension. From the kitchen, I heard Mem, Datt, Sylvia, and Sadie get back down on their knees and Datt continued reading prayers. I thought about the irony of Mem and Datt using prayer as punishment, even though I was relieved that I wasn't part of it this time. Perhaps this was what it was like for Sylvia, who was usually the one exempt from punishment.

Two weeks after I had attended my first Communion Service, the bishop asked all the members to stay seated for a members' meeting. As the children and youth left the service, I realized I was finally going to find out what happens at a members' meeting. I had often wondered what they did behind the closed doors. Now I'd be on the other side of the doors.

The realization of what was about to happen crept up on me slowly. First I noticed that Datt followed the young people out of the service. I thought he might need to go to the barn for a break. Then the bishop talked about "a brother who wants to 'make things right.' He said, "He disciplined a daughter, but he realizes he may have been too harsh and he's sorry for it."

I was thinking that other families must have their troubles too. Then Bishop Dan began relating what this person had to confess. "He wanted the daughter to stay home and she tried to leave, so he punished her." That's when it hit me like a lightning bolt—Datt is making this confession! I felt my face getting flushed red with shame. He had caught Sadie trying to sneak out the Saturday before and beat her about her head and shoulders so she was in no shape to go out.

But Bishop Dan wasn't done. He said, "I believe if the wife and daughters weren't so rebellious, then maybe Sim wouldn't have this problem. So because I don't feel he is entirely to blame, I will take his confession sitting down instead of kneeling, if no one has any objection to that." With that, he asked the deacon to go around to collect the votes for this decision.

I could feel my face becoming crimson, the color of my shame. By asking for a vote about whether Datt should be sitting or kneeling for his confession, Bishop Dan was sidestepping any other issues. I could not object to the confession itself because this wasn't what we were "voting" for. I could not say that the story the bishop told wasn't the whole truth or that this wasn't the first time Datt had become violent. I also could not say that this "pardon" would only help perpetuate Datt's cycle of violence. Because everyone was expected to agree with the bishop, I couldn't say that now. And I couldn't say it later because once Datt had made his confession, then I would be forbidden to ever speak of this again.

The deacon started with the older men and worked his way to the younger men. Then he shuffled over to the oldest women and wove his way through the kitchen, getting one submissive yes after another while a battle raged inside me. I wanted to run from the room and never come back. But I was expected as a member of the church to give my "yes" like everyone else. I didn't know how I could do it. Before I knew it, Deacon

John was standing before me, expecting me to give my voice vote. I opened my mouth to say yes, but nothing came out. Deacon John stepped closer and said, "What?"

I wanted to shout, "I don't agree with any of this. Public shaming is not going to help Datt, and it certainly is not going to help the rest of our family! Now do you hear me?" Instead I forced myself to say yes and the deacon shuffled on to get the last two yeses.

I was barely listening as the bishop said we had an unanimous agreement. He sent Deacon John to bring Datt in. Datt walked in, holding his hat in his hands with his head hanging in shame. His countenance was so meek that a person might wonder if he was capable of violence at all. He had learned the Amish martyr role well.

Datt sat meekly in front of the bishop and recited in German the words that were supposed to absolve him. I was barely aware that Datt didn't have to confess to what he'd done because Bishop Dan had done it for him. Showing remorse was the important part of the confession, and Datt had done an adequate job of that. However, remorse wouldn't be enough to prevent him from doing it again. Bishop Dan forgave Datt, bade him sin no more, and gave him the holy kiss. Datt took his seat among the men, and the bishop dismissed the members' meeting. I felt so ashamed.

I went straight to the washhouse, found my bonnet and shawl, and walked out the lane and down the road toward home. Everything inside me felt numb in disbelief over what had just happened. My shame was turning into a seething rage, and I didn't know what to do with it. I found myself walking faster and faster. Buggies kept going by me. I couldn't let on that I felt like crying, so I decided to take the path through the woods to be alone. I walked past all the familiar landmarks without thinking or feeling until I got into the house. Immediately I started eating whatever I could find—slices of bread with butter and jam, pie, cookies, and popcorn. I ate until I could eat no more. Then I walked out into the woods, purged myself, and covered it with leaves.

After Mem came home, she told me I needed to pop corn for everyone. When most of the family had gotten their bowls of popcorn and dispersed into different parts of the house and yard, I found myself alone with Mem in the kitchen. There was a long moment of silence between us before I asked her, "Has any Amish woman ever disagreed with the bishop in a church matter?"

Mem said, "Not that I know of."

"So she has to agree to whatever happens?"

"She is to tell her husband and he is to relay her concerns to the bishop."

"How is that supposed to work if they are sitting in separate rooms?"

Mem said nothing for a long moment, then said musingly, "I've often wondered that myself."

"I'm not married, so who am I supposed to go to if I disagree?"

"It's supposedly through Datt."

I'd already felt trapped at church, but now I felt like I was locked into a fortress with no hope of escape.

"So I had to say I agreed today, even if I didn't agree with any part of what happened, is that it?" My voice was rising in panic.

"Oh Lomie, you're just making things harder on yourself," Mem said. Her words and tone conveyed both sympathy and exasperation at the same time.

I retreated to my room and lay on my bed, staring at the ceiling. Like so many other times in my life, Mem had opened up the door to understanding my struggle, but then just as decidedly, she'd slammed it shut. Now she was on one side of that door with everyone else in the community, and I was on the other.

How I wished I had the gumption to walk away and leave it all behind. I absentmindedly picked up the *Vermont Life* magazine on my nightstand and turned to the page with the photo of a Cape Cod style home with a birch tree and a maple tree framing each side of the house. The bare branches reached toward the deep blue sky, with the last leaves of late autumn scattered in the green grass at their base. A dirt road stretched into the distance, and billowing white clouds hung above the mountains on the horizon. I willed myself into this scene and imagined what it would be like to travel to the land of my dreams and leave my problems in Ohio.

Ever since I had seen pictures of New England in my seventh-grade geography books in school, I sought out everything I could about the region, especially Vermont. One day I paged through a *Yankee* magazine at work and found an advertisement for *Vermont Life* magazine. I thought about sending for it, but I told myself it would be a waste of my allowance money. Yet a week later when I looked at the ad again, I decided to subscribe.

When I received my first magazine, Mem seemed surprised. We rarely got magazines other than *The Farmer's Almanac* and the Pathway magazines written for Amish families, like *Family Life* and *Young Companion*. Mem asked me why I was spending my money on frivolous things. Later that day, I saw her with the magazine open.

As usual, Datt didn't seem to notice what I did.

Even as I willed myself into the beautiful Vermont scenery in my magazine, it felt like I would always be stuck in the life I had, as if the woods around our house held me in. If only I had the freedom to follow the yearnings of my heart without leaving behind everything and everyone I knew. Then again, maybe I was ready to do just that.

I wondered how my life would turn out. Would I stay and get married to an Amish man, have children, and take my place in the community of my birth? I doubted that. It seemed the young men I longed to get to know wouldn't ask me for dates. Instead, I was asked for dates with young men with smelly feet or roving hands, making me want to turn away when they initiated *schmunzling*.

Yet every Sunday night, when it was time to join the youth in the community for a singing, I attended. I was yearning to meet the right someone. When I thought about my life in the long term, I wondered if that was what I wanted. I couldn't imagine anything else, even though I knew there was a much bigger world out there than the one I was living in. I did not feel like the path to enter into that wide world of freedom was open to me, which left me wishing that I hadn't been born Amish.

Sure enough, it took less than a month for Datt's violence to emerge again. One day when I came home from work, I found the house unusually quiet. When I went upstairs, I found Sylvia and Sadie standing by the cedar chest in Sylvia's room. This was the place where we gathered after Datt's violent episodes to wring our hands and wonder what we should do. I asked what had happened.

I listened as Sadie told the story. She was ironing when Datt stopped rocking in his chair and demanded that she tell him why she combed her hair the way she did. It was a strange question, considering Sadie had been combing her hair the same way for a long time, even though she was pushing her covering back farther than she had before. Sadie didn't know what to say, so she said nothing. He kept saying, "Answer me! Answer me!" Finally Sadie said she didn't know. Then he demanded, "Why don't you know?"

When Sadie didn't answer, Datt jumped up from his rocking chair and hit her over her head, her neck, and her back. She decided she wasn't going to let him know it hurt, so she braced herself and let him hit her. Just as Mem got there, Sadie was beginning to faint. She heard Mem say, "Sim, you have to stop! You're going to kill her!"

Tears choked Sadie's voice. She put her hands over her face. "You know how he gets when he goes crazy."

Sylvia and I nodded. We knew all too well.

I felt trapped by Datt's violence. When he went after someone, there was no fighting back. He was physically strong, but when he got into one of his rages, he was as strong as a bull, and just as wild.

"We have to *do* something!" I said.

"But what?" Sylvia asked. The three of us stood around the cedar chest at the foot end of Sylvia's bed as if we were having a funeral for the hopes that had died there. Our fear of Datt's violence kept us trapped so that we could not even imagine freedom.

I thought about telling Sylvia and Sadie the shame I had felt when Datt had made a confession in church just weeks before, and how he would now likely be making another one. Yet I was afraid I would have to make a public confession if I told them and I was found out. So I held back.

"What if we told someone?" I asked.

"Who?"

"Someone outside the Amish."

"Then we would just have to live with the shame of having other people know," Sadie said.

"As long as we keep it to ourselves, nothing will change," I said.

"But there is no guarantee that anything will change even if we do," Sylvia said.

"That's true, but we know it will *not* change if we don't say anything."

"You always think telling secrets is the answer," Sylvia retorted.

"And it never is," added Sadie.

"Yeah, you wouldn't be happy until the whole world knew our troubles," Sylvia said.

I was crushed. Just when I thought my sisters and I were trying to find a solution to the problem of Datt's violence, they turned on me. I should have known better than to think that we could get along for more than an hour. No matter what happened in the family, I ended up feeling alone and isolated in my perspective.

I retreated to my bedroom and closed the door where I contemplated the situation. I now knew that if I was going to reach into the outside world to get help, I was on my own.

～

When Sylvia started going to the singings a year after I did, I thought she and I might become close again. She was shy and hung back until I taught her how to play party. With her tall figure, blond hair, and light eyes, she drew stares from the young men. The first few times she attended the singings, she rode home with my date and me, or in a taxi we called if no one asked me.

One night, Sylvia and I were playing party together when a young man cut in to dance with Sylvia. Later that night, he sent someone to ask Sylvia for a date, and she accepted. His name was Sonny. He was romantic and talkative. I found myself riding home in a buggy with my younger sister and her date. At nineteen, I suddenly felt old.

Sadie started her *rumspringa* soon after Sylvia, and she began dating one boy after another. I wondered why she was so popular when she was one of *Sim's maet* too. I rode home with her and her dates until she got tired of that. She said I talked too much.

Sadie soon started going steady, and then Sylvia and Sonny also began going steady. I not only felt old but I also felt like I was well on my way to becoming a spinster.

Then one night, I was asked for a date with Sonny's cousin, Donny. It seemed good to have my own ride home again, and I enjoyed our conversation along the way. However, the ride home turned out to be the best part of the date. When we began *schmunzling*, I had the urge to turn my back and go to sleep. As the night dragged on, I was grateful that Donny at least didn't push his luck to see how far he could go.

The following Sunday night, I was asked for another date with Donny. I was surprised. No one had asked me for a second date for a long time. I was flattered, so I said yes. Besides, I needed a ride home. That night Donny's kisses didn't seem so bad.

I continued to enjoy my rides home with Donny for several Sundays. Talking to someone who was interested in what I had to say was a new experience for me. It seemed like he enjoyed our conversations too. Before I knew it, he had driven me home nine Sunday nights in a row. It wasn't like I felt love or attraction for Donny. He was more like a companion than a lover.

One day, Donny called me at work. I had given him the phone numbers at the homes where I cleaned. Donny's voice was nearly inaudible and he was panting. I could barely make out what he was saying. "Hi, this is Donny," he said breathlessly. "I was wondering if it would be all right to go steady."

I was stunned into silence, and I didn't know what to say with Donny's nervous panting in my ear. Going steady was the first step toward marriage, and I couldn't imagine myself as Donny's wife. Nor could I imagine him as my husband. It seemed to me that I should feel at least a little romantic toward Donny or be able to say I loved him. For that matter, Donny had never talked about his feelings for me, either.

Donny interrupted my thoughts when he said, "You don't have to answer me now. You can tell me later."

"Okay," I said. I wanted to add, "I already know what my answer is," but Donny had already hung up.

When I arrived home from work, Sylvia was in the summer kitchen cooking up zucchini with tomatoes for part of our supper. The aroma from the spices she'd added tantalized my appetite, even though I didn't like tomatoes.

Sylvia turned around when I came down the stairs and said, "*Lomieeeee*," with a knowing smile on her face.

My heart sank when I realized that I wouldn't be allowed to make my decision without interference.

"What?" I asked with a straight face.

"You know! Come on, I already know about it."

"About what?"

"Didn't Donny call you at work today?"

"How would you know?"

"Sonny called me at work and told me. You are going to say yes, aren't you?"

"No."

"Why not?"

"Because I don't love him," I said bluntly.

Sylvia looked at me reproachfully and said, "Lomie! You've had nine dates with him already. Why would you do that if you had no feelings for him?"

Sylvia knew just how to make me feel guilty. If I told her that I wanted my own rides home from the singings, she would know that I'd used him for his transportation. So I said, "I was trying to find out if I loved him or not."

"What do you mean by love?"

"Love is what you and Sonny have. I see it in your faces."

"What Sonny and I have is unusual. It's different for everyone, you know. Would you even recognize love?"

As if that wasn't enough to convince me, Sylvia asked, "How do you feel about Sadie and me both going steady when you aren't?"

Sylvia's voice followed me up the stairs, "You may not get another chance like this..."

"It's my decision, not yours!" I called down the stairs.

"I just hope you make the right one!"

Sylvia's words echoed in my mind all the way to my room and for the days that followed.

In the end, I made a choice that would be hard to undo. That Sunday when Donny drove me home, I said yes when I wanted to say no. I was glad it was dark so he wouldn't see the lie on my face. Ready or not, I now had a steady boyfriend.

Over the weeks, I became used to having Donny visit me every Sunday afternoon. I tried to have romantic feelings for him. When Sylvia and Sonny went for walks with a blanket and found a comfortable spot under a tree away from the house, I initiated those kinds of encounters with Donny. One day in October, I even took him for a walk to my happy place by the tall maple next to the natural spring. The maple leaves created a colorful carpet on the ground. Donny and I sat up against the trunk of the big maple. I wanted to sit there next to him and not have to say or do anything, but I couldn't get away from Donny's face in mine, his persistent but empty kisses always in the way. I finally got up and walked toward home with him trailing behind me. After that, the spot by the maple was no longer special to me.

It was common for young people who were going steady to sometimes date on Saturday nights. However, Datt was dead set against us dating on Saturday nights. Nevertheless, Donny and I had made arrangements for him to visit me one Saturday night. Datt didn't say anything when Donny drove in, but I saw the dark look on his face, and I sensed I was in trouble.

Donny and I hadn't been in bed long when I became bored with his *schmunzling*. We hadn't yet explored below the neck, so I guided one of his hands to my chest. Then something happened that I wasn't ready for. He began breathing so heavily that I felt like he was using up all the air around me. I slid out of bed, saying I needed to use the outhouse. I hoped he would calm down in the meantime.

When I came out of the outhouse, I saw someone moving in the darkness. For a second I thought it might be Donny, but then Datt began shouting, telling me how I wasn't supposed to have a boy over on Saturday night, and because I was a member of the church, I should be ashamed of my behavior. I ran to my room. There was a chance that Datt would charge up behind me, though I had never heard of Amish parents interfering with dates. It simply wasn't done. But when Datt got into one of his rants, I couldn't count on a taboo holding him back.

"What's the matter?" Donny asked. I could see him sitting up in bed in the moonlight. He looked like a scrawny teenager. Yet I was glad for his presence.

"Datt is upset that you are here on a Saturday night," I said, trying to catch my breath.

Donny got up and put on his shirt. "Let's go to my house," he said. I thought Datt would be twice as upset with me when I got home. On the other hand, he might have calmed down by then. So running seemed like a reasonable choice.

Donny hitched up his horse in a hurry. He brought the buggy up to the kitchen door. I slipped downstairs in my white nightdress, climbed into the buggy, and we took off. We saw no sign of Datt.

It was a ten-mile ride to Donny's house. I filled him in on Datt's pattern of outbursts. He listened in silence. I longed for him to offer the understanding I so craved. I thought if he could offer empathy, I might be wrong about him. But from his silence, it was clear he didn't want to get involved. I wondered if he would break up with me now, as I rode alongside him in the cool, star-filled summer night. A part of me wished for that, but then I wondered if he was my ticket out of my parents' home. Then a new thought hit me with such clarity, it startled me. *If joining church hadn't made things better for me, then marrying Donny wouldn't either.*

When we got to Donny's house, we spent the rest of the night in his bed, doing the same boring things we usually did. I had learned my lesson about exploring any new territory. I was glad he didn't push me.

The next day was an in-between-church Sunday for both Donny and me. He drove me home in the afternoon and stayed until early Monday morning when he left for home.

A few hours after Donny left, I got up and waited in my room for my ride to arrive. Then I ran downstairs and out the door so Mem and Datt didn't have time to call me back. A man named Mr. Pell drove me to work. I sat in the back seat because I wanted privacy in my turmoil.

I was going to Megan's house that day. I'd been cleaning for her for several months. She had four little ones, and she usually left her children with me so that I had to babysit plus do household tasks. On this day, Megan left me with the children and baskets of ironing to do. I was so upset about the weekend that I wasn't in any shape to do either of the tasks. I spent most of my time in the bathroom crying. I had reached one conclusion. I could no longer bear the fear of Datt's violence. I had no idea what to do, but something had to change.

I was still in the bathroom when Megan came home earlier than I expected. I quickly washed my face and slipped downstairs to iron.

Megan noticed that I had just started the ironing. I thought she would reprimand me, but she looked at me and asked, "Saloma, what is the matter?"

I collapsed into the nearest chair. Aware of the children's stares, I covered my face with my hands and sobbed so hard I couldn't talk. Megan herded her children upstairs to the playroom. She came back downstairs and said, "You need to tell me what this is about."

I had my crying under control by then. I said, "It has nothing to do with you. It has to do with my home life."

"Do you want to tell me about it?"

"My father is violent. He is upset because I had a boyfriend over on Saturday night, and I'm afraid to go home. He thinks we are rebellious, so he hits us when he has an outburst."

Megan looked stunned. She said, "Saloma, I had no idea."

"You didn't? I thought everyone knew about our family."

"Does he ever hit your mother?"

"No, only us. He doesn't like that we're growing up. I think if we all stayed children, he'd be fine. But there is no chance of that happening," I said, my voice dripping with irony.

"You cannot go on living like this," Megan said.

"My sisters and I have said that to each other so many times, but we don't know what to do about it."

"There is a place here in Chesterland called Head Help. I will go upstairs and call them and make an appointment for you to see them next week when you come back to my house. Will you be all right until then?"

I laughed. "I've lived with it so far. I think I can go another week."

Megan went upstairs to make a phone call while I ironed. When she came downstairs she said she'd arranged for me to see a woman named Carol the following week.

I braced myself on the way home, wondering if Datt would attack me. To my surprise, neither one of my parents said a word that night, or any other night. I wonder if Mem talked Datt out of reacting. Having nothing said about it gave me the eerie feeling that I'd dreamed what happened on Saturday night when Donny came to visit me, yet I knew that it had actually happened. And now Donny knew my shame. His silence as I was telling him about my troubles on the way to his house didn't help matters. I wondered what his silence meant. It certainly didn't seem like I could ever count on him to be my advocate. I thought about ending my relationship with him, but I sensed it would be hard to do that.

WRAPPING A PLAN

At the darkest moment comes the light. ~Joseph Campbell

*C*arol wore so many bracelets and necklaces, she rattled when she moved. She had a headful of dark, curly hair. She asked me to describe what happened in my family. I did.

"How old are you?" Carol asked.

"Twenty."

"When do you turn twenty-one?"

"Next June. Why?"

"In the state of Ohio, it is not legal for us to intervene in a family situation when the report comes from someone not of legal age. Do you have any older siblings who could give us permission?"

I felt my hopes getting dashed and I saw them sinking into deep water, like a big stone.

"I have an older brother who is married. He might tell my parents I reported it, which would make it worse for me."

"Is there anyone else?"

"I have an older sister who has left home, but I don't think she would want to get involved."

"Then we need to ask your mother for permission. What is your phone number?"

"We don't have a phone."

"Then this will take longer because whoever writes to your mother will need to wait for her response. I'm not the person to help you. I am going to assign a social worker. Her name is June."

I gave Carol our address and told her how important it was for my mother not to find out that I had told. The letter would need to be written in such a way as not to reveal my identity. I shivered when I imagined the consequences of Mem finding out it was me. I gave Carol the phone numbers where I could be reached, along with my schedule of where I would be each day so June could call me to let me know Mem's response. I didn't think Mem would say yes to the intervention, but there was at least a glimmer of hope. Sometimes she confided to us girls that she didn't know what to do about Datt's outbursts. We'd urge her to get outside help, but she would sigh deeply and say she didn't know who to go to. Then, without warning, Mem would take everything back by saying, "Oh, if you girls weren't so rebellious, then maybe he wouldn't have these problems." We'd point out the times when his rage was triggered by nothing we said or did as if his violence had a life of its own. Mem would purse her lips and not say anything, leaving us with only each other for allies.

A dim hope was better than none at all. So I hoped Mem would accept the help offered to her.

When I arrived home that afternoon, I asked Sylvia and Sadie to come upstairs. Once we'd gathered around the cedar chest, I told them what I'd done. To my surprise, they weren't happy. They questioned me.

"What if Mem finds out it was you?"

"You absolutely may not tell her."

"What if it doesn't work?"

"Then we'll be in the same boat we are now. Nothing else has worked so far."

They grudgingly agreed. They also agreed not to tell Mem that it was me who alerted the social workers.

When Mem received the letter, she would not let us see it, and she didn't tell us anything about the contents. She was only worried about who had "reported us."

I didn't lie. I said to her, "Is it really important that we know who reported it? Isn't it more important that we use this chance to get help for Datt, which could help the whole family?"

Mem's shoulders slumped lower over the potatoes she was peeling. She shook her head and said with her signature sigh, "Oh, I just don't know." I thought Mem was close to saying yes, so I left it at that.

Four days later, June called me at Megan's house and said, "I've received a letter from your mother. Did she tell you what her answer is?"

"No, I didn't even know she'd sent a letter."

"She hasn't said yes. She said she wanted to work through the church."

I didn't know my reaction was audible until June asked, "What's the matter?"

"I know what she means by that, and it hasn't worked yet. It might even be making it worse."

"Do you want to tell me about it?"

"I am forbidden to tell you anything that happens in church."

June paused. "It sounds like your mother was close to saying yes. I can send her another letter if you'd like me to."

"I think it's our only hope," I said, but the light of my hope had dimmed so much, it felt like it was being extinguished.

"I'll do that. I will call you and let you know. Are there any changes in these phone numbers you gave me?"

I said, "They are still the same." Inwardly I was thinking that everything else in my life was still the same too.

I was at the Snyders' house when June called me again. The Snyders had lost their fifteen-year-old daughter in a car accident less than a year before. Pamela's room was being kept exactly as it had been when she was alive. I was cleaning her room when Mrs. Snyder came to the door and said the phone call was for me.

I picked up the black receiver from the white dresser and said,

"Hello." I could hear my heartbeat in my ears. It was June. She said she had gotten another letter from Mem. The answer was still no.

I was quiet until I trusted my voice. I was glad June couldn't see the tears spilling down my cheeks. I asked, "What else can we do?"

"There isn't anything else we can do. When do you turn twenty-one?"

"Next June."

"If there's no change by then, you can give us a call," June said.

I wanted to cry out, "But nine months is the same as never. Even one more month is unbearable, let alone nine!" But like a stoic Amish girl, I said nothing.

"I'm so sorry," June said. Her voice sounded like it was coming from a tunnel as she said, "If you ever need someone to talk to, give me a call."

I wanted to scream, "What good is it to *talk* about things if we can't *do* anything about them?" Instead, I meekly thanked her and said goodbye before hanging up. I couldn't hold back my sobs any longer.

I lay down on Pamela's bed. I realized Mrs. Snyder could walk in and find me there, but I had to take that risk. At that moment, I could not stand on my own two feet.

I wished I could take Pamela's place. I didn't understand why God took away the Snyders' daughter when they had loved her so much, and yet I had to live a life devoid of love from my family.

Before Mem had said no to June, I hadn't allowed myself to think about any other options for getting out of this situation. Now I was forced to. I could think of only two—suicide or leaving the Amish. First I considered suicide. I wondered if death could be any worse than my life. I considered how I might manage suicide. Maybe I could run out in front of a speeding car. But what if I managed to get maimed and didn't die?

I knew I didn't have the guts to go through with suicide. It was probably just as well, I decided, because I'd go straight to hell if I did. But according to Amish beliefs, I would go to hell if I left the Amish, too. Then a daring thought came to me: "If I am going to hell for leaving the Amish, I will at least have a lifetime on earth *before* I go to hell. And besides, what if the preachers are wrong?"

Feelings of excitement and adventure rose in my chest as I imagined choosing a whole new life for myself, away from my family and all its troubles. Before I got up from Pamela's bed, I resolved one thing in my mind. I could no longer think of what was good for the family. I now had to think about what was good for me.

~

Several days after I received the devastating phone call from June, I was on my way to the mailbox when I walked by Datt as he was sawing a piece of wood in half between two sawhorses. Mem had asked him to get firewood to take the chill off the living room where she was setting up the galvanized bathtub for bath night. Datt didn't look up from his sawing as he said, "Lomie, take these into the house."

"No. I'm getting the mail right now," I retorted.

Datt looked at me, his dark eyes startled. I knew my mistake was made. I had never dared say an outright no to Datt before, nor had I dared to show anger toward him.

Datt was too shocked to respond. I used that moment to run into the house, down the stairs, and out the north basement door. I headed for the cornfield behind the barn, and into the woods beyond, before looking back to see if Datt was pursuing me. He wasn't.

When I reached the woods, I found a thicket and sat down on a stump. There was no sign of pursuit for a long time. Then I heard Mem's voice calling me. I didn't answer, knowing full well that I was making things worse for myself. I knew one thing for sure. I needed time to think. I had never talked to Datt that way, and I wasn't about to find out what my punishment was going to be.

Mem stopped calling me. I stayed in the woods, thinking about making an escape. I thought about walking out to Forest Road and up to Route 322 and hitchhiking, just to get away. But then I realized I would be putting myself in danger. What if a man who wasn't to be trusted came along and picked me up?

When the sun was low over the woods, I told myself this was my last chance of walking in the direction of escape while I still had light, but my legs wouldn't allow me to. With no coat, no money, and only the clothes on my back, I didn't think I was prepared to make a getaway yet. Over the previous five years, I had saved four hundred dollars that I'd tucked away into a bank account. I'd been adding to my savings more often since I'd talked with the social workers. I tried not to feel guilty when I skimmed several dollars off before handing my wages to Mem to be thrown into the black pit.

As the sun was setting, sending a chill over the woods, I vowed I would leave, but I would do it in a way that would not jeopardize my safety or well-being.

Where would I go? I closed my eyes and asked myself where I would want to live if I could live anywhere. My eyes opened wide when the answer came. I had dreamed of going to Vermont for years. I could make this dream come true. Instead of waking and finding myself back in Mem and Datt's house, I could see Lake Champlain and Mount Mansfield for real.

I asked myself, how would I get there? I'd always wanted to travel by train. Maybe I could go to Vermont by train. But how would I get to the train station?

Megan came to mind. I wondered if she would help me leave.

I thought about where I would live. I remembered a woman I worked for who was thinking about leaving her husband, and she'd talked about living in a YWCA that helped women in transition. I had tucked that into my memory to recall if I needed it someday. That day had come. I wondered if there were any YWCAs in Vermont. I decided to find out.

It was dark now—really dark. And cold. Leaves rustled nearby. Maybe it was a raccoon going out to feed on the corn on the edge of the field. Still, it made me uneasy. I took comfort in the knowledge that there were no bears, coyotes, or wolves in our woods. But it could be Datt. I sat motionless, listening. The rustle did not come again.

I considered telling Sylvia or Sadie of my plans. Perhaps one of them would want to come with me. I decided to think about it.

Long after dark, I wrapped my plan like a present, tucked it away deep inside me, and slipped quietly into the basement. The house was still. It was Saturday night and I needed to take a shower. I heated water on the oilstove as quietly as I could, mixed it with cold in the watering can, and hung it on a nail on the ceiling. I sponged down my body, then let the warm water flow down over me. I turned this way, then that. Feeling the warm water on my body was bliss. I was sorry when the can was empty. I dried off, wrapped myself in towels, tiptoed up the stairs, slid into my nightdress, and climbed into the warm bed next to Sadie. I sighed, thinking I could at least sleep in the next morning since it was our in-between-church Sunday. I was surprised that there had been no ambush. I fell into a deep sleep.

~

Sylvia and Sadie stood over my bed, demanding that I get up. I was glad I didn't need to listen to them and put my head back on my pillow. Sadie's voice was urgent, "Lomie, you have to get up. Mem and Datt said so!"

I opened my eyes. Then Sylvia really woke me when she said, "If you don't get up, we're going to tell Mem you called the social workers."

I sat up and glared at them. "You promised you wouldn't! That would only make things worse!"

"You made it worse yesterday when you talked to Datt in an angry voice. Then you made it even worse when you didn't come home."

"Why? Is Datt the owner of anger around here?"

"What do you mean?"

"He can get angry and hit us whenever he feels like it, but we can't even use an angry voice?"

"He was in a good mood until you set him off. If he gets triggered, it will be your fault."

"Whose side are you on? Why is it a terrible thing if you get chased out in the cold, but it's all my fault when it happens to me?"

"I didn't provoke him!" Sadie snapped.

"I thought we were going to stick together." I looked them square in the face—first Sylvia, then Sadie.

They were silent for a long moment. Then Sylvia said, "We want what's best for the family, that's all. We're going downstairs. If you're not down there in ten minutes, we're going to tell Mem you called the social workers."

With that, Sylvia and Sadie left the room.

I got up and dressed slowly. Anger was taking over where sadness usually lived. I thought, So much for asking *them* if they want to go with me! I thought about all the times Sadie had snuck out of the house and we'd covered for her. Sylvia had snuck out the window when Datt had forbidden her to go out, and we hadn't told. Now they were both being so righteous!

I combed the front of my hair and put on my *kopp*. I said to myself, Yes, we women and girls need to wear a covering over our heads to show we are submissive to our men—all because God made Adam before Eve. At least that's what the men say. They like to make these rules and pretend God did.

As I pinned my dress at the waist, I pricked myself. "Stupid pins," I muttered. "Men get to wear buttons on their shirts and we have to wear pins because buttons might be too fancy for women. Too fancy indeed!"

I went down the stairs and opened the door. There at the round oak table sat Datt with his Bible open in front of him. Mem sat next to him, and beside her sat Sylvia and Sadie, sharing a Testament. Simon and Katherine sat in their places with downcast eyes. There was an empty spot with an open Testament. As I stood there surveying the scene, they looked at me like a room full of judges.

Mem demanded, *"Huck ahna!*—sit down!"

I thought about not. But there were too many of them and only one of me. For a quick moment, I wished I had gone out to the highway the night before. Even though I wanted to run from the room, I sat down. Mem said, "We are going to read scriptures before breakfast this morning."

I glared across the table at Sylvia and Sadie. They were the same two people who'd been caught using sign language during prayer time one night. Now they were using scripture to bring me under Datt's control? They were traitors, and I would *not* be telling them I was leaving!

When it was my turn to read a verse in German, I sat there for a long moment. Mem said, "Lomie!" in that solid voice of hers that carried her warning if I didn't obey. I read, but I didn't care what I was reading or what it meant. I wanted to get through it.

The reading went on long enough to establish their dominance over me, but nothing was said about what had happened.

After breakfast, I slipped back into the woods. I thought about how I would get to a phone to call Megan. I couldn't go to the Hadlocks or the Weavers because they would tell my parents. The Carters across the road allowed us to use their phone for emergencies when they weren't home. I would have to go down through the green metal hatchway to their basement that they left unlocked and go up the stairs. They had a whole pack of elkhounds in their house. If the dogs weren't in their cages, they might not let me into the house. If the Carters came home, I'd have a hard time explaining why I was there.

I watched for the chance. When I saw Mrs. Carter leave, I snuck over and slipped into the basement, leaving the door open for light. The dogs started barking as I went up the stairs. I carefully opened the door. They were all penned. The animal odor was so strong, I struggled to breathe as I stepped into the hallway. I waited for the dogs to stop barking before reaching for the phone and dialing Megan's number. My heart beat faster with each ring. At last there was a click and then Megan's voice said, "Hello?"

"Hello, Megan? This is Saloma."

"Hi Saloma, what's up?" She sounded cheerful, with no idea what I was about to ask.

I drew a deep breath. "I was wondering if you would help me leave home." I paused and added, "Things have gotten worse."

"Of course I will," she said. "Where are you now?"

"I'm at the neighbors'."

"Do they know what you're doing?"

"No, they aren't home. They said we could use the phone in emergencies."

"Uh-oh. What if they come home? We'd better plan fast. Can you come to my house?"

"Yes."

"Good. Don't come directly to my house. I will pick you up in front of the drug store in the mall. Do you know where I mean?"

"Yes."

"When do you want to do this?"

"Right now," I wanted to say. But I said, "Whenever it's good for you."

"The Tuesday after next I'm getting ready for my sister to arrive from France. Maybe you could babysit the children when my sister is here."

"That's fine," I said, wondering how I would survive another nine days.

"Okay, I'll see you then."

I hung up. Before I could begin to grasp what I'd done, the dogs started barking again. I heard the key in the door click, and then Mrs. Carter walked in.

"What's going on?" she asked.

To my surprise, my voice sounded normal. "I hope you don't mind, but I needed to use the phone. It was a local call."

"Is everything okay?"

I couldn't say it was an emergency. So I said, "I was in a pinch with work arrangements. I had a mix-up."

"I don't mind if you use the phone, but I'd rather you do it when I'm here unless there is an emergency."

"I'm sorry. It won't happen again," I said as I made my exit. My heart was thumping hard with the humiliation of having gotten caught. But I was also excited that I had a plan for leaving home. Now I only had to figure out how to implement it.

OUT OF THE WOODS

Vermont tradition is based on the idea that group life should leave each person as free as possible to arrange his own life. This freedom is the only climate in which (we feel) a human being may create his own happiness.
~Dorothy Canfield Fisher

*C*hurch was being held at the Yoders', which was a five-mile walk. Usually I tried to have a conversation with Sylvia and Sadie, but on this Sunday I walked with them in silence, lost in a world of my own. I was thinking, "I am about to attend my last Amish church service."

Sylvia interrupted my thoughts. "So Lomie, why are you so quiet today?"

Sadie said, "Yeah, I didn't think you could be this quiet. Did the cat bite your tongue?"

I decided not to respond. When we got to church, Sylvia and Sadie acted like they were best friends with each other and not related to me. I didn't care. I looked around and wondered if I would miss anyone there. I didn't think I would.

The slow German chants that were sung in church that day gave me a feeling of ancestral memory, as if I had been there when the early

Anabaptists wrote and first sang these songs during the time of the Reformation in Switzerland and Germany. I'd heard the stories of when they were imprisoned for their religious beliefs, and how they sang the songs from their prison cells as a way of staying connected to one another and their faith. I had a sense of both the past and the future as the chant continued all around me. I sensed that these songs would endure for many more generations. As we sang the second song of every service that we called the *Loblied*—Praise Song—I felt connected to Amish churches elsewhere who were singing this same song at the same time as we were.

I realized I'd always taken the church singing for granted before. Then I thought, now is not the time to be thinking of this. I reminded myself about why I'd decided to leave, which meant I had to leave behind the good, right along with the bad. As the preachers had warned many times, I simply could not have it both ways.

When the singing concluded, the first preacher stood up. I crossed my arms over my knees and put my head down on my arms as a way of having privacy for my thoughts about what I would be doing in two days. That is, if Sylvia and Sadie didn't discover my plan and tell on me. Then I would be ruined. I would be overwhelmed with others trying to talk me out of leaving—the bishop, the ministers, uncles and aunts, neighbors, and especially Joe and the rest of the family. If I made it, I could not tell anyone where I was. Otherwise, the letters and phone calls from people trying to convince me to come back would be overpowering. I wondered if they would send a vanload of people all the way to Vermont to pick me up. Or maybe they would be glad to get rid of a troublemaker.

On the way home, Sylvia and Sadie acted differently toward me. They seemed to be testing me to see if they could draw me out. But no matter how hard they tried, I kept my plan secure in its hiding place like a pearl inside an oyster on the ocean floor. I walked alongside my sisters while remaining alone and private.

When we arrived home, we popped corn, and then our boyfriends came. When Donny walked into my room partway through the afternoon, I realized this might be the last time I'd see him. I felt guilty that my plan didn't include telling him face-to-face that I didn't want to go steady with him anymore. But I sensed that it would be a difficult thing to do, and I had already decided to leave the Amish and him at the same time.

"Do you want to go to the singing tonight?" I asked that evening while we were sitting on the edge of my bed.

"Well, I suppose we could. I'm a little concerned about the distance my horse would have to go."

I remembered how Joe used that excuse when Emma wanted to go to a singing and he didn't.

"We don't have to. I was just thinking it would be nice for a change. It's been a while since we've gone," I said. I was thinking how it would be my last one.

"How about next week? We've been invited to my friend Eddie's for supper, remember? There's going to be a bunch of us, and then a singing afterward."

I remembered. I felt a pang of regret when I thought about never being a part of the youth gatherings again.

"That will be fine," I said, thinking that maybe his horse would have more pep next week. Then I wondered if he would still go, once he found out I'd left.

That is, if I made it.

The next morning, I asked Mem if she would like to go to Middlefield and split the cost of the taxi with me. She said yes. She went to Spector's store to buy material for a dress for herself, and I walked immediately to the bank and withdrew the contents of my savings account. With the money I had skimmed off the earnings I gave Mem and Datt and the savings, I had $450 to make this journey. Then I went to the dime store and bought new underwear. I would be buying fancy clothes later, but I figured I may as well buy my underwear in a familiar place because that would be one thing I wouldn't need to change. It felt comforting that I would be changing on the outside, but inside I would still be the same.

When I got home, I walked to the mailbox. An autumn breeze caught my dress and blew it against my legs. Oak leaves lifted and circled in a little eddy, then floated back down to the ground. I was so excited, I felt like one of those leaves. By this time tomorrow, I could dance in a circle just like those leaves, and no one would be there to criticize me.

I thought more about my name. I would have to change it. Saloma would stand out too much. I had narrowed my choices—Heidi, Maria, Julia, or Linda. I had always wanted Sue for a middle name. Not only had I gotten an old-fashioned Amish first name when I was born, but Datt's mother didn't believe in middle names, so none of us got any. Now I could name myself anything I wanted.

Lamb's wool clouds floated in the sky above the neighbors' field. I looked up and drew strength from the blue around them. Malinda Sue Miller. I liked it. I could see myself fitting into that name. Julia or Maria were both too glamorous for me, and Heidi didn't fit me either.

I went upstairs and packed my little blue overnight suitcase as full as I could with my underwear and slips. I put my money into a pocket on the inside of the suitcase, along with my comb and brush, and a few dozen pictures that Joe and Sylvia had taken with a camera they'd had on the sly. Then I hid the packed suitcase in my closet behind my dresses.

I couldn't sleep all night. I tried not to toss and turn or wake Sylvia, who was sleeping in the same bed. I kept thinking about the little suitcase only a few feet away behind the closet door. I played the scene in my mind over and over. I'd wait in my room in my gray dress, coat, white scarf, and boots until Mr. Pell drove in the lane. Mem would certainly announce when he came. Then by the sound of her voice, I would know whether she was in the living room or the kitchen. If she was in the living room, I would go quickly through the kitchen and out the door before she discovered I had a suitcase in my hand. If she was in the kitchen, I would tell her I was babysitting overnight at the place where I worked. This would also give me the extra day I needed to get out of town before anyone found out what I was doing.

I got up earlier than usual, but not so early that anyone would suspect anything. The yellow car drove in. Mem announced it from the kitchen. I went quickly down the stairs and came face-to-face with her. She was sweeping the gray speckled linoleum under the drop leaf table in front of the kitchen windows. When she saw me, she stopped and looked pointedly at the suitcase in my hand.

I said, "I'm babysitting tonight at the place where I work."

Mem looked at me hard, then at the suitcase, and realized she had no choice in this one. "Well, just don't let it happen too often."

"I won't," I said. I hurried down the steps and out the door before she could call me back.

As Mr. Pell drove out the lane past the kitchen window, I saw Mem looking out at me. Without thinking about it, my hand went up and I gave her a wave. Then a stab of guilt went through me as I wondered if I would ever see her again. I knew she'd be devastated when she found out that I'd left. I also knew that if I started feeling sorry for her, I would not be able to leave. Before I allowed my feelings to surface, I set my jaw and said to myself, "She gave me no choice." The car kept going. I am not running away blindly, I told myself. I had made plans and had money. I would be all right.

Mr. Pell wanted to drive me to wherever I was going to be working that day, but I insisted he drop me off in front of the drugstore. He did that after saying for the second time, "I can drive you right to work like I usually do."

"No, that's okay. I will be doing some shopping," I said. He finally relented when he realized I wasn't budging.

I was early. I went into a shoe store and bought a pair of beige shoes. Then I went into the drugstore next door and bought a pair of pantyhose. The clerks gave me strange looks. Amish women didn't normally buy sheer stockings. I said nothing to explain myself.

Megan arrived with her station wagon full of children. She looked amazed that I was there with a suitcase. I got in for the short ride to her house, and I was relieved that she hadn't changed her mind about helping me. As soon as we got to her home, she sent the children to the playroom and we started planning.

"You did it!" she said. "You left! What was it like this morning? Do they have any idea?"

I didn't want to talk about it. Briefly, I told her what I'd told Mem about babysitting overnight, and then I said that the first thing I wanted to do was cut my hair.

"Is that necessary?" she asked. "Many women have long hair."

"My hair looks like a horse's tail when it's down," I said, "because I've been putting it up in barrettes and it is all broken."

"Why don't you go up and take a shower, and when your hair dries, I will take a look at it."

Megan took one look at my hair and said, "You are right, it does look like a horse's tail." She picked up the phone and made an appointment at her hairdresser's that afternoon. "We can take you clothes shopping afterwards," she said. "Now, do you have any idea where you want to go?"

"I'd to go to Vermont," I said.

"Oh? Do you know someone there?"

"No."

"Then why Vermont?"

"It's where I've always wanted to go, so I figured since I'm running away, I may as well go to someplace I like."

"How do you know about Vermont?"

"I remember reading about it and seeing pictures in geography books in school."

Megan looked at me with a sideways smile on her face.

"I also have been getting *Vermont Life* magazines," I said to assure her I knew at least a little about Vermont.

Megan laughed.

"You don't think that's a good idea?" I asked.

"No, I think it's fine. I am just amazed that you are so clear about this. So, how will you get there?"

"I was thinking of taking a train if there are connections."

"Where in Vermont do you want to go?"

"I heard about YWCA places that house women in transition. I want to find out where in Vermont they might be located. I'd rather live in the country than a city."

"We could call the Chamber of Commerce in Vermont. But some YWCAs don't have rooms for rent, so be sure to ask them if they do."

"How am I going to pay you for the call?"

"You may use my phone as much as you need to and I will pay for it. That will be my gift to you," Megan said.

"I don't know how I will ever thank you. I couldn't be doing this without your help."

"I'm glad you called me," Megan said with a sincere smile.

I called information to get the number for the Chamber of Commerce in Vermont. I called them and asked where in Vermont they had YWCAs that housed women. The woman I spoke to said there was one in Rutland and one in Burlington. Then she double-checked that and said the only one that was a residential YWCA in all of Vermont was in Burlington. She gave me that phone number.

I called the Y and talked to Mrs. Orr, the director there. She said there was a room available for a week and that something might become available for longer. It would cost eight dollars a week. I made reservations, beginning the next day.

Next I called the train station and asked for the cost of a one-way ticket to Burlington, Vermont. The ticket agent said the best way to get to Burlington was to take the train to Port Kent on the New York side of Lake Champlain across from Burlington, then take a ferry across the lake. I said that sounded fine. I booked a ticket for the next night, leaving Cleveland at 11:20. The ticket cost forty dollars.

After lunch, Megan took me to have my hair cut. The salon was a small but bright shop off the main street, and the man who greeted us at the door took us to a station in the far back. I took off my *kopp* and pulled my hair free of the barrettes and pins that held it up. The man did not comment on the gray Amish dress I was wearing. He was only looking at my hair.

"What have you been doing to your hair?" he asked as soon as I'd sat down in a padded chair.

"Putting it up in barrettes," I said faintly.

"But what about this?" he asked. He picked up the broken strands of hair in a circle around my head where my covering had hidden it up until now.

"I've been using a rubber band as a hairband."

"You should never use a rubber band in your hair. You can see, right here," and he picked up the strands, "where you broke the hair and it's all frizzy. Now you are going to need to grow it all out before it will become healthy again."

"I won't use rubber bands anymore," I promised.

"How much do you want me to cut?" he asked.

"I'd like it to be as long as possible, but still have it look good."

He shook his head slowly. "I'm going to need to cut at least up to this point." He laid his finger across my hair, just below my shoulders.

My hair was the length of my back.

I gulped, and then told him to go ahead and cut it. As he snipped and the horse's tail fell to the floor, all I could think about was the Bible verse that said it was a sin for a woman to be shorn and shaven. That's how I felt when he was done, shorn and shaven. But it was only one of the many Amish sins I would commit that day.

That night I lay in a single bed in one of the children's rooms, and I couldn't sleep. I kept feeling my hair loose on the pillow around me. I thought about the clothing lying on the chair beside the bed. I'd bought a green wool skirt and jacket and a cream-colored turtleneck top to go with it. I had paid over $25 for the outfit. That left less than $400 for my journey.

I still worried that I would not be able to leave before I was found out. Mem and my sisters did not know where I was working that day, and it would be tomorrow evening before they missed me.

In the dim light of the nightlight, I tossed and turned. I got a fluttering feeling in my stomach. I couldn't tell if it came from fear or excitement—perhaps both. I finally fell asleep in the darkest hours of early morning.

The following day, Megan told me that she wanted her husband, Peter, to talk with me about what to do and what not to do when I was traveling. She herded the children out of the kitchen, and Peter sat across the table from me. I felt self-conscious as he gave me all the don'ts. "If a man wants you to go with him to his apartment, don't go. If a guy talks to you and you feel uncomfortable, tell him to leave you alone."

I had planned to go by my instincts, but now I was wondering if they would be reliable. Peter made me feel as though there might be more "bad guys" out in the world than I had thought.

Megan wanted me to write to Mem to let her know I was all right. I wanted to leave and not have any way for them to know where I was. But on the other hand, I didn't want them to think I'd been kidnapped. So I let Megan talk me into writing a short note:

I'm writing to you to let you know I am all right. I'm leaving because of Datt's violence. I can't live like this anymore. You had the chance to get help

*for him, and you didn't. I will not be coming back until he does get help, so
don't try to find me.*

I didn't add that I wouldn't be coming back even if he did get help. I
asked Megan to mail my letter the next day so that I would have left town
by the time Mem received it.

Megan's sister and brother-in-law arrived from France that evening.
Megan had told me that her sister and her husband were very wealthy,
and I realized from the way she talked that she wanted very much to
make a good impression on them.

My job was to keep the children occupied while Megan, Peter, the
esteemed sister, and her husband ate dinner in the dining room with the
door closed.

I put the children to bed at eight o'clock. Then I took a shower,
combed my shorn hair and pinned it back with barrettes, got dressed in
my new clothes, and packed a white suitcase that Megan gave me that was
bigger than the one I'd brought from home. She also gave me several
sweaters and other pieces of clothing. I felt bareheaded as I walked
downstairs into the living room with a suitcase in each hand.

Peter looked at me and his eyes sparkled. "Well, Saloma, I must say
you look very attractive and pretty."

"Thank you," I said. I could feel myself blushing. I wasn't used to
compliments about my appearance.

We started out for the station early. Peter wove his way through the
heavy Cleveland traffic, but we got there in plenty of time. He waited
with me, even though I told him if he wanted to go back home to their
company, I would be fine.

I purchased the ticket. Then I stood on the platform with Peter,
waiting for the train. When it pulled in, Peter handed me an envelope and
said it wasn't much, but it was his and Megan's way of wishing me well.

"Oh, thank you," I said, meaning it sincerely. "You've already helped
me out so much. I can't ever repay you for all you and Megan have done."

Peter gave me a goodbye hug and kissed me in a way that made me
focus on picking up my two suitcases and boarding the train. His hand
lingered on my back. I was completely confused. Peter, who had warned

me about men with bad intentions, had given me a kiss like that—on the lips? I realized something I hadn't known before. My Amish clothes and appearance had been a shield, and without them, I was vulnerable. It seemed to me that Peter had been the first one to take advantage of that. Would there be others? As I stepped up into the train, I wondered what I was getting myself into. But it was too late to turn back now.

INTO DAYBREAK

We delight in the beauty of the butterfly, but rarely admit the changes it has gone through to achieve that beauty. ~Maya Angelou

When I saw the crowded train, I focused on finding a seat. All except one of the double seats had at least one person in them. The empty one had a pack on it. I decided to take my chances. I put my luggage on the rack above and scooted into the seat next to the pack.

A tall man stopped in the aisle beside me. He had thin, blond hair with a tinge of red and a balding spot at the crown of his head, though he looked like he might be in his late twenties.

"Were you sitting here?" I asked him.

"Yes, but you are welcome to take this seat next to mine," he said.

I let him into the seat by the window.

He stuck his pack in the rack above. "I'm John," he said, shaking my hand.

"My name is Linda," I said with such confidence that anyone listening would never have guessed this was the first time I had used my new name.

"Hello, Linda," he said.

Just then the train began to move. My heart pounded to the beat of the wheels on the rails. I stood up and waved to Peter, and he waved back, and then he and the platform were gone and the train picked up speed and rushed into the darkness. Everything swayed and vibrated so that I felt it in my bones. My first train ride was as thrilling as I'd imagined.

"Is he your father?" John asked.

"No," I said, sitting back down. "He's a friend."

"Where are you traveling to?"

"I'm going to Burlington, Vermont." I expected him to be surprised.

John said, "I'm going to Boston to visit a few friends of mine. We usually get together about once every six months. I haven't seen them in a while, so I'm going there for the week. How long will you be in Burlington?"

"I don't know yet."

John looked at me as if he expected me to clarify what I meant.

For a split second, I wondered whether John was the kind of man Peter had warned me about. Then I remembered how Peter had kissed me. I felt so relieved to be on my way to freedom, I decided to take the chance that my instincts were right and that it would be safe to tell John. I quietly said, "I'm running away from home."

John got a surprised look on his face as his mouth formed an O.

"Not only am I leaving my family, but I am also leaving the Amish," I said.

John looked twice as surprised. "Wow. That must take a lot of courage," he said.

I shrugged and nodded.

With a kind smile he said, "I've had some contact with Amish folks. I'm an intern at the Children's Hospital, and occasionally some Amish children need care from us."

I hoped he wouldn't mention our conversation to any Amish people. Somehow I felt safe in the feeling that he wouldn't.

"So, what prompts you to leave?" John asked.

The story flowed out from me naturally, like water over rocks in a brook. I told him about Datt, about my brothers and sisters, about my love of Vermont, and why I finally decided to leave.

"This really must take a lot of courage for you," John said again.

"Not really. I think running away from my problems is less courageous than sticking it out at home."

"It sounds like it was intolerable for you, though."

"It was." I kept my voice even. I was aware of having no covering on my head and a skirt that didn't cover my knees when I sat down. I couldn't believe I was talking so intimately with a stranger.

John and I talked for a long time. I found myself combing my hair with my fingers and pulling strands away from my neck. At some point, I said I should get some rest since the last few nights I'd hardly slept. He said, "You're welcome to lean against me if you want to."

"Oh, no, that's okay," I said, shifting my body away from his.

"Okay, that's fine," he said. I could tell he wasn't offended. I sensed it would have been fine, yet it felt wrong to be that intimate with someone who had been a stranger when I first boarded the train.

We had been quiet for a few minutes when the conductor came and offered me a seat by myself in the car up ahead. I followed him, telling John I would be back in the morning to get my luggage.

The double seat by myself felt lonely. The train car was quiet with people sleeping. I noticed they had blankets and pillows. I wondered where they'd gotten them. The conductor came by with one of each and offered them to me. I thanked him and leaned up against the seat with the pillow and wrapped the blanket around me. I looked out at the dark November landscape. Signs in a town we went through indicated we were in New York State.

While I'd been talking to John, I hadn't thought about what was happening back in my parents' house. Tonight Mem would know that I was gone. I wondered if she'd be sitting in the living room under the hissing of the gas lantern, crying into her handkerchief. Or was she moving toward her bedroom in the flickering light of the lantern, after she'd turned it off, but before it died out completely? I was glad I was safely on the train with no turning back. I was also glad I wasn't there to see Mem cry. Then I realized for the first time in my life that Mem might have brought some of her sorrow on herself. I couldn't take this journey and feel sorry for her too.

Would they let Donny know I was gone once they got my letter? Or would they tell him when he came to visit me on Sunday afternoon? Then I reminded myself that by the next day, the news would be all over the community. I was relieved to think I wouldn't have to be with Donny ever again, and I wouldn't have to "tell him off" as the Amish called breaking up with someone. I don't know how I could have told him because of the way he avoided talking about anything personal. I realized I had talked with John about more personal things in a few hours than I had with Donny in the five months I'd known him. Somewhere in the turmoil of my thoughts, I drifted into the place between waking and dreaming where thoughts and dreams mingled.

When I awoke, the train was traveling into a red morning sun shining over the brown November fields. I thought about Datt's saying, "Red sky in the morning is a sailor's warning." I imagined he was sitting on his hickory rocking chair in the living room with the sun coming through the east windows. Was Mem up, starting the fire in the cookstove and getting ready to make breakfast?

I looked out into the morning for a long time. What would it be like in Burlington, Vermont? Would the people be friendly? What would I do for work? Where would I live after my week at the YWCA?

I was hungry and thirsty. I wished for a cold glass of orange juice. I wondered what time it was, and I decided to go visit John. I hoped he was awake. I walked through the door at the end of my car, across the little metal bridge between cars, trying not to look through the gap in the floors at the tracks rushing by underneath. I stepped into the car where John was sitting. His head was back and his eyes were closed. I thought about going back to my seat, but that was too lonely. I decided to go and get my luggage from the rack above him.

John opened his eyes when I reached up into the rack. He seemed surprised and sleepy. I apologized for disturbing him and offered to get the suitcases later, but he said, "No, that's fine. Would you like to sit down for a bit?"

"Sure," I said and sat down much too quickly. John looked a bit startled and blinked a few times to wake up. "I can come back later," I said as I started to get up.

"No, it's fine, really. I'm awake."

John got an orange out of his pack and peeled it. He offered me slices of it. I took them. They were juicy and sweet. I found it wasn't as easy to talk with him as it had been earlier, so when we got close to Albany where I would switch trains, I said goodbye. He offered me his address and said he would like to hear how things turn out for me. I accepted his address and assured him I would write. I took my luggage back to my seat.

I had a five-hour wait in Albany. I thought about going to a store to shop for clothes, but I was afraid I would get lost. I stayed in the station and tried to sleep on a hard, white, plastic chair. But I was afraid that I would miss my train, and every time I dozed off, I would jump awake again. After several hours had passed, I walked restlessly around the station and bought a hamburger. Finally in mid-afternoon, I boarded a train bound for Port Kent.

The conductor shook his head in puzzlement at my ticket. As I sat down, I heard him mumble something about "Port Kent?" and give me a strange look.

Did he know I was a runaway?

The train began moving. I breathed more easily. Surely if he was going to report me, he wouldn't have done anything to show that he was suspicious.

I had a double seat to myself this time, and I relaxed into the swaying and vibrating. Even though I was tired, I felt my confidence building. I had gotten through the train switch all by myself as though I'd done it many times. Maybe I would be all right.

Then, just as I was starting to feel relaxed and sleepy at last, the conductor came by and asked to check my ticket again. I gave it to him. He stuck it up in the rack above my head and walked down the aisle, shaking his head and muttering under his breath, "Port Kent... Port Kent..."

Two women from across the aisle looked at me. "Why is he so worried about your ticket?" one of them asked.

Maybe because I'm a runaway, I felt like saying. But I shrugged and said I didn't know. They fussed and said they thought he should leave me alone, that I was very well-dressed for a young woman when few young women dressed this way anymore. To take the focus off me, I asked them where they were traveling to, and they said they were just coming home from being on the *Phil Donahue Show* the day before. I'd often watched that show while I was cleaning and had thought about how glamorous it would be to be on television.

The train began traveling through mountains that were covered with a carpet of freshly fallen leaves beneath bare trees. As dusk gathered, I started to feel alone and lonely. The only home I'd ever known was far away. The occasional whistle from the train intensified my loneliness. The song by Hank Williams, "I'm So Lonesome I Could Cry," came to mind. It had been one of my favorite songs when I listened to country music on the radio at the houses where I cleaned. Now, if I were to hear Hank Williams wail out that song, I would probably cry.

The dark mountains loomed above and around the train as it curved through the valleys. Partly because I wanted to talk to someone, but mostly because I wanted to know, I stopped the conductor when he walked by and asked him what mountains we were going through.

"The Adirondacks," he answered. He looked at me for a minute. Then he blurted out, "I don't mean to be rude, but what *are* you going to do in Port Kent? That is a nothing place with no phones, no restaurants, and no places to stay. It's only a stop on the tracks in the middle of the woods!"

I didn't know whether to be relieved or scared by what the conductor said. "The ticket agent in Ohio told me I could take a ferry across the lake to Burlington, Vermont, from Port Kent. She said I could walk to the ferry ramp from the train stop," I said.

He shook his head soberly. "That ferry was discontinued twelve days ago."

It was dark out now. I couldn't see the mountains anymore. I imagined myself getting off the train, stranded in the dark woods with my two suitcases. It felt as though someone had dropped something heavy in the bottom of my stomach.

"So how can I get to Burlington?" I asked.

"If you want to get there by train, you would have to go up to Montreal in Canada, then back down to Essex Junction in Vermont."

"How much would that cost?" I asked.

"I don't know. I could find out for you. But there is another couple at the end of the car who have tickets for Port Kent. Let me ask them if they're going to Vermont."

"I would be glad to pay for a ride," I said.

"Just a minute, I'll ask." With that, he approached an elderly couple, and I heard him ask if they were going to Burlington.

The woman nodded.

"How are you getting there from Port Kent?" he asked.

"Our daughter," the woman said in a foreign accent. "She will drive to the Charlotte ferry."

"There is a young woman on the train who needs a ride to Burlington. Would you give her one? She's willing to pay for gas."

"No! No! Can't do that, she's a stranger!" said the woman, shaking her head.

"She is a very nice young lady and she doesn't have a way to get to Burlington ..."

"No, no, can't do that, she's a stranger," she repeated.

The conductor came back to me and said, "Have your luggage ready and we'll just see." I trusted the kindness in his tone.

I was standing in the aisle with my suitcases in hand when the train stopped and the door opened. A woman called, "Hi Mom! Hi Dad!" and began helping her parents down the train steps. The conductor leaned out the door and said, "There's a young woman on the train who needs a ride to Burlington. Will you give her one?"

"Sure, come along!" said the daughter with a welcoming wave of her arm.

"Go! Go!" the conductor said, nearly pushing me from the train and handing me my two suitcases. Then the door closed and the train moved on down the tracks.

I looked at the tall trees and dark woods around me. I had no choice but to follow the family down the driveway to the little white car parked there. The mother was saying, "You can't do that, she's a stranger!"

"Oh Mom, I'm a Vermonter!" said the daughter as she opened the trunk of her car and put in her parents' luggage. She gestured for me to do the same.

"You can sit in the back," she said. I climbed in next to her mother and her eight-year-old son. He looked at me in wide-eyed silence.

"So what are you going to do in Vermont?" the daughter asked me as she started driving.

"I—I don't know," I said, feeling the same panic setting in that I'd felt at first with John. Here I was, surrounded by strangers in a strange car on a strange road. I wished that lying came naturally to me. But I had no other story prepared, so I told her the truth, "I'm leaving home. I'm going to stay at the YWCA and find work."

"See, I told you!" the mother snapped. "Now you've got a runaway in your car!"

"Oh, mother," the woman laughed. "You're too much." To my relief, she didn't ask me any more questions.

I kept silent. We drove through the woods until we came to a ferry crossing between Essex, New York, and Charlotte, Vermont.

When I booked the ticket, it had sounded romantic to enter Vermont for the first time by ferry on Lake Champlain at night, but I was too distracted by my situation to enjoy it now. I insisted on giving the Vermonter ten dollars for the ride. She didn't want to take any money. Then she asked, "How about five dollars?" I insisted on ten.

When we drove off the ferry on the Vermont side, I wanted to savor the moment. As we headed north on Route 7 toward Burlington, I kept telling myself I was in Vermont. I wanted to pinch myself to make sure I wouldn't wake up in my parents' home.

The woman in the back seat kept talking to her daughter in a foreign language. I realized the mother was using English whenever she wanted me to understand the insults she hurled at me. She did it again as we were driving down Main Street. Her daughter asked if she wanted to get something to eat at McDonald's.

"No, get rid of her first!" the mother demanded.

Lake Champlain looked dark in the distance beyond the buildings. Big houses lined Main Street. I spotted number 278 and the daughter pulled into the driveway of the old brick building. She got out and helped me with my luggage. "I am so sorry about my mother," she said.

"I'm sorry for you. Looks like I've made your visit with your parents difficult."

"Don't you worry, it would've happened anyway. When my brother put them on the train in California, he warned them not to talk to strangers. I think my mother has taken that too far. Please call me when you can. I'd like to know how you're doing. My name is Sprite and I'm in the phone book."

When I stepped up onto the front porch of the stately brick building on Main Street that housed the YWCA, my long journey from home was finally at an end. I was hungry and travel-weary, but I was so grateful to have made it to Vermont.

I rang the doorbell. A woman with a pleasant smile came to the door and let me in. She introduced herself as Ana Mae and showed me to a room behind the back staircase, next to the kitchen. It was small with a faded gray carpet and sparsely furnished with a dresser, a nightstand, and a single bed. But it was a room of my own, so it might as well have been a room in a mansion. I kicked off my shoes and stretched out on the bed with my clothes on. Lying down had never felt so blissful.

I'd noticed as I'd come through the kitchen that the clock said it was 9:10. Exactly twenty-four hours ago, I'd been taking a shower at Megan and Peter's house. I couldn't have made it to the YWCA without the help of others. I closed my eyes and thanked God for the angels along my way. I realized that I could pray and believe in God in whatever way I chose. There was no one telling me that what I believed was wrong. In the Amish way of thinking people are not angels, but I remembered how Megan and Peter had helped me to leave, how John had allowed my self-confidence to surface, how the conductor had rescued me from being stranded in the woods, and how the Vermonter in her little white car had delivered me to my new home. They were all angels to me.

Then I slid effortlessly under a soft blanket of sleep.

I awoke sometime later to the sound of voices in the kitchen and the smell of toast. Someone was having a late-night snack. I was famished. I turned on the light and combed my hair. Then I stepped into the kitchen where three women were eating at the counter. We introduced ourselves. Maureen had long red hair and lively hazel eyes. Christine wore thick glasses that kept sliding down her nose and long dark hair hung down her back. Bernetta was a tall, slender African-American woman who was a quiet observer.

Maureen offered me a piece of toast and I gratefully accepted. As we were sitting on stools at the counter, Maureen asked where I was from. One question led to another.

"How did you get here?"

"Why did you pick Vermont?"

"How did you know about this YWCA?"

"You only went through eighth grade? I would never have guessed, you speak so well."

As I told my story, more of the women residents joined the circle to listen in. Seeing the eagerness on these women's faces and hearing their questions spurred me on. Instead of seeing my life as unbearable and mundane, as I had when I was still living with my parents, I now saw it as unique.

There was a pause, then Maureen asked, "So what are you going to do now?"

First I'd like to find out if I can stay here longer than a week."

"Of course," Maureen said. "The director isn't going to put you out on the street. You can apply for permanent residency and stay as long as you like."

"That's a relief! I was really worried about that. As to what I will do for work—I'd love to be a waitress, but I've only cleaned houses. I might have to start with that."

"Do you have a social security number?"

"No."

"You'll need one before you can get a full-time job. The social security office is on Pearl Street right downtown. I can give you directions."

Ana Mae offered to take me there the next day. I thanked her and said I wasn't used to finding my way around a city.

Maureen laughed and said, "This is not a big city. You'll soon find your way around." She gave me a sideways mischievous grin and said, "You are going to have so much fun!"

I wondered if she would be a bad influence on me. I realized I would need to balance my newfound freedom with common sense so I wouldn't lose myself in this adventure.

I smiled back and said, "I know it!"

Everyone became quiet for a minute. Then Ana Mae said, "I'll show you where the bed linens and towels are."

I made my bed and then ran a deep bath in the clawfoot tub in the bathroom above the back stairs. As I lay in the bath, deep enough to cover my whole body, I wondered what was going on back at my parents' house. I could imagine Joe there, telling Mem and Datt, "Don't worry, she'll come back," in his self-assured way. I liked the feeling of Joe not knowing where I was any more than the rest of them. For the first time in my life, he had no control over me.

Only a few weeks ago I'd been sitting in Datt's woods, wanting to run away, yet feeling as if Datt's trees were holding me in. I thought they were stronger than me with their roots growing so deep, just as I thought the Amish traditions were strong enough to hold me in the community.

But here I am, I thought. No one would tell me what to do the next day. I would decide that on my own. Now, as I sank into the warm water with only my head above it, the bliss of it all was like coming home to myself—a place where I had never been before.

The next morning I stepped out onto the front porch, breathed in the crisp autumn air, and looked out across Lake Champlain sparkling under the November sun. The Adirondacks on the opposite shore framed the lake, and fluffy clouds hung in the blue sky above. I realized no one in my family or community knew where I was or that I had changed my name. Everyone in my new world would know me as Linda. I waited for the feelings of remorse and guilt to set in, but they didn't. Instead, I breathed in the air of freedom. The lake represented my future—both exhilarating and terrifyingly open.

I wondered what Mem was doing. I could imagine her moving slowly and sadly around the kitchen, from the counter to the oil stove and back again, with her fair freckled skin flushed from crying, her light blue eyes moist with tears. Causing Mem tears had always made me feel guilty. Instilling guilt was one of the tools she used to make me give in—to her, to Datt, to Joe, to the church—anything to get me to submit. She'd refused the offer of help from the social workers, even though she acted as if she was at her wit's end about Datt's violence.

I turned to walk up the hill. Maureen had told me that I would be able to see Mount Mansfield from the top of Main Street. I would walk there and see the mountain before I'd go to the social security office, the used clothing store, and the grocery store. I was used to walking since that was often my form of transportation back in my Amish world, but I'd never walked with such purpose before. I was stepping boldly into my new experiences.

At the crown of the hill, I stopped in my tracks. There stretched Mount Mansfield across the horizon, with snow covering its top. I thought of the psalm, "I will lift up mine eyes unto the hills, from whence cometh my help (KJV)." White cotton clouds hovered above the mountain in a light blue sky. I imagined the clouds were angels, there to watch over me. Breathing in my newfound freedom and the fresh Vermont air was like waking up inside one of the photos of *Vermont Life*. I wrapped the white sweater Megan had given me around myself and looked into the blue between clouds, drawing strength from the sky's expanse.

I was finally free. Back in my parents' home, I'd been like a butterfly caught inside a jar—I could see freedom, yet it was beyond my reach. I had struggled against my confinement like a butterfly beating its wings against transparent prison walls. Now my eyes filled with tears of joy. No longer confined, I was as free as a butterfly in the meadows of my childhood. This was the beginning of my new life as Linda and it was even better than I could have imagined.

AFTERWORD

Go confidently in the direction of your dreams. Live the life you have imagined. ~Henry David Thoreau

On that long-ago day when I waved to Mem standing in the kitchen with a broom in hand, I was overcome with guilt. Back then I was sure that my reason for leaving was to escape my father's violence. I now realize that to develop a sense of self, I had to separate from Mem to stop her from annexing my will to her own or allowing her to determine the path my life would take.

Despite my guilt about Mem, I reveled in my newfound freedom in Vermont. I found a job as a waitress, bought new clothes, prepared to take college courses, and established a social life. I began dating a young toymaker named David. We dated for seven blissful weeks, dining in restaurants and dancing in the bars. I cooked meals at the Y, and David took me driving around the countryside of Vermont. Then came the best date of all when David took me to my first concert at the Ira Allen Chapel at the University of Vermont.

A week later, a vanload of Amish arrived unannounced at my front door. The sense of being able to make my own choices evaporated instantly when I found out who was in the van. They may as well have brought the whole community with them. The bishop and his wife, my

261

uncle and his wife, Joe, Sylvia, and Emma's sister Ada had come to Vermont with a mission. They knew, as I did, that I would not be able to stand up to them. I was too bound by kin and culture to resist them, so I returned.

Back in my original community, I felt more conflicted than ever—between loyalty to my parents and community and my longing for the freedom I had tasted in Vermont.

I taught in an Amish school for two years, trying to fit myself into my Amish culture. In the meantime, David from Vermont kept trying to continue the romance we'd started. I kept telling him our relationship was impossible since I was Amish and he was not. Yet I kept yearning for David's company and for the freedom in Vermont I associated with him. Eventually, I accepted the hand of love he offered me. When I finally decided to leave again, he drove to Ohio to take me back to my beloved state of Vermont and all its freedom.

As I made the transition out of my Amish world, I felt like a cultural refugee for years before gradually integrating into mainstream society.

In 1982, a year and a half after I left the second time, I experienced the happiest day of my life. It was the day I married my beloved David. We became parents for the first time a year and a half later when our son Paul was born. Three years later, our second son Tim was born.

My life would not be what it is today had I not sought counseling. Before I left Ohio the second time, I'd been in counseling with Rachel Harrer, who supported me during the years I was in such turmoil with indecision. When I finally decided to leave for the second time, she revealed to me that she had once lived the life of a nun. When I asked why she hadn't told me sooner, she said she felt it would make my decision too easy. It was a powerful confirmation that she knew my plight so intimately.

When I left the community for the second time, I thought I would be fine without counseling, and I was when my sons were still babies and toddlers. I loved to nurture and care for them, and did so with aplomb. I also loved the quiet afternoons when they were taking a nap and I could engage in activities that were for me, separate from being a mother. I wrote in my journal, wrote letters, and read. One afternoon, after reading stories to the boys and settling them down for their naps, I heard something going on in their room. When I opened the door, I found Paul jumping on his bed instead of sleeping. I felt such a rage rise in me. Before I could stop myself, I grabbed him and spanked him hard, several times. In the middle of it, I left him and ran into the other room, sobbing.

David heard what was going on from downstairs in his toy shop and came running upstairs. Both Paul and I were crying. Instead of going to Paul, David came to me and held me, asking, "Are you all right?"

"No," I sobbed. "I need help or I'm going to do to my children what was done to me."

After calming down, I apologized to Paul and told him that I should not have hurt him. I comforted him and put him down for his nap.

Within a week, I was sitting before my next counselor, Brookes Cowan. For the next four years, I worked with her doing "inner child work" to confront the pain and losses I'd experienced. There were times when I said to Brookes, "There is no bottom to this."

She would assure me, "There is a bottom to it, and you will find it." She also said, "Sometimes the only way out is through."

She was right. I eventually did find the bottom of my grief and sorrow. Once I had cried my way "through" it, I found myself feeling like a different person.

I've sought counseling several more times since then, but the therapy I did with Brookes was the most intensive and life-changing. It allowed me to examine how I wanted to parent my children instead of perpetuating the unhealthy family patterns I most certainly would have passed on without this healing work.

During the three most intense years of therapy, I had no contact with my family or my community. I needed the 600 miles of distance between them and my chosen life in Vermont.

After three years of keeping my emotional and physical distance from my family, I reestablished my family relationships by visiting and writing letters. At that point, I had an insatiable desire to know more about Mem and Datt before they became my parents. I knew more about Datt's family than I knew about Mem's.

During my therapy, I often had the feeling that my pain was greater than what I could attribute to my own wounds. I felt I was grieving for what had been lost in the generations before me, and I sensed that the sorrow was coming from Mem's side of the family. When I asked her, she said, "Oh, you must mean Datt's family. My family—we're a happy-go-lucky bunch." Mem wanted that to be the beginning, middle, and end of her family's story.

To learn more about Mem's family, I decided to start with something I'd heard about. Her mother, Grandma Saloma, had lost her mother Lizzie when Saloma was a young woman. I wanted to know more, but Mem would not relinquish what she knew. So I embarked on a search of my own by visiting the area where Grandma Saloma had grown up. I discovered from newspaper articles stored at the local library that her mother, Lizzie, became ill with influenza during the pandemic. Two weeks after contracting influenza, Lizzie fell into a coma-like sleep that puzzled doctors from Pittsburgh to Philadelphia. Then, on April 19, 1919, she died amid such violent convulsions that her bed broke down. Grandma Saloma was nineteen years old.

I have pieced together more of the story. As the eldest daughter, Saloma was expected to hold the family together. But her father was a hopeless alcoholic who would use whatever money he had to go into town and buy alcohol. The family lived in poverty.

Grandma Saloma rebelled and left her family to marry my grandfather in Ohio. Other Amish families then took in her younger siblings, and Saloma's alcoholic father came to live with her and her new husband, my grandfather, Joe.

Visiting the area where Grandma Saloma had lived, I found out where the Amish cemetery was. I walked into this graveyard that was narrow and deep, and I wondered how I would find my great-grandmother Lizzie's grave among so many. I slowly walked down the middle of the graveyard and stopped under a weeping willow tree. I looked down and saw I had stopped by her gravestone. I felt chills up and down my spine and tears spilled down my cheeks. As I looked out over the surrounding hills, I imagined the funeral scene—Amish people clad in black, leaning into an April wind, with a slight rain falling. Grief and sorrow so heavy that they weighed down all those present. Wide-eyed children standing by the open hole in the ground that was about to swallow up their mother's body. Nineteen-year-old Saloma feeling choked by her grief, holding her eight-month-old sister. Saloma would have known it was up to her to carry on with the responsibilities she'd always shared with her mother.

Before the day was out, Grandma Saloma saw her father handing over eight-month-old Mattie to a childless aunt to raise. I wondered if she'd felt conflicted between the sorrow of losing her little sister and relief that her responsibilities had been lessened, even by a little bit. She had eight other siblings to care for, including her older brother who was "special."

As I stood under that weeping willow tree, I felt as if I had been there on that long-ago day and was now recalling it.

I looked for a gravestone bearing my great-grandfather's name, but I couldn't see one. Then I discovered a fieldstone to the immediate left of my great-grandmother's with a few nearly illegible letters carved on it—not even his whole name, Emanuel Byler. There were only enough letters to indicate that this was his grave. His death date was there, but not his birth date. This was in contrast to Great-grandma Lizzie's gravestone, which was by no means fancy, but at least it was a real gravestone, with her whole name, Lizzie (Detweiler) Byler, along with her birth date and death date carved on it. I wondered if Emanuel had died in disgrace and no one cared enough to properly mark his grave. I felt the sadness of such a family tragedy.

After discovering all this about my Grandma Saloma's family, I wondered if there was any connection to those sleepless nights of my childhood when I worried about what would happen to us children if Mem died. In her later years, I told Mem about my fears and she admitted she'd worried the same thing about her mother when she was young. With memories and patterns like these, the idea of inherited family trauma seems completely plausible.

After I'd left home the second time, I had acquired a GED and I'd taken several college courses in Burlington, Vermont. When I became pregnant, I decided I would not try to divide myself between being a mother and being a student. But I promised myself that one day I would go back to school. That time came when both my sons were in high school. I was in my early forties when I again enrolled in community college courses. I kept hearing about the Ada Comstock program for adult students at Smith College and decided to apply. I was accepted with nearly a full scholarship.

When I entered Smith College, my lifelong dream of earning a college education was finally being realized. Each class discussion, each paper I wrote, and each day on the Smith College campus felt like I'd stepped into a dream and stayed for a while.

Every course at Smith opened and expanded my mind and my thinking. I explored the connection between thought and language. I contemplated the interplay between the concept of destiny and freedom of choice. I wondered whether the universe is finite or infinite. I was exposed to the idea that there are an infinite number of mysteries in the universe, while also trying to comprehend the concept of nothingness. I realized that ethics is not only a religious concept, but also a philosophical one. I learned a new language, which was also the language of my ancestors. And then came the crowning experience of my Smith education when I studied in Hamburg, Germany for a semester.

At fifty, I graduated from Smith College with a major in German Studies and a minor in Philosophy. A year later, David and I moved from Vermont to Western Massachusetts, where we bought and restored a 1930s house in the village of Sunderland.

We were living in that house when I finally had my first book published. I embarked on speaking tours with David that took us to twenty-seven states. I was interviewed for the PBS documentaries, "The Amish" and "The Amish: Shunned" on *American Experience*. I also had my second book published during this time.

David and I lived in the home we loved for nine years before moving to the Shenandoah Valley in Virginia where we live now. We are grateful for a good rapport and a loving relationship with our sons, Paul and Tim. We are entering our elder years, so we know we have fewer days ahead of us than behind us. We have the years behind us to reminisce about, and we have travels and other adventures ahead of us to look forward to. We are grateful for the simple joys of our home life like taking walks, watching birds, and gazing upon beautiful sunsets that allow us to contemplate the wonders of our world and the mysteries of the one beyond.

When I was younger, I used to wonder how my life would have turned out if I had gotten an earlier start in developing a career. Would I have had the chance to become a philosophy professor? Maybe. These days I don't wish for a life I don't have. Instead, I wonder if perhaps I am living exactly the life I was meant to live. After all, growing old with the love of my life is a joy all its own. When I contemplate what my life would have been like if I had stayed in my Amish community, I feel blessed indeed.

APPENDIX

Notes on Amish Customs

Like many traditional cultures in the world, Amish practices and customs have their roots deep in their ancestry, so that even the leaders of the communities don't remember how and why these practices came about. What they do know is that these centuries-old traditions have defined their culture, and that they have provided cohesion. Below I explain several of their customs to the best of my ability.

Transportation: Go by Car, or by Horse and Buggy?

The horse and buggy is an icon of Amish life, and it represents a slower-paced lifestyle. In the stricter communities, horse-drawn vehicles are always used for local transportation, while trains are used for long distances. However, in most communities, the Amish will hire their "English" neighbors to drive them to where they want to go, and pay the driver by the mile. They call these "taxis." The most common way for men to travel to their workplace, especially those who are craftsmen working at various worksites, is to hire a taxi driver. For other weekday trips, it is often a personal decision whether to travel by car or by horse and buggy, though it is very much frowned upon to arrive at an Amish church service in a car. Church members are expected to walk or take a buggy to church. In some communities, it is also acceptable to use bicycles for transportation.

In the Amish way of thinking, it's different to ride in cars than to own them. One Amish man was asked why this was so, and he replied with this question: "When you take a plane, do you buy a ticket or the plane?" While that may be humorous, it doesn't answer the question. I don't know of any Amish person who can answer this question definitively. I know I can't.

Naming Practices

Because the Amish don't have much variety in either first or last names, it is rare to have a unique first and last name in a given community. Even though Saloma was not that common, I was not the only Saloma Miller in the community. There was another girl in my Amish school with my name. To differentiate between us, our father's names were used before our own: I was called "Sim's Lomie" ("Simon's Saloma") and the other Saloma was "John's Lomie." The apostrophe is used for those who are not yet married. When a woman marries, she takes her husband's name before her own, but the apostrophe is dropped as if the husband's name becomes a prefix rather than a mark of her belonging to him. If I were to go by Amish naming practices, I would be "David Saloma."

The men with common names will take their father's name before their own. However, there are times when one has to go back several generations. For instance, there was more than one Joe's Joe, one of them being my Uncle Joe. So he was called Moses's Joe's Joe. There are times when it is too cumbersome to go back that many generations, in which case the wife's name is used as a prefix. There was a man in my community known as "Ada Joe" and his wife was known as "Joe Ada."

There is another way that Amish naming practices differ from the mainstream culture. It is common to use the first name of the father in the family and add an "s" to his name to indicate the whole family. If someone in the mainstream culture were to visit us, they would likely say that they are visiting "The Furlong Family" while the Amish would say they are visiting "Davids." If David's name were common in the community, they might say they are visiting "Saloma Davids." Now that

I've been out of the community for this long, I understand how strange this sounds to those in the mainstream culture. Back when I was a part of the community, it seemed quite natural.

Kopp or Bonnet, What's the Difference?

Most Amish women and girls wear a *kopp*—hair covering—indoors their whole lives long. In most communities, girls will wear black *koppa*, until they reach adolescence, except for special occasions when they wear white *koppa*, such as for funerals. However, this is different in Lancaster County where girls will wear no covering until they reach adolescence.

Amish girls wear dresses that button down their backs until they reach adolescence when they begin wearing a "front-closing" dress, fastened with straight pins. At that time, a girl begins wearing a white covering for everyday and a black one for church on Sundays. The day a woman marries, she changes her black covering for a white one right after the wedding ceremony.

When women and girls go out into public, it is expected in most communities that they wear a bonnet in addition to their *kopp*. In some communities it is becoming more common for young women, during their dating years, to sometimes go places without a bonnet. However, they must always wear a bonnet to church, weddings, and funerals. In the stricter communities, women and girls are expected to wear bonnets whenever they are in public.

Amish Courting Practices

When I was young, bed courtship was practiced in my community. This meant that a young man would ask a young woman for a date, drive her to her home, put up his horse, and find his way to her upstairs bedroom where he would remove his hat, shoes, and outer shirt. It was acceptable to kiss and hug and neck, called *schmunzling*, but they were not supposed to have intercourse.

Back in the old country it was called "bundling." Reportedly, when our Anabaptist ancestors were hiding from authorities, they hid in the upstairs rooms of their homes during their dates. There would be a board down the middle of the bed to keep the man and woman separated. This left them together in a warm place to visit without getting them into carnal trouble.

In the pioneer days when many of the Amish communities were being established here in this country, sleeping spaces were not nearly as private as they tend to be in the present day. In fact, in stagecoach inns (not only Amish), it was common for innkeepers to sell half a bed. So in the middle of the night, a person might find himself sleeping next to a total stranger.

Bed courtship is not practiced in every Amish community. Many new communities are established expressly so that they can get away from it. I suspect some communities don't admit that they still practice it, especially those that were established back when the practice was common.

Needless to say, bed courtship often leads to pregnancy before marriage. I believe most Amish elders would rather a young woman become pregnant before marriage than leave the community. After all, there are ways of "remedying" the situation of pregnancy before marriage, including planning a hasty wedding before the pregnancy shows. Such a remedy traps her in marriage.

If both partners are members of the church, they plan their wedding to take place before the pregnancy becomes obvious. If one or both of them are not yet members of the church, they have to act quickly to become members before they can get married.

Becoming a member normally takes from spring to fall. First the youth need to take instructions to join the church and become baptized. Church is held every two weeks in each district. The youth take a summer of instruction before they are baptized.

If a young woman gets pregnant before she (or her partner) is a member of the church, this process must be accelerated. They will need to take instructions in their own church district on their usual church Sundays, in addition to a neighboring church district on alternate Sundays. This way a person can get through the process in half the time it normally takes.

Even if a woman doesn't become pregnant and a couple decides they want to get married, they have to go before the elders of the church to ask permission. Though I never experienced this myself, reportedly when young people ask permission for marriage, they are admonished by the church elders that the flesh is weak and are asked if they have stayed "free of sin" during their courtship. If they have not, they are asked to make a public confession before they are granted permission to marry.

These practices puzzle me. If the "flesh is weak," then why tempt it by allowing two young people to go to bed together? And why the hands-off approach until someone gets pregnant or asks for permission to marry, and then bring on the public shaming rituals? This system seems designed to keep the youth in the community.

Shunning: Amish Style

The Amish practice of shunning does not mean that those who leave are shut out of their family and culture for the rest of their lives with no contact. Even in the strictest of Amish communities, this is not usually the case.

There are as many nuances to Amish shunning as there are Amish families. Each community has its own level of strictness. Then each family within each community has their own level of shunning for any sons or daughters who leave.

Shunning is designed, in their view, to reform the one who sinned (normally by leaving the community) by withholding the family and community relationships. The one being shunned for leaving often experiences the practice as rejection, and it induces guilt and shame—guilt that we left our poor parents feeling like they didn't raise us right, or else we would have stayed Amish, and shame for causing our family and friends grief. Worst of all is that our family and original community members think of us as sinners who are damned.

Amish-style shunning offers the "wayward" redemption if they will only return and take up their rightful place in their family and community. This causes more inner conflict than if relations were severed altogether because we experience the loss of our family several times over.

For the most part Amish shunning means that the one being shunned may not eat with their family members. Those who are upholding the shunning may not accept gifts from the one being shunned, nor may they do business with that person. My family and community members would not ride in my car with me, even though they were allowed to ride in someone else's car. My parents also never visited my home after I left.

In some stricter communities, those who shun are not allowed to take anything from the hand of the shunned. Those who have left are not welcome to attend a funeral if a family member dies. This is one of the cruelest forms of shunning, much like the stories we heard growing up of our martyred ancestors in Germany and Switzerland, when the authorities would steal the bodies of the deceased to deprive the loved ones of their grieving rituals as a means of convincing them to return to the state churches.

There is enough variation in Amish shunning that I can best describe it by my own experience. During my first visits home after I left the final time, David and I were allowed to eat with my family. My parents were criticized for that, so the next time we visited we sat at a separate table only about six inches away from the family table. Not only were my parents criticized for that, but they also had to make a confession in church for not adhering to stricter shunning. After that they stopped eating with us altogether.

This is the ambiguous part of shunning. My parents didn't think there was anything wrong with eating at separate tables until they were asked to make a public confession. A more popular family in my community might have gotten away without any consequences for this. By punishing my parents for eating with me and having them tell me about the punishment, the church elders heaped even more guilt on me than if my parents had refused to eat with us from the start.

Now that my parents are both deceased and I don't have many connections to my original community, I feel free to live my life as I see fit.

ACKNOWLEDGMENTS

I thank all who helped bring this book about. Much gratitude goes to all you readers who kept reminding me that you are waiting for my next book. You are the reason this book matters. I hope these stories will connect you with your own memories.

I want to thank all my friends in Vermont who were there when I was developing my writing skills: members and teachers of my writing classes and groups, those who read drafts of my writing along the way, and other friends who supported my endeavors.

This book might never have come about without my late friend, Marie Houle. In 2016, a year before she left this world, she told me she'd read both of my published books and asked if I was writing another. When I said I wasn't, she said, "Saloma, you have been given a gift—for writing—and you may not *squander* that gift!" I was moved by her reminder that I have a responsibility to accept and develop the talents I was given.

My appreciation goes to friend and coach Russ Eanes for his advice during the self-publishing process; to Pamela Johnson from TechPro Publications for designing the book cover; to Marjorie Turner Hollman for her content editing; to Frances B. King for her copyediting; and to April Sachs for proofreading.

I am grateful to Kathie Weaver Kurtz and Esther Stenson for their thoughtful critiques and moral support throughout the writing of this book, and for their ongoing support of my writing.

My deepest gratitude goes to my husband David who has read several drafts of everything I've written. He has a knack for coming up with good titles, which is where *Liberating Lomie* came from. His love and support over the years mean everything to me.